WE THE COURT

We The Court

THE EUROPEAN COURT OF JUSTICE AND THE EUROPEAN ECONOMIC CONSTITUTION

A Critical Reading of Article 30 of the EC Treaty

MIGUEL POIARES MADURO

HART PUBLISHING
OXFORD
1998

Hart Publishing
Oxford
UK

Distributed in the United States by
Northwestern University Press
625 Colfax, Evanston
Illinois 60208–4210 USA

Distributed in Australia and New Zealand by
Federation Press
PO Box 45, Annandale
NSW 203 Australia

Distributed in the Netherlands, Belgium and Luxembourg by
Intersentia, Churchillaan 108
B2900 Schoten, Antwerp
Belgium

Hart Publishing is a specialist legal publisher based in Oxford, England. To order further copies of this book or to request a list of other publications please write to:
Hart Publishing, 19 Whitehouse Road, Oxford, OX1 4PA
Telephone: +44 (0)1865 434459 Fax: +44 (0)1865 794882
email: hartpub@janep.demon.co.uk

British Library Cataloguing in Publication Data
Data Available

ISBN 1–901362–25–6 (cloth)

Typeset in 10/12 Sabon
by Set All, (Abingdon)
Printed in Great Britain on acid-free paper
by Bookcraft, Midsomer Norton, Somerset

Foreword

Francis Snyder and Christian Joerges

In the European Community the determination of policies, the adoption of legislation and judicial decision-making raise two related dilemmas. The first dilemma concerns the controversial nature of the economic order, more precisely its constitutional status. Should policy-makers and law-makers, including judges, treat "market integration" as an end in itself, thus shielding the economic system against political manipulation and state intervention? The second dilemma is characteristic of any divided-powers system or any system of multi-level governance. When politics is preferred over the autonomy of the economic sphere, which level of governance should take action? In the context of the European Union, there is also a third dilemma: are the dichotomous distinctions between the state and the market and between national and supranational at all adequate when it comes to conceptualising Europe's emerging polity?

These types of queries have been explored for a number of years in a series of interdisciplinary seminars given within the framework of the Law Department at the European University Institute (EUI) in Florence. This book results from the conjunction of these seminars, the intellectual challenges which the process of European integration presents, and—last but not least—the imagination, creativity, dedication and patience of an outstanding young scholar. Without any doubt this book will also inform future seminars, at the EUI and elsewhere, in a kind of dialectical process.

Miguel Poiares here comes to grips with some of the most difficult issues in European Community (and European Union) law. Article 30 represents in many respects the core of the European Community Treaty. Poiares' stimulating analysis makes this Treaty article come alive, both its widely known legal aspects as well as new constitutional dimensions. It traces the development by the European Court of Justice of what the author calls 'majoritarian activism'. Such a judicial strategy, whether intended or unintended, raises special questions in an evolving legal system and would-be polity such as the European Union. For example, how can the judicial process take account of participants in the political process from other Member States? What legal and political models should guide our discussions of the European Union's future? To address these questions, this book uses a constitutional approach that is based in an innovative way on a comparative institutional analysis. This analysis redesigns the tensions between the European Community's political aspirations on the one hand and its reliance on economic integration on the other.

This innovative work thus addresses some of the most intractable, yet most stimulating issues on the current agenda of European legal scholarship. It should be recommended reading for all students of European Union law. It should also attract the interest of the judiciary and political scientists who wish to understand better the specific features of the role of law in the process of integration. By reflecting on the world to which they have contributed so much, it illuminates not only the past but also the present and the future of European integration.

Contents

Table of Cases

Introduction

This book takes as its starting point the relation between Article 30 of the EC Treaty (the general rule on the free movement of goods) and the European Economic Constitution. On the one hand, it examines Article 30 in the context of the constitutional dilemmas facing the European Union, particularly the balance of powers to be defined between Member States and the Union, between public power and the market, and between the legitimacy of Community law *vis-à-vis* that of national law. On the other hand, it reviews different conceptions of the European Economic Constitution by analysing the role of Article 30 in the review of market regulation.

When reviewing national measures with an effect on trade under Article 30, the European Court of Justice must both decide whether there should be regulation and, if so, who will have the power to regulate. Thus, the Court has, through Article 30, defined many of the essential foundations of the European Economic Constitution. The extent of regulatory powers left to Member States will largely depend on the scope given to Article 30. In the same way, the criteria followed in upholding or striking down national measures brought under review through Article 30 will be reflected in the level of market regulation. The decision to review national regulations and, if so, according to which criteria, implies choices regarding the division of competences between the Member States and the Union. It also presupposes choices concerning the constitutional limits to State or public intervention in the market.

Article 30 also reflects and depends upon constitutional conceptions of the legitimacy of Community law. In reviewing national regulations the Court is faced with the problem of imposing the (debated) legitimacy of Community law upon national law, which has been instituted according to traditional democratic mechanisms. Article 30 has helped to legitimise this use of Community law through the protection of individual rights; at times it has even appeared to support theories of legitimation founded on the protection of individual economic freedoms against public power. In contrast to the latter, Article 30 has also led to calls for greater competences to be granted to the Union and, consequently, for the development of traditional majoritarian democracy in the European Union (mainly in the form of an extension of powers of the European Parliament). Whether Article 30 should be used as part of these means of legitimising Community law, and whether it can help highlight new forms of legitimation, is an issue that cannot be ignored.

Chapter 1 will explain and review the constitutional development of the European Union from the perspective of the way in which the European Court of Justice has built up both its legitimacy and that of Community law, while at the same time shaping and being shaped by the legal and constitutional discourse of European integration. It will be shown how the constitutionalisation of European law and its legitimacy and that of the Court of Justice are linked with the adoption of formal reasoning, the development of individual rights and the promotion of a legal discourse with national and Community actors. It will also be argued that these elements are essential in explaining the present model of the European Economic Constitution. The widening of the scope of Community "market rules" (notably Article 30) involved in the process of "integration through law" has extended the supervision of Community law over practically the entire area of national regulatory law. Those rules have played an essential role in the legitimation of Community law and its process of constitutionalisation. As a consequence, the logic of market integration dominates the European Constitution and its supremacy over national law. Broadly, this created or enhanced a "political deficit" or "constitutional deficit" in the construction of the Community legal order: the spillover of Community "market rules" into virtually all other areas of the law has remained "prisoner" of formal reasoning and the constitutional limits of the Treaties; the functional use of market integration rules and the associated litigation have been the object of a limited community of interests and actors; there has been no political discourse developed at the supra-national level.

In Chapter 2, the classical readings of Article 30 (discrimination, typological and cost/benefit tests) will be reviewed and criticised. It will be argued that underlying the classical discussions between cost/benefit analysis and anti-protectionism are two basic understandings of the European Economic Constitution. One conception argues for a constitutional interpretation of free movement and competition rules as limiting public intervention in the market. It is the neo-liberal or ordo-liberal conception of the European Constitution as protecting economic freedom and free competition. The other conception relates Community law to classical anti-protectionism trade law. The discussion will highlight the constitutional dimension and institutional choices inherent in the application of Article 30.

In Chapter 3, the aim is to identify the main features of the present model of the European Economic Constitution developed by the European Court of Justice. It will be noted that, though the case law of the Court of Justice has led to deregulation, this is so only from a national perspective and does not correspond to a neo-liberal construction of the European Constitution by the Court of Justice. Instead, the outcome of the decisions of the European Court of Justice in the review of national and Community legislation fits with a "European majority policy". The Court's approach to the European Economic Constitution has revealed a peculiar type of activism: defined in this book as majoritarian activism. The broad scope given to market integration rules (notably Article 30) in the review of national regulations was not intended to control the degree of public intervention in the market but to bring about harmonisation among national rules through the judicial process. This different type of activism will be related to the institutional alternatives to the Court in regulating the common market. These institutional alternatives are the European Union political process and the market. Finally, the changes taking place in these institutional alternatives will be related with the recent developments in the case law of the European Court of Justice. The comparative institutional analysis undertaken will also help in highlighting two different judicial approaches for State regulation in the market in the context of federal or quasi-federal systems: market-building and market-maintenance.

Chapter 4 moves from the descriptive to the normative analysis of the European Economic Constitution and Article 30. It identifies three models for the European Constitution in the European constitutional debates and the proposals regarding the present constitutional and democratic deficits. These models also correspond to different forms of regulation taking place in the common market. The European Economic Constitution is linked to the continuous interplay between the Constitutional models of centralisation, competition and decentralisation. These models are then related to different visions of the European Economic Constitution and its legitimation. The first argues that negative integration, deriving from the application of market integration rules, must be followed by positive integration which is legitimised through the development of traditional democratic mechanisms in the European Union. The second argues for the constitutionalisation of negative integration. No traditional democratic developments are required for the European Union institutions. No transferral of powers to those institutions takes place. The market is conceived as the best source of legitimation of the European Economic Constitution. The goal is to protect market freedom and individual rights against public power. The third vision still sees the highest source of legitimacy in national democratic legitimacy. The legitimacy of the European Economic Constitution derives therefrom and is thus conditioned. No other form of constitutional legitimacy that can be opposed to national democratic processes is foreseeable or even defensible in the European Union at this stage. All these visions of the European Economic Constitution, their legitimacy and the regulatory models which embodied them present problems and potential institutional malfunctions which are reviewed in the book.

Chapter 5 argues that the future of the European Constitution will probably lie in a permanent discourse involving these different models. What lawyers should do is to concentrate on the shaping of this discourse and on developing constitutional criteria to choose among those models and their different institutions (the European Union political process, the market and the State). For this, it is essential to work on the notion of the legitimacy of European law. This will be related with different European goals and institutional frameworks. While analysing Article 30 of the EC Treaty from the point of view of the European Economic Constitution, the argument in favour of European law as a tool to promote participation and representation of all European Union citizens in the national political processes will be advanced;

and finally a test developed to be applied in the review of national measures under Article 30, arguing that the European Court of Justice should only review national regulatory policies where there is a suspicion of representative malfunction in the national political processes with regard to nationals of other Member States.

The interdisciplinary approach followed in the book attempts to provide the ground for a contextual analysis of Article 30 addressing the broader constitutional questions of the EU. Pretentiously, the book presents itself as different from traditional and classical approaches to EU law. I pompously quote John Cale and Lou Reed's critique of classicism (In Songs for Drella) to justify myself:

> The trouble with a classicist, he looks at a tree
> that's all he sees, he paints a tree
> The trouble with a classicist, he looks at the sky
> he doesn't ask why, he just paints a sky
>
> John Cale and Lou Reed
> from *Songs for Drella*

Small parts of Chapters 3 and 5 were published as articles in the European Law Journal and the Irish Journal of European Law. Chapter 4 is based on a paper presented in Madison in 1992 in the seminar of Professor Neil Komesar on law and economics and comparative institutional analysis.

The book stems from the author's PhD thesis defended at the European University Institute, Florence, at the end of 1996. I am especially indebted to my two supervisors: Francis Snyder (with whom I later developed an invaluable friendship) and Christian Joerges. They have done much more than supervising my thesis. They have challenged and changed my way of seeing and thinking the law. They have also give me a tremendous personal support throughout my research and at the beginning of my academic career. Their imprint on this thesis is visible in the inter-disciplinary approached followed and the way in which problems of legitimacy and the relation between Community law and national law are addressed. However, they do not necessarily share the views expressed in this book. The same applies to other people from which comments and support I have greatly benefited. In particular, I would like to thank Joseph Weiler whose supportive comments have meant a lot to me. His sharp points and critiques have also played a crucial role in making a book out of my ideas. I am also very grateful to Francisco Lucas Pires and Stephen Weatherhill and to others who have commented or discussed different parts of this book at different stages of its writing. I would like to mention the names of Antonio Estella, Carlos Padros, Carlos Pinto Correia, Carol Harlow, Fin Traff, Jeronimo Maillo, Karl-Heinz Ladeur, Martin Shapiro, Mary Volcansek, Massimo La Torre, Mark Jeffery (who has revised much of my English), Nicholas Bernard, Nuno Piçarra, Renaud Dehousse, Rossa Phelan and William Whitford. The editorial team at Hart Publishing has done a wonderful job in revising my English and made clear ideas that were previously inadequately expressed.

I also own an enormous debt to Neil Komesar. Throughout this book I make an extensive use of the Comparative Institutional Analysis developed by Komesar and thoroughly discussed in his book: *Imperfect Alternatives – Choosing Institutions in Law, Economic and Public Policy* (Chicago and London, The University of Chicago Press, 1994). I have benefited greatly from his numerous, and never superficial, comments both on my understanding of Comparative Institutional Analysis and, in general, on the topics discussed on the book. His external perspective to Community law has also helped me to reassess and review many of my working assumptions. Naturally, he is in no way responsible for the use of Comparative Institutional Analysis made in this book, though I, pretentiously, hope to contribute to the "legal revolution" that he has started.

A particular word of gratitude is also due to Silvana Sciarra. I have learned a lot while working with her in topics not directly concerning this book. Her support, understanding and advice have been fundamental to me in the last years of my thesis and in preparing the publication of this book. She has been an example to me both as an academic and as a person. Also thanks to many other persons, colleagues and friends at the European University Institute and Madison: Notker, Akas, Caterina, Suzana, Antonina, Veronique, Jacobien, Marcelo, Miguel, Adolfo, João, Antonio, Sylvaine, Claire, Ana, Piera, Manel, Marlies, Evie, Jaime, Kim, Erin, Allison, Stephan, Miguel, Pedro, Susan, Majteld and Emir (whose help on my research was essential to this book). Some friends have been particularly close to me, during my days in Florence: Maria, Gil, Gianni (and the entire Galli family, especially my teacher of Italian literature, Nori), Nuno, Alexandre, Pedro, Eva, Monica, Angela, Marta and Luciano (who is also the only person to share my political beliefs!).

My gratitude also extends to my friends in Portugal: Margarida, Paulos, Teresas, Miguel, Sara. I am particularly grateful to all those with whom I shared legal and non-legal discussions and support, which have fulfilled some of the best moments of my life: Quimpe, Margarida, David, Julio and Alexandra. I would like to single out my close friend Rui Batista for his invaluable friendship and for the numerous hours of endless discussions on any imaginable topic (including those of this book). Many thanks also to Imî for the support given in the last stages of this book. My final words must go to all my family. In particular to the support and patience of my mother, my sister and my brother and the enthusiasm of my nephews. I owe a lifetime of gratitude to many other people. At a early age, I learned much from my uncle and especially my father. This book is dedicated to their memory.

1

The Creation

THE CONSTITUTIONALISATION OF COMMUNITY LAW: THE LEGITIMACY OF THE EUROPEAN COURT OF JUSTICE AND COMMUNITY LAW

In its early days the European Court of Justice was faced with two main challenges: to ensure its own effectiveness and the effectiveness of Community law in general while, at the same time, avoiding any involvement in national and political conflicts that might undermine both its own judicial credibility and the credibility of Community law. The steps taken by the Court in the interpretation of the Treaties and in the definition of its own role are largely a consequence of those constraints, as well as of the determination of its judges to accord to Community law a status distinct from that of international law. I will not address here the issue of how the Court has done this; instead, I will concentrate on how, in doing it, the Court has developed a certain conception of Community constitutional law and of its own legitimacy; how it adopted a particular form of legal reasoning; how it shaped, and was itself shaped by, the European legal discourse; and the impact this has had in the European Economic Constitution and Article 30 of the EC Treaty.

One of the first moves the Court made was to construct Community law as the Community's own legal system.[1] This implied the creation of an entire legal framework and led to the constitutionalisation of the treaties, with well-known principles such as supremacy, direct effect, a system of jurisdictional guarantees and a framework of horizontal and vertical separation of powers.[2] In a classical article on Community law, Eric Stein has identified in the cases dealing with direct effect, supremacy and external relations the creation of European constitutional law.[3] A similar description is given by Hancher who follows Weiler in referring to direct effect, supremacy, implied powers and human rights but compares these elements of Community law with

[1] See Case 6/64, *Costa* v. *Enel* [1964] ECR 585. See also Case 26/62, *Van Gend en Loos* [1963] ECR 1 and Case 14/68, *Walt Wilhelm* [1969] ECR 1.

[2] For a more detailed analysis see, for example: K. Lenaerts, "Constitutionalism and the Many Faces of Federalism", (1990) 38 *American Journal of Comparative Law*, 205; G.F. Mancini, "The making of a constitution for Europe", (1989) 26 *CMLRev*, 595; E. Stein, "Lawyers, Judges and the Making of a Transnational Constitution", (1981) *American Journal of International Law*, 1 (or "Giuristi, Giudici e la creazione di una Constituzione Transnazionale", in *Un nuovo diritto per l'Europa* (Milano, Giuffre, 1991)); and J. Weiler, "The Transformation of Europe", (1990–91) 100 *The Yale Law Journal*, 2403 and "The Reformation of European Constitutionalism", (1997) 35 *JCMS*, 97.

[3] Stein, (n.2 above), at 3 *et seq*.

international law. All those elements of Community law can also be found in international law; what makes Community legal order unique is their combined impact on the development of legal remedies and enforcement.[4] The different constitutional readings of Community law claim that the Treaties have acquired a constitutional status and that constitutional doctrines best explain Community law and its development. According to Weiler:

> "The constitutional thesis claims that in critical aspects the Community has evolved and behaves as if its founding instrument were not a Treaty governed by international law but, to use the language of the European Court of Justice, a constitutional charter governed by a form of constitutional law".[5]

Formalist international lawyers may argue that a Treaty will remain a Treaty no matter how close its operation and effects resemble those of a Constitution and how deeply rooted it will be recognised and applied in national legal orders. But this will be a debate about words. The relevant point is that, not only does Community law have constitutional effects and constitutional doctrines, the discourse that dominates its construction and relation with national legal orders is a constitutional discourse.[6] Conflicts of competences, separation of powers, fundamental rights: these are all constitutional concepts that form the cornerstone of the legal and political debates on the European Union and Community law. Moreover, these are the concepts that have driven the European Court of Justice approach to Community law.

The classical literature on the constitutionalisation of Community law has described how the case law of the Court developed a constitutional infrastructure with individual and fundamental rights, enforcement mechanisms, an institutional rule of law (eg separation of powers) and an autonomous and hierarchical legal order.[7] But if the "body" is well known, its "soul" is still, to a large extent, a mystery. In this chapter the focus will be on the interplay between the constitutionalisation of Community law and market integration rules and the impact of this process and the constraints therein in the European Economic Constitution.

In this first stage, the main need was to create a legal infrastructure capable of making Community law operate directly in national legal orders and upon individuals. At the same time, the Court had to establish its authority with respect to other Community and national institutions. Thus, the construction of an entire conceptual apparatus of procedural and institutional principles and rules was required.

[4] The impact is broader and stronger; domestic remedies complement international remedies; and the presumption of international law in favour of State sovereignty has been reversed. L. Hancher, "Constitutionalism, The Community Court and International Law", (1994) 25 *Netherlands Book of International Law*, 259, at 265–6.

[5] The Reformation of European Constitutionalism (n.2 above), at 96.

[6] See Weiler, ibid.

[7] See references in n.2 above.

A further step taken to enhance the effectiveness and legitimacy of Community law was the "subjectivation" of the Treaties. By "subjectivation" it is meant here the move from a state-based interpretation of the Treaties into an individual-based interpretation. The Treaties are not simply to be interpreted as an agreement between States, but as having been created for the "peoples of Europe": Community rules are directed towards individuals and can be invoked by them. The "subjectivation" of Community law provided a particularly strong instrument for ensuring the implementation and the effectiveness of Community law in national legal orders. It also presented Community law as a source of new rights for nationals of all Member States. Decisions of the Court are not seen as deciding conflicts among states, but as protecting individuals from states: even, in some cases, from their own home-state.

A further important element in securing the legitimacy and authority of both the European Court of Justice and EC law was co-operation with national courts. This was also enhanced by the individual rights flowing from the European Economic Constitution (notably free movement rules). The role played by national courts in requesting rulings from the ECJ and in applying these rulings[8] provided ECJ decisions with the same authority of national court decisions and gave these decisions added values of both neutrality and of legitimacy in being "sanctioned" by a court of the State against which the judgment had gone. As stated by Weiler:

> "When European Community Law is spoken through the mouths of the national judiciary it will also have the teeth that can be found in such a mouth and will usually enjoy whatever enforcement value that national law will have on that occasion".[9]

Finally, an equally important element in the constitutionalisation of the Treaties and the legitimacy of the Court and Community law was the Court's co-ordination of its efforts and strategy with those of the European Commission. Eric Stein, in reviewing the relevant cases in the construction of the constitutional structure of the Communities, reached the conclusion that the Court was guided by the Commission in the direction of greater legal integration, and speaks of a close alliance between the Court and the Commission.[10] This alliance was relevant, for example, in defining the agenda for legal integration, and in the selective enforcement of Community law

[8] Why national courts were willing and available to do so is another question. See, J.H.H. Weiler, "Journey to an Unknown Destination: A Retrospective and Prospective of the European Court of Justice in the Arena of Political Integration", (1993) 31 *JCMS*, 417, at 423 and A.-M. Burley, and W. Mattli, "Europe Before the Court: A Political Theory of Legal Integration", (1993) 47 *International Organization*, 41, at 62.

[9] Weiler, (n.8 above), at 422. See, also, from the same author, "A Quiet Revolution: The European Court of Justice and Its Interlocutors", (1994) 26 *Comparative Political Studies*, 510, at 519.

[10] See E. Stein, *Un nuovo diritto per l'Europa* (n.2 above), especially at 17–43. In the same sense, S. Cassese, "La Costituzione Europea", (1991) *Quaderni Costituzionali*, 487, at 494.

which rather than being directed towards addressing the most important violations of Community law, was intended to create a "habit of obedience" towards Community law. In the first years of the EC Treaty, the Commission carefully decided which actions should be brought against the Member States. The controlling principle was that it was better not to bring an action against a State, notwithstanding the importance of the violation of Community law involved, if the Commission and Court were convinced that the Member State would not comply with the Court decision. Instead, it was preferable to bring before the Court less important issues, where Member States could be expected to comply with the Court's decisions.[11] This is part of what Volcansek calls "the political aspects of judging".[12] According to this author:

> "Decisions that may be legally 'right' but are ignored, defied or evaded are not politically desirable. No Court would consciously, one would presume, create a line of jurisprudence with foreknowledge that it would have no effect".[13]

The approach of developing Community law while creating a "habit of obedience" is also visible in the way the legal principles laid down by the Court are sometimes only given full effect in decisions following those in which they are first identified,[14] and in the "step by step" approach taken in the legal construction of the Community constitutional order, each decision following as the logical consequence of the previous one.[15] Reactions against the Court's legal principles are softened by the time delay and, most importantly, decisions are legitimised by being grounded in settled precedents.

Naturally, in this process of legitimation, an essential element was the way in which decisions were argued and justified. First, the legal reasoning of the Court of Justice should correspond, as much as possible, to the traditional understanding of judicial reasoning. Secondly, such reasoning has to convey the impression of neutrality necessary to establish the judicial authority of the Court of Justice and to safeguard legal integration. The natural consequence of this is the adoption of a model of formal reasoning in the justification process of the decisions of the European Court of Justice. Formal reasoning

[11] Oral information given by Michel Gaudet, head of the legal service of the EEC Commission in the first years of the Treaty, in a seminar at the European University Institute, Florence, on 11 March 1993.

[12] Mary L. Volcansek, "Supranational Courts in a Political Context", in Volcansek (ed.), *Supranational Courts and the Legalization of Politics* (Gainesville, University Press of Florida, forthcoming), at 10.

[13] Ibid.

[14] Case 8/74, *Dassonville* [1974] ECR 837, concerning free movement of goods, is a good example of this (see the analysis of the Court's case law in Chapter 2. The same is the case with *Cassis de Dijon* (Case 120/78, *Rewe-Zentral AG* v. *Bundesmonopolverwaltung für Branntwein* [1979] ECR 649, discussed below), where the Court introduced what came to be identified as the principle of mutual recognition in a manner incidental and not essential to the decision it took, thus signalling more a principle of future application. In this sense, see K.J. Alter, and S. Meunier-Aitsahalia, "Judicial Politics in the European Community—European Integration and the Pathbreaking *Cassis de Dijon* Decision", (1994) 26 *Comparative Political Studies*, 535, at 539.

[15] See Burley and Mattli, "Europe Before the Court" (n.8 above), at 66.

corresponds to the traditional conception of legal reasoning and of the judicial role. It bases the authority and legitimacy of Court decisions on recognition of, and not on the creation of, the law. In the same manner, by presenting courts as merely the appliers of a pre-existing law, formal reasoning denies discretion, isolates judicial decisions from extra-legal considerations and confers upon those decisions an appearance of neutrality. Courts are thus distinguished from political bodies which exercise discretion for policy reasons in the same way that law is distinguished from politics. In the words of Burley and Mattli:

> "At a minimum, the margin of insulation necessary to promote integration requires that judges themselves appear to be practising law rather than politics. Their political freedom of action thus depends on a minimal degree of fidelity to both substantive law and the methodological constraints imposed by legal reasoning. In a word, the staunch insistence on legal realities as distinct from political realities may in fact be a political tool".[16]

It is this that promoted the use of law as, in the words of the same authors, a "mask for politics"[17] in European integration.[18] Therein lies part of the dilemma of the European Court of Justice[19] caught between the need to secure legitimacy, according to the traditional adhesion to the rule of law, and the political role and strategy that it has had to develop to promote market integration and the constitutionalisation of Community law. In turn, the Court has benefited from an advantage in its search for legitimacy if compared with national constitutional courts. National courts are traditionally contrasted with the democratic legitimacy of national parliaments *vis-à-vis* their lack of accountability. The European Court's constitutional activism was not faced with a traditional democratic representative body at the EU level[20] and it has been directed mainly at national decisions that do not represent the majority in European terms. This is part of the peculiar nature of European judicial activism that will be highlighted throughout this book. Contrary to the traditional conception of judicial activism addressed to the protection of minorities against the democratic majority will, European judicial activism can better be described as majoritarian activism: promoting the rights and policies of the larger European political community (the majority) against the "selfish" or autonomous (depending on the point of view) decisions of national polities (the minorities).

[16] Ibid, at 45. See, also, Weiler, "Journey to an Unknown Destination" (n.8 above), mainly at 427.

[17] Burley and Mattli, "Europe Before the Court" (n.8 above), at 44.

[18] According to another commentator: "In the Communities, politics has to hide and disguise itself as law": F.L. Pires, "Justiça Constitucional e Príncipio da Maioria", in *Legitimidade e Legitimação da Justiça Constitucional*, Colóquio no 10º Aniversário do Tribunal Constitucional, (Coimbra Editora, 1995), at the end. Author's translation; in the original: "*Nas Comunidades quem tem que se esconder e se disfarça como direito é a política*".

[19] Volcansek, "Supranational Courts in a Political Context" (n.12 above), at 11.

[20] Ibid, at 11.

In the following sections some of the previous points will be developed in addressing the different elements that have affected and constrained the judicial creation of the European Economic Constitution.

THE EUROPEAN COURT AMONG REASONS, RULES AND INSTITUTIONS

Studies on the Court of Justice have departed from recognising its role in promoting "integration through law"[21] and constitutionalising the Treaties. Generally, authors tend either to describe the legal instruments and effects of this constitutionalisation or to review the role of the Court in the dynamics of European integration.[22] Different points are stressed by different approaches: from the importance of rules and formal legal reasoning (what Burley and Mattli call legalism theories[23]) to the importance of contextual and institutional analysis (Weiler's explanation of how legal supra-nationalism was made possible by the presence of inter-governamentalism in the Community decision-making process);[24] from remarking a predominant role of state interests in the integration process (understood as mirroring State preferences and bargaining power)[25] to noting the importance of the process of functional interdependence in institutional building (functionalism)[26] and the role of institutional and individual actors in making use of the integration process and institutions therefrom to promote their interests and fuel integration (neo-functionalism).[27]

Inspiration can be draw from all these sources in drafting a framework of analysis capable of embracing the different elements of the legal and constitutional discourse of European integration that help explain the conception of its judicial role adopted by the Court and the way in which it constructed its own legitimacy and that of Community law. This, in turn, will help to explain the judicial model of the European Economic Constitution. To this purpose

[21] This is the title of a project undertaken at the European University Institute in the 1980s and which resulted in a series of books edited by Mauro Cappelletti, Monica Seccombe and Joseph Weiler (published by Walter de Gruyter).

[22] The different legal and political science theories assessing the impact of the European Court of Justice in European integration, are reviewed by Burley and Mattli, "Europe Before the Court" (n.8 above), at 45–52.

[23] Ibid, at 45.

[24] J. Weiler, "The Community System: The Dual Chracter of Supranationalism", 1 (1981) *Yearbook of European Law*, 267.

[25] See: A. Moravcsik, "Negotiating the Single European Act: National Interests and Conventional Statecraft in the European Community", (1991) 45 *International Organization*, 19, and "Preferences and Power in the European Community: A Liberal Intergovernamentalist Approach", (1993) 31 *JCMS*, 473; G. Garret, "International Cooperation and Institutional Choice: the European Community's Internal Market", (1992) 46 *International Organization*, 533.

[26] See Pentland, "Political Theories of Integration: Between Science and Ideology", in Lasok and Soldatos (eds.), *The European Communities in Action* (Bruxelles, Bruylant, 1981), at 550–4.

[27] Ibid, at 554–8 and Burley and Mattli, "Europe Before the Court" (n.8 above), at 52.

the analysis must take into account three different levels: rules, reasons and institutions. Judicial action departs from rules, their interpretation and application. But courts are also simultaneously empowered and constrained by rules. Applying and interpreting rules is a rational process (or, at least, presented as such) in which reasons play an important role. These reasons, in their turn, are both given to an audience and dependent on the "suggestions" and constraints placed by actors in the judicial process.[28]

From a more strict legal perspective, all these different levels can be identified with the three levels involved in the justification of judicial decisions. The first level determines what is a valid legal answer in a certain legal system. This is part of the process of legal reasoning. But legal reasoning may offer us more than one valid legal answer. The choice among the different valid legal answers requires criteria that constitute the second level of justification.[29] The third level of justification is that of legal discourse, that determines how critique and acceptance of the decisions will take place.

However, rules, reasons and institutions are also present in a political approach to the judicial process. In this case, rules are constraints in the actions of courts as political and social actors; rules are also institutionalised forms of decision-making and inputs and outcomes of dispute-resolution.[30] Rules also require reasons in dispute resolution.[31] Under a political approach to the judicial process, reasons are both what allows the transformation of the outcomes of dispute resolution and political bargaining into rules and what is necessary to promote political change through the application and interpretation of rules in the judicial process. Finally, a fundamental role is also given to institutions and individuals as actors of the judicial process, constraining and promoting its use.

All this is well known, though rarely assumed by all those working in this area. For long, the role of law and the European Court of Justice in the integration process was either ignored or merely understood as a functional outcome of the technical operation of a closed normative system. In 1982, Weiler wrote that, among non-lawyers, there was "a common but often misguided conceptualization of the role of law":

> "Law is seen primarily, if not exclusively, as having an instrumental function: the translation into operational language of the policies decided upon by political organs so that these may be put into action; in short, a technical-serviant role. The

[28] According to Aarnio, interpretation can be seen as a dialogue in which different interpreters participate presenting arguments and counter-arguments: A. Aarnio, "On Rational Acceptability —Some Remarks on Legal Justification", in Nerhot (ed.) *Law, Interpretation and Reality* (Dordrecht, Kluwer Academic Publishers, 1980), at 78.

[29] MacCormick calls this the problem of interpretation that cannot be solved through deductive juustification: N. MacCormick, *Legal Reasoning and Legal Theory* (Oxford, Clarendon Press, 1978), at 68.

[30] See A. Stone, *Judicialization and the Construction of Governance*, EUI Working Papers RSC No. 96/59, (Florence, 1996), mainly at 4–6.

[31] See ibid.

Court is often regarded as being merely the organ of a closed self-referring technical system which has been charged with the interpretation of the system's own complex rules and adjudication in the case of breach".[32]

In the same year Shapiro depicted the attitude of lawyers to the European constitution as "constitutional law without constitutional politics":

> "the Community as a juristic idea; the written constitution as a sacred text; the professional commentary as a legal truth; the case law as the inevitable working out of correct implications of the constitutional text; and the constitutional court as a disembodied voice of right reason and constitutional teleology".[33]

These were the orthodox approaches of lawyers and political scientists while the Court was constructing the constitutional structure of the European Community. This constitution-making occurred in a setting wonderfully depicted by Eric Stein, in his well known sentence describing the Court has "tucked away in the fairyland Duchy of Luxembourg and blessed with benign neglect by the powers that be and the mass media".[34] Since those days, the Court and its process of constitutionalisation of the Treaties, have been the object of growing attention by both lawyers and political scientists. Sometimes, but rarely, this scrutiny has even been extremely critical, pointing to the lack of legitimacy of the Court in pursuing what is seen as a political role in favour of integration.[35] However, while lawyers have focused their attention on conceptualising and systematising that process of constitutionalisation and, in some cases, discussed its legitimacy by looking, almost exclusively, at the legal texts, political scientists, in their turn, tend to consider the Court and the law as mere instruments of political action directed towards integration and appear to ignore the normative questions of legitimacy and the autonomous constraints imposed by law and the judicial process on courts and other actors.[36]

To capture fully the process of constitutionalisation of Community law and understand the model of the European Economic Constitution one must go beyond formal conceptions of the law and the judicial role depicting that process and its outcomes simply as the mechanical consequence of legal

[32] J. Weiler, "Community, Member States and European Integration: Is the Law Relevant?", (1982) 25 *JCMS*, 39, at 39–40.

[33] M. Shapiro, "Comparative Law and Comparative Politics", (1980) 53 *Southern California Law Review*, 537, at 538.

[34] E. Stein, "Lawyers, Judges and the Making of a Transnational Constitution", (1981) 75 *American Journal of International Law*, 1.

[35] See H. Rasmussen, "Between Self-Restraint and Activism: A Judicial Policy for the European Court", (1988) 13 *ELR*, 28, and *On Law and Policy in the European Court of Justice* (Dordrecht, Martinus Nijhoff Publishers, 1986); Coppel and O'Neill, "The European Court of Justice: Taking Rights Seriously", (1992) 29 *CMLRev*, 669; and references given in Schepel and Wesseling, "The Legal Community: Judges, Lawyers, Officials and Clerks in the Writing of Europe", (1997) 3 *ELJ*, 165, at n.115.

[36] See C. Joerges, "Taking the Law Seriously: On Political Science and the Role of Law in the Process of European Integration", (1996) 2 *ELJ*, 105, mainly at 118–21.

interpretation and adjudication. But one must also not limit oneself to an instrumental and functional vision of law as a mere instrument of a larger political process, and must take into account the independent normative power of the law and the constraints of legal reasoning and legal discourse. Rules, reasons and institutions (including individual actors making use of the judicial process) are, thus, both conditions of the legitimacy of the Court and instruments and constraints of its role in the process of political and economic integration.

A normative assessment of the role of the Court must depart from the very nature of Community law itself and the legal reasoning adopted by the Court in its interpretation and application. It must also address the way the Court responds and promotes a discourse with the actors in the judicial process and with alternative institutions whose jurisdiction may conflict with that of the Court in interpreting Community law. At the same time, all these elements are also necessary factors to be taken into account in a political theory of legal integration. The nature of Community law and its influence in the role of the Court; the legal reasoning adopted in interpreting Community law and legitimising judicial action; and the relation with other actors in the national and European judicial and political processes, are all functions of the process of integration. One must look into all these elements to explain fully the process of constitutionalisation of Community law and the European economic constitutional model arising from it.

In the same way that legal reasoning and legal discourse can be seen as the pillars of the judicial self-construction of legitimacy, it must also be recalled that this internal perspective has to be complemented by an external perspective. In other words, legal reasoning and legal discourse cannot be seen simply from the internal perspective of the Court as mechanisms of decision-making, implementation and enforcement of judicial decisions. They are also to be seen and understood through the constraints imposed by other actors and institutions on the Court. In many cases, and, as will be discussed below, this is particularly so in the European Union system, the relation between the Court and other institutions is not ruled by a clear hierarchy. The consequence is that the result of this legal discourse between the Court and other institutions depends on the bargaining power of institutions and their management of contingent conflicts—a process easily explicable if one understands the process of interpretation and application of the norms also as a process of institutional choice. This is notably so in cases of constitutional review or in the adjudication of competences typical of divided-power systems. In these cases, one is not simply choosing among different interpretations of a norm but is also choosing among the institutions with jurisdiction to interpret the norm. When a Court declares that a certain legislation is unconstitutional it is denying an exercise of discretion by the legislator while ascertaining its own exercise of discretion in the interpretation of the constitutional norm at stake. In doing so, it restricts the jurisdiction of the legislator and expands its own. Since the jurisdiction of the courts and the legislator are not totally constitutionally determined, constitutional review always involves an institutional choice on who is constitutionally entitled to exercise discretion in that case. This also implies a constitutional conflict of jurisdiction that is traditionally embraced by the legal scholarship debates on the degrees, forms and criteria of judicial activism *vis-à-vis* the legislator. Moreover, such a conflict of jurisdiction and legitimacy is intentionally expected by the constitutional doctrine of checks and balances. At the same time, if it is true that, within the formal legal architecture of Constitutions, courts are usually given the final interpretative authority of the law (at least where there are some forms of judicial constitutional review), it is also true that, in real life, courts, including constitutional courts, are constrained by other sources and forms of power in the hands of institutions such as legislative bodies.

This discursive nature of institutional choice is even more so in the case of the European Union in which no clear hierarchical relation exists between national and Community institutions. In this case, the institutional choices mentioned are the result of a legal discourse in which different institutions participate without one institution retaining final interpretative authority. Even if, from the perspective of the Community legal system, the Court of Justice may appear as the final interpretative authority, in reality it depends and interacts with other institutions that within the logic of their internal legal systems are attributed the same authority. Thus, it is important to look at legal discourse both from the perspective of the Court's autonomous construction of the law and from an external perspective, that puts that autonomous construction of the law within the context of a discourse taking place with other institutions.

Here, the focus will be on how the characteristics and constraints of this process of constitutional creation through legal reasoning and legal discourse have favoured certain developments in the European Economic Constitution.

FRAMING THE CONSTITUTION I: LEGAL REASONING

When a Court is called upon to hear a case it must make a decision. Although a lawyer may defend more than one possible answer, a Court is expected to present its decision as the only decision—as the law. Law is both what the Court applies and what the Court decides. In the traditional understanding, the facts of the law (judicial decisions) will always correspond to the norms of law. This vision of law makes facts (judicial decisions) correspond to norms by negating discretion in the application and interpretation of norms. Legal reasoning is limited in this case to formal reasoning. However, it is now undisputed that this approach does not reflect the open texture and indeterminacy of the law,[37] an indeterminacy that is shared by Community law, in which it is, moreover, probably enhanced. Sources of indeterminacy or uncertainty in Community law are multiple.[38]

A fact that contributed largely to the crisis of formal reasoning was the extension of the "rule of law" to domains traditionally out of its range of action. The growth of administrative and constitutional law and the increase of social and economic regulation led to a change in the character of the law or, at least, to a change in the way in which law was conceived. Moreover, such branches of law are often characterised by the use of general principles and by the adoption of broad aims that exarcebate the linguistic indeterminacy of the law. The increase on social and economic regulation, in turn, gave rise to constant conflicts between the law and the environment in which the law is supposed to act. In Community law such a process is enhanced by the interplay of different legal and social cultures. The conflicts and contradictions between the aims of the law and the social systems it invades are bound to be reflected in the interpretation and application of the law. This is particularly so in the case of Community law, originally conceived of as market integration law and later raised to the status of "higher law" spilling over into other social and political areas in different national systems.

At the same time, the incapacity to reach decisions in the political forum has left judicial institutions with the responsibility for solving political conflicts. Sometimes this is even a conscious choice taken by political actors, either to avoid political conflicts or to confer on political decisions the legitimacy of the law. The law-making process in the European Union and the plurality of national and ideological interests therein, emphasises these problems:

[37] In the words of the classical legal philosopher Hart: "it is a feature of the human predicament (and so of the legislative one) that we labour under two connected handicaps whenever we seek to regulate, unambiguously and in advance, some sphere of conduct by means of general standards to be used without further official direction on particular occasions. The first handicap is our relative ignorance of fact: the second is our relative indeterminacy of aim", *The Concept of Law* (Oxford, Clarendon Press, 1961) (rep. from 1972), 125. Another well-known philosopher, Alexy, presents four reasons why "in many cases the singular normative statement which expresses a judgment resolving a legal dispute is not a logical conclusion derived from formulations of legal norms presupposed to be valid taken together with statements of fact which are assumed or proven to be true". These reasons are: "(1) the vagueness of legal language, (2) the possibility of conflict between norms, (3) the fact that there are cases requiring a legal statement which do not fall under any existing valid norm, and finally (4) the possibility, in special cases, of a decision which is contrary to the wording of the statute": R. Alexy, *A Theory of Legal Argumentation* (Clarendon Press, Oxford, 1989), 1, footnotes omitted. For other well-known opinions see Perelman, *Le Champ de l'argumentation*, (Bruxelles, Presses Universitaires de Bruxelles, 1970), at 143, and MacCormick, *Legal Reasoning and Legal Theory* (Oxford, Clarendon Press, 1978), at 68 . Note that none of these authors belongs to the school of Critical Legal Studies: to recognise the indeterminacy of the law, one does not need to go as far as Unger in saying that "it is always possible to find in actual legal materials radically inconsistent clues about the range of application of each of the models and indeed about the identity of the models themselves": R.M. Unger, *The Critical Legal Studies Movement*, (Cambridge/Massachusetts, Harvard University Press, 1983), 10.

[38] See T. Hartley, "Five Forms of Uncertainty in European Community Law", (1996) 55 *Cambridge Law Journal*, 265.

deadlocks in the legislative process lead the Court to intervene and supplement the work of the Community legislative process; and the lack of consensus among States leads them to adopt multi-meaning normative statements; "agreement is reached in the form of words when there is no agreement on what the words mean".[39] Thus political conflicts are shifted into the realm of judicial litigation. According to a former Court of Justice judge, Lord Mackenzie Stuart:

> "There has been a failure to take Community action where action is required . . . The result, so far as the Court is concerned, is that, from time to time, it has had to resolve problems in the absence of important guide-lines or, indeed, even of adequate rules of law relevant to the matter in hand. In the extreme case . . . it has been known for those who sought to negotiate a text, and who have been unable to agree, to settle for an ambiguous expression in the hope that the court would one day be able to resolve the ambiguity".[40]

In the absence of a political forum at the supra-national level,[41] political conflicts and the ideological moulding of constitutional law and politics is left in the hands of the judiciary. In consequence, the model of the Economic Constitution will depend, to a large extent, on those "feeding" the judicial process, who tend to vary, in participation and representation, from those "feeding" the political process.

Indeterminacy means that competitive interpretations of the law are possible and that the Court must choose among them. This implies an exercise of judicial discretion The use of this discretion takes many forms that can be found in the case law of the Court. The most visible form of judicial discretion lies in deciding between different possible major premises and applying them to the specific circumstances of a case. A very good example of vague Community law language requiring interpretative choices is precisely the reference in Article 30 EC to "measures having equivalent effect" to quantitative restrictions. We could describe this as substantive discretion, the same being the case when the Court decides upon different possible grounds on which to review a case by subsuming it under one of several possible norms. In some cases these conflicts of norms are clear, but quite often that is not the case, such as when something is classified as capital or goods[42] for the purposes of the rules of free movement, or when abortion is considered as covered by the definition of services given in Article 60.[43] The conception of Community law as an independent legal order and its constitutionalisation have also required a high degree of discretionary powers and legal construction beyond existing

[39] See T. Hartley, "Five Forms of Uncertainty in European Community Law", (1996) 55 *Cambridge Law Journal*, at 273.

[40] Lord Mackenzie Stuart, *The European Communities and the Rule of Law*, The Hamlyn Lectures, (London, Stevens & Sons, 1977), at 81.

[41] See Shapiro, "Comparative Law and Comparative Politics" (n.33), at 541.

[42] See Case 7/78, *Thompson*, [1978] ECR 2247.

[43] This has been one of the most discussed conclusions of the Court in the "Irish abortion" case, Case C–159/90, *SPUC* [1991] ECR I–4685.

norms: two possible examples are the protection of fundamental rights[44] and the liability of Member States for damages arising from the breach of Community law first established in *Francovich*.[45] A further form of discretion is what could be called selective input. Unlike the US Supreme Court, the Court of Justice does not have the prerogative to choose the cases it wants to deal with. However, it can determine its agenda in other ways. One form of "agenda setting" by the Court comes from the close co-operation with the Commission mentioned above. Another relates to the way in which Article 177 of the EC Treaty (references from national courts) is conceived: the Court can determine what, for the effects of Article 177, is a court or a tribunal of a Member State; it can decide the interpretation to give to a question from a national court; and it can define the boundary between an interpretation of the law (which it is empowered to do under that Article) and a decision upon a case (which it is prevented from taking). There are many ways in which the Court can manage its workload and set its "legal agenda", deciding if and how it wants to take up an issue presented to it by a national court. However, perhaps the most relevant form of selective input is the determination of the boundaries of its jurisdiction and the scope of Community law. A good example is the concept of "purely internal situations" developed by the Court: for example, national rules prohibited under the free movement rules are only so in their application to imports or foreigner nationals (except if home nationals have previously exercised free movement to another Member State). This reduces the scope of Community law and mitigates the deregulatory impact of the Court's decisions. A final form of discretion regards the consequences and follow up of judicial decisions (selective output), for example, by the greater or lesser discretion left to national courts in the application of Community law[46] or by imposing time limits on the effects of its judicial decisions.[47]

[44] See Case 44/79, *Hauer* [1979] ECR 3727. In *Hauer* a Community Regulation was challenged on the grounds of its alleged incompatibility with the right to property and the right freely to pursue trade and professional activities, protected by the German Constitution (Grundgesetz). The Court, however, considered that in order to protect the substantive unity and efficacy of Community law, a measure passed by Community institutions could only be judged in the light of Community law. It did not however used Community free movement rules in reviewing that legislation as some would argue (see below the economic due process approaches to Article 30 discussed throughout this book) but instead found support in the general legal principles of Community law in which was included the protection of fundamental rights. For the construction of this, the Court "draw[s] inspiration from constitutional traditions common to Member States" and from "international treaties for the protection of human rights on which the Member States have collaborated or of which they are signatories" (para 16).

[45] Joined Cases C–6/90 and C–9/90, *Francovich* [1991] ECR I–5357. Recently developed in Joined Cases C–46/93 and C–48/93, *Brasserie du Pêcheur* [1996] ECR I–1029.

[46] The answers given by the ECJ to national courts, under Article 177, on the interpretation of Community law are generally quite specific, and in many cases appear closer to a decision of the case, through an application of Community law to the facts presented by the national Court, than to a simple interpretation of Community rules. However, sometimes, the Court has left a great margin of discretion to national courts in the approach taken to the cases in hand, and in the interpretation of Community rules. A good example are the "Sunday Trading" cases. See, Chapter 3 below.

[47] That was the case, for example, in Case 43/75, *Defrenne* v. *Sabena* [1976] ECR 455 where

What is remarkable in the Court's case law is that the conflicts of values inherent in the exercise of discretion and the choices made thereon are not made explicit, but remain hidden behind formal reasoning. Under the formal conception of legal reasoning, judicial decisions do no more than apply a pre-existing rule to a concrete situation: this rule is the criterion of validity for the judicial decision. One can say that formal reasoning presents the solution to a certain case as the logical conclusion of an assumed premise. The measurement of validity is thus the measurement of correctness. The conclusion is either true or false, depending on whether it conforms to the logical requirements. There is no choice between conflicting values; and nor is there more than one valid answer.

Formal reasoning may be necessary (for example, to secure certainty and equality under the law), but it is no longer sufficient. Because formal arguments no longer provide all the legal answers, a justification based on formal arguments is, in many cases, no longer legitimate justification. Judicial neutrality, with reference to an ideal "robot-court", associated with syllogistic reasoning in the application and interpretation of law, does not correspond to the present complexity of the judicial process and the exercise of discretion it entails. This is by now a non-contentious assertion. The exercise of judicial discretion requires a different type of justification which MacCormick has called "second-order justification" involving "justifying choices; choices between the rival rulings which are possible".[48]

That has rarely been the case in the European Court of Justice case law, especially that regarding free movement rules and the European Economic Constitution. In part this has been accompanied by the formal approach to Community law adopted by the broader legal community of lawyers and academics.[49] The references to the legal formalism in the Court's reasoning have grown with the *Keck* decision in which the Court was seen both as creating an arbitrary and formal distinction between two different types of State measures and as not clearly identifying the reversal of its previous case law.[50] However, formalism has been a consistent element in the Court's case law, presenting the developments in Community law as a logical consequence of the Treaty rules and not as a result of any choice or exercise of discretion by the Court. This

the Court, having declared the direct effect of Article 119, restricted the retroactive effects of its judgment. The economic effects of the potential avalanche of actions brought to courts under the direct effect of Article 119, was decisive in convincing the ECJ to *condone* what itself considered as an illegal behaviour when ruling that: "the direct effect of Article 119 cannot be relied on in order to support claims concerning pay periods prior to the date of this judgment, except as regards those workers who have already brought legal proceedings or made an equivalent claim" (para 75).

[48] MacCormick, *Legal Reasoning* (n.37 above), at 101.

[49] See Shapiro, "Comparative Law and Comparative Politics" (n.33 above), and Schepel and Wesseling, "The Legal Community: Judges, Lawyers, Officials and Clerks in the Writing", (1997) 3 *European Law Journal*, 165.

[50] Joined Cases C–267 and C–268/91, *Keck and Mithouard* [1993] ECR I–6097. See the discussion in Chapter 3 below.

also prevented the Court seeing itself involved in the conflicts of value arising from the application of free movement rules to a large area of national economic, social and cultural policies. If one looks at *Dassonville,*[51] the leading case in free movement of goods, we find no "second-order justification". It is a clear example of formal reasoning. As is now well known, the main issue in *Dassonville* was the validity under Community law of a Belgian provision requiring that imported goods bearing a designation of origin should be accompanied by a certificate of origin. In answering to the question raised by the national court, the European Court interpreted first the notion of **measures having equivalent effect to quantitative restrictions** in Article 30 of the EC Treaty. The Court decided the major premise to be followed in its interpretation and application of the notion of measures of equivalent effect. It did not provide any arguments for the choice implied in that step of its reasoning. The Court stated:

> "All trading rules enacted by Member States which are capable of hindering, directly or indirectly, actually or potentially, intra-Community trade are to be considered as measures having an effect equivalent to quantitative restrictions".

The first question that comes to mind is *why* "all trading rules enacted by Member States which are capable of hindering, directly or indirectly, actually or potentially, intra-Community trade are to be considered as measures having an effect equivalent to quantitative restrictions"? No answer is provided by the Court in this respect. That Article 30 provided a choice among different major premises can be seen in various doctrinal debates on the topic. Is it not possible to argue that only measures discriminating against imported products are covered by Article 30?; has not the Court itself provided different interpretations of Article 30?;[52] does not the interpretation of Article 30 involve an allocation of competences between the EU and the Member States and a balance between different economic, social and cultural values?; if so, should that not be part of the Court's reasoning?; ought not, also, the Court to justify why different interpretations have been given to the various free movement rules?[53]

[51] Case 8/74, *Dassonville*, [1974] ECR 731.

[52] For some examples before *Dassonville*, see: Case 60/63R, *Albatros* v. *Sopéco* [1965] ECR 29; Case 25/67, *Fink-Frucht* v. *Hauptzollamt München* [1968] ECR 231; Case 7/68, *Commission* v. *Italy*, [1968] ECR 617. More difficult to assess is the decision in Joined Cases 51–54/71, *International Fruit Company* [1971] ECR 1106. In these cases it is quite unclear, however, what is for the ECJ the relevant criterion in the interpretation of Article 30. The Court considers as invalid under Articles 30 and 34 a national provision "which requires, even purely as a formality, import or export licences or any other similar procedure". For Alfonso Mattera, in *Le Marché Unique Européen* (Paris, Jupiter, 1988), 440, this decision establishes the irrelevance of the discriminatory criterion, as the Court abstained from looking at the treatment given to national products and did not inquire as to the discriminatory or non-discriminatory character of the measures involved. However, it is possible to argue that it is precisely because exports or imports licences are by their very nature discriminatory (they only apply to exports or imports) that the Court did not allow them.

[53] Case 15/79, *Groenveld* [1979] ECR 3409, which dealt mainly with Article 34, the wording of which is exactly the same as that of Article 30. In *Groenveld* the Court used, in the

The adoption of formal reasoning as a model of justification in the Court's decisions[54] is, in part, a consequence of legal traditions in Member States that are, nevertheless, becoming outdated. For the European Court of Justice, the adoption of formal reasoning responded to the need to establish its judicial authority by preserving an image of neutrality and impartiality.[55] Paradoxically, however, inadequate formal justification enhances judicial discretion. The exercise of discretion by the Court is hidden under the cover of syllogistic reasoning that presents the decisions of the Court as the only possible legal decisions. At the same time the critique of judicial decisions tends to be limited to the realm of formal law.

This may, in part, explain why academic commentators have been for so long so deferential towards the Court and why their work has consisted mainly of an exegesis of the Court's case law. According to Weiler:

> "The overall response, of academia—political science, economics and law—to the judicially-driven constitutional revolution has ranged from indifference and equanimity to celebration . . . Even more interesting was the almost non-critical approach and tradition developed by European Community law".[56]

In this sense, as already mentioned, legal writers have adopted "the case-law as the inevitable working out of the correct implications of the constitutional text".[57] In part, this is a consequence of the legal formalism in which the decisions were vested.[58] Due to the self-referential nature of legal formalism, it is difficult to enter into a critical discourse. What has happened is that academic authors have presented their own ideas as if they were the Court's

interpretation of Article 34, the very same formal reasoning that was present in the interpretation of Article 30 in *Dassonville,* but with opposite results: "Article 34 of EEC Treaty provides that 'quantitative restrictions on exports, and all measures having equivalent effect, shall be prohibited between Member States'. That provision concerns national measures which have as their specific object or effect the restriction of patterns of exports and thereby the establishment of a difference in treatment between the domestic trade of a Member State and its export trade in such a way as to provide a particular advantage for national production or for the domestic market of the State in question at the expense of the production or of the trade of other Member States" (paras 7 and 8).

This was subsequently confirmed in other decisions. See, for example, Case 155/80, *Oebel* [1981] ECR 1993 (para 15) and Case 286/81, *Oosthoek's* [1982] ECR 4575 (para 13).

[54] This is not an undisputed opinion. Bengoetxea, in what is, to the author's knowledge, the only attempt to date of a legal theory analysis of the Court's case law, makes a very favourable review of the Court's legal reasoning. See J. Bengeotxea, *The Legal Reasoning of the European Court of Justice* (Oxford, Clarendon Press, 1993).

[55] In this sense, Weiler, "Journey to an Unknown Destination" (n.8 above), at 423–4.

[56] Weiler, "Journey to an Unknown Destination" (n.8 above), at 431 and 432.

[57] Shapiro, "Comparative Law and Comparative Politics" (n.33 above), at 538.

[58] Schepel and Wesseling ("The Legal Community" (n.49 above)) have also called attention to the rather "incestuous" character of much of Community law legal writing, that tends to be dominated by those working at Community institutions. This can be considered, at the same time, as a consequence and an enhancing factor of the self-referential character of Community law and the limited community of interests and actors having the information and organisation required to participate effectively in EU legal discourse.

own interpretation, thus hoping to enhance the chances of these ideas being adopted as the "official" line of the Court.[59]

The main consequence of formal reasoning is that the internal logic of legal rules is made the determinant factor of interpretation, independent of the context. Conflicts of values in the application of these rules are either ignored or assumed not to exist. In reality, such conflicts of value are inevitable in judicial decisions and the consequence of formal reasoning is simply that the balance of such values undertaken by the Court is either hidden or unconsciously made.[60] This is the more so in a field such as Community law, where the scope of free movement rules has been extended much beyond its natural area. A specific legal logic is transplanted to new fields without contextualisation; in other words, without being adapted to its new functions. The Court's expansion of Community law jurisdiction through free movement rules, elevated market integration to the controlling rationale in the new areas of the law covered by the supremacy of Community law. In the words of Judge Pescatore it was "the economic and juridical union, as *the supreme objective*, that provided the decisive grounds for a great number of decisions concerning the problems raised by the establishment of the Common Market".[61] Another well known former judge of the Court has described this as an "instrumentalist" approach, becoming increasingly apparent in cases like *Cassis de Dijon* and *Reyners*.[62] The extensive interpretation of the four freedoms, necessary for achieving the common market and legal integration, led to an overflow of market integration law into political and social spheres. This was instrumental in the general process to which Burley and Mattli refer as substantial penetration of EC law,[63] and Sabino Cassese as "*'comunitarizazione' di funzione nazionali*".[64] The consequence of this spill-over of Community economic rules, with their own particular internal logic, into all areas of national regulation, was the promotion of negative integration.[65] In reality, the effect

[59] The exceptions, in turn, tend to be rather strong critiques on the "general policy" of the Court, seen as instrumental activism in favour of integration. See references given in n.35 above.

[60] A danger which Holmes, the famous American Justice of the Supreme Court. has long ago highlighted: "I think that judges themselves have failed adequately to recognize their duty of weighing considerations of social advantage. The duty is inevitable, and the result of the often proclaimed judicial aversion to deal with such considerations is simply to leave the very ground and foundation of judgments inarticulate, and often unconscious": "The Path of the Law", (1897) 10 *Harvard Law Review*, 457, at 467.

[61] In the original: "l'unite economique et juridique, comme objectif supreme, qui a fourni les themes decisifs d'un grand nombre d'arrets portant sur les problemes souleves par la mise en ouevre du marche commun": Pescatore, *Le droit de l'integration* (Genève, A.W. Sijthoff—Leiden, 1972), at 81 (translation by the author—emphasis added).

[62] T. Koopmans, "The Role of Law in the Next Stage of European Integration", (1986) *International and Comparative Law Quarterly*, 925, at 927.

[63] "Europe Before the Court" (n.8 above), at 43.

[64] "La Costituzione Europea" (n.10 above), at 487.

[65] Negative integration can be described as the process of integration through deregulation at the national level or, in other words, by eliminating State legislation which restricts market integration. This is opposed to positive integration where market integration is promoted through the enactment of harmonised legislation at the Community level. The functionalist view of

intended was to increase Community powers over those areas ("communitarizzazione" or, as will be used later, europeanisation).

This expansion of market rules into other areas of the law is not, as implied by formal reasoning, a neutral policy. It involves choices between conflicting values. The Court is bound either to balance such values without admitting that it is so doing or to ignore such conflicts and the consequences that a formal application of the rules has upon them. This has been perfectly depicted by Paul Davies:

> "two different hypotheses about the Court's approach to justification and the balancing of Community and Member State policies could explain the decisions handed down. The first is that the overt situation reflects the actual situation i.e. that no balancing is going on within the Court . . . the Court simply decided what interpretation of Community law is required by the policy of market integration . . . The national social policies (and indeed any other Member State policies) then are either struck down or escape intact as an incidental consequence of the prior decision taken by the Court as to the scope of Community law
>
> The alternative analysis is that there is a balancing process going on in the Court but that it is not an overt but rather hidden one . . . the balancing process is hidden behind the Court's decisions on the scope of the Treaty articles".[66]

The use of formal reasoning explains why conflicts of values and morals, such as those involved in cases on "abortion" or "pornography", are ignored or appear to be so. In the USA, formal reasoning has been criticised as closely associated with a vision of judicial neutrality based on inaction *vis-à-vis* both the status quo as defined by the common law, and the distribution of wealth which it protects.[67]. It has also been argued that in *Dassonville*, for example, the Court of Justice adopted a similar vision of "normality".[68] Translated into current European jargon, this means that deregulation will be the substantive outcome of the balancing of values hidden in the application of the Treaty rules on the Common Market. However, as will be argued in Chapter 3, there is not a "*laissez faire*" policy guiding the decisions of the Court; rather, cases have been decided from a majoritarian point of view, taking the European Union as the relevant political community.

European integration expected that negative integration would be followed by positive integration but that was not to happen because of the deadlocks in the Community decision-making process (responsible for the promotion of positive integration). See A.R. Leitão, "Quelques réflexions politco-juridiques autour de l'élimination des mesures d'effet équivalent: unité du marché commun, principe logique ou principe organique?", (1986) *Revue du Marché Commun*, 21, at 23.

[66] P. Davies, "Market Integration and Social Policy in the Court of Justice", (1995) 24 *Industrial Law Journal*, 49, at 67.

[67] See D. Kennedy, "Form and Substance in Private Law Adjudication", (1976) 89 *Harvard Law Review*, 1685, mainly at 1754 and 1755; and C.R. Sunstein, "Lochner's Legacy", (1987) 87 *Columbia Law Review*, 873, at 874.

[68] According to Joel Paul: "The assumption of market normalcy is implicit in the European Court of Justice's landmark judgment in *Dassonville*. The Court's judgment treated the market as the normal state which exists prior to the distortion of national laws": "Free Trade, Regulatory Competition and the Autonomous Market Fallacy", (1994/95) 1 *Columbia Journal of European Law*, 29, at 39.

The explanation of the use of formal reasoning by the Court of Justice lies in the concerns over legitimacy discussed above. Formal reasoning corresponded to the traditional understanding of the Court's legitimacy. It allowed the expansion of Community law to be presented as a logical process of legal reasoning. It also allowed for the political effects and conflicts of values arising from that expansion to be hidden in the legal language and, in this way, insulated from political and social conflicts.

This also helps in explaining the adoption of a majoritarian approach. If the intention was not to implement a specific economic vision but to promote a process of europeanisation of regulatory law, what could fit better with this than the review of national regulations under "European" criteria? The increased scope of free movement rules, supported by formal reasoning, was tempered with a majoritarian (in a European scale) review of State regulation. This also permitted the Court to avoid entering into complex policy judgements (which could be open to criticism) regarding conflicting values in the application of those rules. It was another form of securing legitimacy while promoting market integration. Formal reasoning was the legal authority behind the Court's expansion of the scope of Community law rules and of market integration; the majoritarian approach was the policy authority behind the outcome of the Court's decisions.

FRAMING THE CONSTITUTION II: LITIGATION

Litigation is the core of legal discourse when approached from an internal perspective of the legal system. From an internal point of view, legal discourse concerns the way in which the Court structures the judicial process, in defining the actors, the arguments and the competences therein. The structuring of the European legal discourse by the Court played a relevant role in the legitimation of European Community law and its process of constitutionalisation. At the same time, the nature of Community law and the litigation it has generated have had an important impact on the model of the European Economic Constitution. On the one hand, the broad scope and the uncertainty of free movement provisions have promoted litigation and offered new grounds of challenge to legislation by individuals. Community law has been a new source of legal arguments even in a purely national context. On the other hand, the self-referential nature of Community law previously highlighted, the resources and information needed to use it, and its functional link to market integration, have all shaped Community litigation. This, in turn, being the fuel of the process of constitutionalisation, played a fundamental role in shaping the European Economic Constitution.

The broad scope given by the European Court of Justice to Article 30 in the review of national measures[69] has promoted European legal discourse and

[69] See Chapter 3 below.

served in both the legitimation of Community law and the constitutional construction of Community law.

Article 30 of the EC Treaty is one of the general principles of Community law. According to former Judge Everling, it was necessary for the Court in its formative years to lay down some general, broad principles which it could limit later; Judge Everling cites Article 30 as a concrete example of this.[70] In this sense, the broad scope given to Article 30 in reviewing State measures was important not only as a means of establishing that Community law has a general supervisory power over national law, but also in defining the hierarchy among those legal orders for the purposes of Community law.[71] For this to occur the Court could not allow Community law to be dependent upon the will of the Member States. It needed other interlocutors in its relations with national legal orders. In this sense, the wide scope given to Article 30 was important in establishing and enhancing a direct discourse with national courts and individuals. The direct effect of Article 30, and its broad scope in reviewing almost any national regulation, made it one of the main instruments of communication with national courts and individuals. It became a leading instrument in what Volcansek has characterised as "a pattern of positive reinforcement for national courts seeking preliminary rullings".[72] Furthermore, the nature of the subject matter to be discussed under Article 30 EC is economic and commercial: this could be expected to result in national economic actors exerting strong pressures on national courts to enforce the conditions for competition offered by the EC Treaty. Following on a French report by Jens Plötner, Alec Stone advanced the thesis that "the more a court is faced with commercial litigation, the more pressure a court comes under to function as a Community court".[73] Thus, an enhanced Article 30 will allow private interests to push more strongly in favour of European integration, as anticipated by the neo-functionalist vision of Europe: a conclusion which is reinforced, in terms of litigation, by a correlation recently highlighted by Golub, between the importance of trade and the number of Article 177

[70] U. Everling, "The Court of Justice as a Decision Making Authority", in Michigan Law Review (ed.), *The Art of Governance: Festschrift in Honor of Eric Stein*, Baden-Baden, Nomos Verlagsgesellschaft, 1987), 156, at 162–3.

[71] According to Mauro Cappelletti and David Golay: "Legal integration in the federal or transnational union requires initially, therefore, acceptance of a legal hierarchy . . . Maintaining the supremacy of the federal or transnational law, must be therefore, the initial contribution of the judiciary to legal integration in the federal or transnational union": M. Cappelletti, and D. Golay, *Judicial Review, Transnational and Federal: Its Impact on Integration*, EUI Working Paper (Florence, Sept. 1981), at 3, or The Judicial Branch in the Federal and Transnational Union: Its Impact on Integration, in M. Cappelletti, M. Seccombe, J. Weiler (eds.), *Integration Through Law*, vol 1, book 2, (Berlin, New York, Walter de Gruyter, 1986), 261–351.

[72] In her words: "the Court of Justice accepted all conceivable requests from national courts and invited wide participation": M.L. Volcansek, *Judicial Politics in Europe* (New York, Lang, 1986), at 265.

[73] A. Stone, *Constitutional Dialogues in the European Community*, EUI Working Paper RSC 95/38, (Florence, 1995), at 26. See also, the report by J. Plötner, *The European Court and National Courts — Doctrine and Jurisprudence: Legal Change in its Social Context, Report on France*, EUI Working Paper RSC 95/28, (Florence, 1995), mainly at 27.

references to the European Court.[74] To sum up one could say, along with Burley and Mattli, that "the Court created a pro-community constituency of private individuals by giving them a direct stake in promulgation and implementation of Community law",[75] and that Article 30 (together with other free movement rules) played a key role in this.

This also promoted co-operation and discourse with national courts, helping to establish the autonomy and authority of Community law. National courts are responsible for the effective integration of Community law into national legal orders; in ensuring its ranking as supreme to national law; and in accepting and applying the principles of direct effect and of supremacy. Direct effect makes Community law part of national legal orders; supremacy places it first in the hierarchy of national legal orders. In the words of Weiler: "the combination of the two doctrines means that Community norms that produce direct effects are not merely the Law of the Land but the 'Higher Law' of the Land".[76] Article 30 is not simply an example of this process. Given the broad interpretation made of it by the European Court, it allowed a particular kind of discourse to be developed with national courts, involving the entire spectrum of the national legal order. First, it was, as stated, one of the main channels of communication with national courts and individuals. It has always been one of the Articles of the EC Treaty most used in Article 177 references to the Court. Secondly, due to the broad scope for review of national regulations, it was one of the main instruments in the process of giving national courts powers of judicial review (empowerment), an aspect that several authors identify as very important in understanding the co-operation between national courts and the European Court.[77]

The second important aim to be achieved in promoting legal discourse through Article 30 is that of legitimation. By enhancing the participation of individuals, the Court established a new source of legitimation both for itself and for Community law. Legitimation will no longer come exclusively from States indirectly, but will lie in a direct relation with the "peoples of Europe". The broad scope granted to Article 30 allowed an ever-growing participation

[74] J. Golub, "Judicial Cooperation Between National Courts and the European Court of Justice: the Politics and Patterns of Preliminary References", Paper presented at the 37th Annual Convention of the International Studies Association, (San Diego, CA), 16–20 April 1996, at 7–10 and 15.

[75] Burley and Mattli, "Europe Before the Court" (n.8 above), at 60. In the same sense, J.H.H. Weiler, "A Quiet Revolution" (n.9 above), at 521.

[76] "The transformation of Europe", (1990–91) 100 *Yale Law Journal*, 2403, at 2415.

[77] According to Weiler, the key idea, is that: "Lower courts and their judges were given the facility to engage with the highest jurisdiction in the Community and, even more remarkable, to gain the power of judicial review over executive and legislative branches even in those jurisdictions where such judicial power was weak or non-existent", J.H.H. Weiler, "Journey to an Unknown Destination" (n.8 above), at 425. Also, in "A Quiet Revolution" (n.9 above), at 523. Reviewing different national reports on the issue, see: K. Alter, *The European Court and National Courts — Doctrine and Jurisprudence: Legal Change in its Social Context, Explaining National Court Acceptance of European Court Jurisprudence. A Critical Evaluation of Theories of Legal Integration*, EUI Working Paper RSC No. 95/27 (Florence, 1995), at 16–17.

of individuals, and an ever-growing acknowledgement of the new rights and voice brought to them by Community law.[78] According to Ole Due, former President of the Court:

> "it is remarkable . . . that those judgements which are often described as landmarks have generally contributed to promoting integration and at the same time to protecting the legal position of individual citizens and undertakings vis-à-vis both the authorities of the Member States and the Community institutions".[79]

Even if one does not to share the view that the legitimacy of European law is founded on individual rights as opposed to all forms of public power,[80] one must recognise the importance of granting new rights to individuals as a form of legitimation; and even as a way to gain social legitimacy in compensation for the loss of formal legitimacy resulting from the developments in the integration process (the classic democratic deficit).[81]

The establishment of this dialogue between national courts and individuals on the one hand and the European Court of Justice on the other could not be restrained to a single direction. Litigation was the fuel of the process of constitutionalisation but, at the same time, moulded the Economic Constitution arising from that process. Many of the important developments in the European Economic Constitution and Article 30 have been triggered by individuals and national courts. So, as formal constitutions are mainly a product of the representation and participation in the political process, so too is the European Economic Constitution, to a large extent, a result of participation and representation in the European judicial process. This may explain developments towards deregulation at national level arising from the European Economic Constitution. The litigation that has supported and promoted such a constitution has been based on market integration rules (notably Article 30) and affected by the role of repeated litigants and the information costs typical of a new legal order characterised by s strong self-referential character. Thus, it is not surprising for companies to have started much of the discovery process of the new constitution and to have lead to some of its most important developments. The same has not been the case with other actors'

[78] According to Keeling and Mancini: "the consequence is a vicious circle. More and more Europeans are aware that a law higher than the statutes enacted by Parliaments bestows upon them rights which are, in the last analysis, protected by the body interpreting the law. This growing awareness increases the visibility of the Court . . . and the legitimacy thus aquired by the Court reverberates in the law which the Court administers and enlarges expectations which ordinary people found on its provisions": "Democracy and the European Court of Justice", (1994) 57 *MLR*, 175, at 187.

[79] O. Due, "The Law-making Role of the European Court of Justice Considered in Particular from the Perspective of Individuals and Undertakings", (1994) 63 *Nordic Journal of International Law*, 123, at 126.

[80] E.J. Mestmäcker, "On the Legitimacy of European Law", 58 RabelsZ 1994, 615, at 631–2.

[81] On the relation between social legitimacy and formal legitimacy in the Community, see J.H.H. Weiler, "Problems of Legitimacy in Post 1992 Europe", 46 Aussenwirschaft 1991, 411, at 416.

promotion of other Community rules.[82] Litigation actors have given "life" to the constitutional "body" created by the Court but, in doing this, they have also impacted on the "soul".

The patterns of Community law litigation on Article 30 EC and other Community rules in pushing for policy changes, even if purely at a national level, are rather visible. Article 30 is the "European defence" of domestic actors against national policies.[83] One example of this are the "Sunday Trading" cases, through which a group of national litigants has managed to change national political and legal outcomes deregulating, at least for some years, Sunday trading.[84] Also, according to Alter and Meunier-Aitsahalia, the famous *Cassis de Dijon* case "was selected as a test case by the plaintiff's lawyer to . . . provoke harmonization of the alcohol industry".[85] One can highlight some "professional" litigants of Community law such as Denkavit, a company that has managed to bring cases before the European Court of Justice 21 times. There are other well known cases in the realm of Article 30 EC: Leclerc, in France, has challenged national regulations on TV advertising and on fixed prices for books and fuel, through both Article 30 EC and the competition rules of the Treaty; another well known Article 30 EC litigant is GB-INNO which has litigated at least four relevant cases in the area of free movement of goods and the European Economic Constitution.[86] In challenging such diverse and "neutral" (in terms of trade impact) regulations, these litigants have had a real effect on the Court's case law on Article 30 EC. They have also raised the possibility of new trends in European Community law, such as that of an interconnected use of free movement and competition rules. On the one hand, this helps the legitimacy of Community law which provides individuals with new rights *vis-à-vis* national political processes and gives them an important "voice" in the discourse shaping the European Economic Constitution. It may also help in promoting legislative innovation at national level and challenging national regulatory regimes dominated by special interests. On the other hand, not only may Community law undermine national democratic legitimacy, it may undermine its own legitimacy due to the amount and type of litigation brought by the wide scope of free movement rules. Moreover, the "voice" given to individuals is not necessarily the same. Powerful corporations, for instance, tend to be "repeat players"[87] and thus are

[82] With regard to social provisions, see C. Ball, "The Making of a Transnational Capitalist Society: The Court of Justice, Social Policy, and Individual Rights Under the European Community's Legal Order", (1996) 37 Harvard International Law Journal, 307, at 319.

[83] See, R. Rawlings, "The Eurolaw Game: Deductions from a Saga", (1993) 20 *Journal of Law and Society*, 309, mainly at 332.

[84] Ibid, at 313.

[85] Alter and Meunier-Aitsahalia, "Judicial Politics in the European Community—European Integration and the Pathbreaking Cassis de Dijon Decision" (1994) 26 Comparative Political Studies, 535.

[86] See Chapter 3 below.

[87] See the example of Sunday trading: Rawlings, "The Eurolaw Game" (n.84 above), at 309 and 315.

able to use and participate in the European legal discourse to a much higher degree than individuals. As a consequence, the European Economic Constitution may be perceived as a biased process. This can be presented as another form of "democratic deficit". Perhaps, more than a democratic deficit, it would be more appropriate to speak of a constitutional deficit: the spill-over of market integration rules into virtually all areas of the law has remained "prisoner" of formal reasoning and the constitutional limits of the Treaties; the functional use of market integration rules and the associated litigation have been the object of a limited community of interests and actors; there has been no political discourse developed at the supra-national level; the logic of market integration dominates the European Economic Constitution and its supremacy over national law. This has created or deepened a constitutional deficit in the European Union constitutional order.

FRAMING THE CONSTITUTION III: LEGAL DISCOURSE AND LEGAL PLURALISM

National courts have not been passive instruments in the "Europeanisation" of national legal orders. They have been active participants in the construction of the Community legal order, and, moreover, they have entered into a true discourse with the Court of Justice beyond any hierarchical construction of the law. In this latter sense, national courts have been essential participants in the legal discourse as seen from the external point of view.

Law has always been conceived as hierarchically organised. There was always something—a "grundnorm", "a set of rules of recognition", or positivised natural law—conceived of as the "higher law" of the legal system: the criterion of validity for all other legal norms. The internal conception of the Community legal order was also made to fit this model by the European Court of Justice. Community primary law will be the "higher law" of the Union,[88] the criterion of validity of secondary rules and decisions as well as that of all national legal rules and decisions within its scope. Moreover, the Court of Justice is the higher court of this legal system and therefore enjoys the monopoly of interpretation of the rules.[89] However, a different perspective is taken by national legal orders and national constitutions. Here, Community law owes its supremacy to its reception by a higher national law (normally constitutions). The higher law remains, in the national legal orders, the national constitution and the "*kompetenz/kompetenz*" (to decide the conflicts of jurisdiction between legal orders) belongs to national constitutional courts. This

[88] One can even rank some rules higher than others; raised to the status of material limits on the revision of the Treaty on European Union; but that discussion will not be entered into in here.

[89] See below as to the problems raised by the exclusion of its jurisdiction in some areas of the Treaty on the European Union.

is the logic behind the German Constitutional Court decision on Maastricht,[90] which is shared by many other constitutional courts and by many national constitutional doctrines. In this way, the "*kompetenz/kompetenz*" problem, when viewed from a perspective outside both national and Community legal orders, requires a conception of the law which is no longer dependent upon a hierarchical construction. In reality both the European Court of Justice and national courts are aware that neither of them has absolute power or supremacy over the other, and in this way, they are encouraged to engage in a discourse.

A pluralist construction of the relations between the European Union legal order and national legal orders has as yet only been sketched out in an article by Neil MacCormick.[91] In this article, adopting Hart's concept of "rules of recognition", MacCormick noted that national and European legal orders could well have different rules of recognition, without the different rules necessarily clashing with each other. For example, the supremacy of Community law over a national rule may be recognised either directly through the doctrine of supremacy as set up by the European Court or by founding such supremacy on national constitutional law reception. Conflicts will be contingent since each legal order, and institutions thereof, perceives and avoids conflicts the cost of which would be higher than a compromise. This is visible in the dialogue that has been taking place between national courts (notably constitutional courts) and the European Court of Justice in the area of fundamental rights.[92] A dialogue recognised by Bruno de Witte:

> "The relationship between Community law and the national constitutions is not to be settled according to unilateral principles of hierarchy . . . Both the Court of Justice and the national constitutional and Supreme Courts could recognise that the relationship can be seen from two different, but equally legitimate, perspectives and that there is now a plurality of "supreme texts" in Europe".[93]

It is not, however, intended to develop here any such analysis of European legal discourse.[94] The aim is simply to note how the existence of this legal discourse constrains the European Court of Justice and affects its case law on Article 30. Moreover, effective constraints do not simply flow from a discourse with national courts or other national institutions. They also arise from a discourse with the political and legislative actors of the Community.

[90] It stated: "the German Federal Constitutional Court must examine the question of whether or not legal instruments of European institutions and governmental entities may be considered to remain within the bounds of the sovereign rights accorded to them, or whether they may be considered to exceed those bounds": (para C-I–3, unofficial translation from (1994) 33 *International Legal Materials*, 395).

[91] R.N. MacCormick, "Beyond the Sovereign State", (1993) 56 *MLR*, 1.

[92] See for example, B. de Witte, "Community Law and National Constitutional Values", (1991/2) *LIEI*, 1, at 22; Mancini, "The Making of a Constitution" (n.2 above), at 608; T. de la Mare, *Judicial Cross-Fertilisation in the European Community*, (Thesis submitted for the degree of LLM at the European University Institute, 28 February 1995, 22).

[93] B. de Witte, "Community Law", (n. 92 above) at 22.

[94] For a more developed analysis of this type see de la Mare, *Judicial Cross-Fertilisation* (n.92 above).

An example of a discourse with national courts in the realm of Article 30 can be seen again in the "Sunday Trading" cases. In the first of these cases which concerned the validity of legislation restricting trade on Sundays, the Court, though appearing to uphold the restrictions, was not very decisive and clear in its answer, preferring to leave this political "hot potato" to national courts by putting in their hands the assessment of whether or not "the effects of specific national rules do in fact remain within . . . the effects intrinsic to trade rules" and do not "exceed what is necessary to achieve the aim in view".[95] This led to different decisions being taken by different British courts in the assessment of the proportionality of such regulations.[96] This created a threat to uniformity that was reflected in the further references to the Court, and in the Court's clarification of its position in *Marchandise*[97] and *Conforama*,[98] two cases regarding similar French and Belgium legislation. The discourse with national courts becomes particularly evident when the British regulations are again sent for review in the Court of Justice by the House of Lords. The drafting of the questions by the House of Lords clearly expresses its dissatisfaction with the previous European Court decision that, as noted, had left the "hot potato" in the hands of national courts and led to growing litigation and contrasting decisions on the subject of Sunday trading in the British judicial system. The questions were:

> "1. Whether the effect of the Court of Justice's rulings in Cases C–312 *Conforama* and C–332/89 *Marchandise* is to determine that the prohibition contained in Article 30 of the EEC Treaty does not apply to national rules, such as those in issue in Case 145/88 *Torfaen Borough Council* v. *B & Q plc*, which prohibit retailers from opening their premises on Sunday for the serving of costumers with certain goods;
>
> 2. If not, whether it is nevertheless immediately apparent, whether or not evidence is adduced, that the restrictive effects on intra-Community trade which may result from national rules such as those of Question 1 above do not exceed the "effects intrinsic to rules of that kind", as that phrase is used in the ruling of the Court of Justice in Case 145/88;
>
> 3. If not, on what criteria and by reference to what, if any, factual or other evidence the national court must determine the question whether or not the restrictive effects on intra-Community trade which may result from national rules such as those in Question 1 above exceed "the effects intrinsic to national rules of that kind" within the meaning of that phrase as used in the ruling of the Court in Case 145/88".

The House of Lords declared its lack of satisfaction with a role that it saw as political[99] and demanded a clear answer from the European Court, in effect, pushing the responsibility of the decision back to the Court of Justice.

[95] Case C–145/88, *Torfaen Borough Council* [1989] ECR 3851, paras 15–16.

[96] See a review in A. Arnull, "What shall we do on Sunday?", (1991) 16 *ELR*, 112.

[97] Case C–322/89, *Marchandise* [1991] ECR I–1027.

[98] Case C–312/89, *Conforama* [1991] ECR I–997.

[99] See Rawlings, "The Eurolaw Game" (n.84 above), at 318.

And it succeeded, since the Court, finally and clearly stated that such legislation was valid under Article 30 of the Treaty.

The shaping of the Court's case law by a legal discourse which it does not control, but where it is instead often dependent on other institutions, is also visible in its relations with the Community legislative and political processes. A good example of this is the reaction of the Community legislative process to the *Cassis de Dijon*[100] decision of the Court, in which, in order to break down existing restrictions to trade, it introduced a principle of mutual recognition among national regulations, tempered by a rule of reason or mandatory requirements. The reaction of the Community legislative process—the communication on *Cassis de Dijon* and the white paper from the Commission; the new approach to harmonisation; and, the internal market programme in general—cannot be seen exclusively as a reflection of the Court's policy as laid down in *Cassis de Dijon*.[101] It also shows the Community political process regaining control over the internal market programme.[102] According to Berlin, as long as the "lawmakers" of the European Union (Council, Commission and Parliament) stand united in the control of the single market they "could adopt measures limiting the exercise of the major freedoms contained in the Treaties for the sake of the Community public wealth" without fear of Court intervention.[103] The policy developed by the Community legislative process was quite different from a straightforward follow-up to the Court's establishment of the principle of mutual recognition;[104] but it is also undisputed that the Court's decision had a decisive impact in the development of the internal market programme. Thus, the retaking of control by the Community political process was not done at the cost of a direct confrontation with the Court. Similarly, the Court has not pushed the principle of mutual recognition advanced in *Cassis de Dijon* to its limits: aware of the strong opposition of some politicians and interest groups to a general application of this principle, the Court maintained a close link with the rule of reason and other exceptions to the principle.[105] Moreover, it has reconciled the application of mutual recognition with the interests of the Member States through the majoritarian approach (from a European standpoint) followed in reviewing State regulations under Article 30 EC, as will be described in Chapter 3.

[100] Case 120/78, *Rewe-Zentral AG* v. *Bundesmonopolverwaltung für Branntwein* [1979] ECR 649.

[101] On these reactions see Alter and Meunier-Aitsahalia, Judicial Politics n.85.

[102] See M. van Empel, "The 1992 Programme: Interaction Between Legislator and Judiciary", (1992/2) *LIEI*, 1, at 5 and A. Easson, "Legal Approaches to European Integration: The Role of Court and Legislator in the Completion of the European Common Market", (1989) *Revue d'Integration Europeén*, 101, at 101–2.

[103] D. Berlin, "Interactions Between the Lawmaker and the Judiciary within the EC", (1992/2) *LIEI*, 17, at 44.

[104] Alter and Meunier-Aitsahalia, Judicial Politics n.85, at 554.

[105] Ibid, at 547.

In addition, the specificity of the European legal discourse may well help in understanding current developments in the Court's case law, such as those highlighted in the *Keck* decision on Article 30 EC.[106] The Court has been under attack for excessive activism in law-making, both in the political debates over Maastricht, and in judicial decisions such as those of the German Constitutional Court.[107] These "visions" of the Court were reflected in the exclusion of European Court of Justice jurisdiction from the third pillar under the Treaty of the European Union and in the limits imposed on the potential effects of the *Barber* decision.[108] Moreover, even academic criticism is increasing.[109] The present aspects of self-restraint shown in the Court's case law are to some extent an answer by the Court to the pressures placed on it by the European legal discourse. This has been recognised by a judge of the Court.[110] The recognition of a European legal discourse between the Court and other actors implies, however, two further and important changes in the way in which we conceive the case law of the Court and the way in which the Court itself sees and constructs its own role. It requires a comparative institutional analysis. Judicial decisions imply institutional choices that require all institutional alternatives to be taken into account. In a context of legal discourse, institutional choices deserve particular attention and a proper framework, such as comparative institutional analysis. This will also help us in understanding and structuring the process of constitutional creation as the product of a larger community of actors and not simply a direct result of the European Court's European vision. Legal discourse also requires us to understand judicial decisions in view of institutional alternatives to the courts. This may explain variations in the European Court of Justice case law with regard to the free movement of goods. These two perspectives will be developed throughout this book.

[106] See Chapter 3 below.

[107] See, for example, S. Boom, "The European Union After the Maastricht Decision: Will Germany Be the 'Virginia of Europe'?", (1995) 43 *The American Journal of Comparative Law*, 177.

[108] Protocol Concerning Article 119 of the Treaty Establishing the European Community.

[109] Weiler, "Journey to an Unknown Destination" (n.8 above), at 443–4, and Schepel and Wesseling, "The Legal Community" (n.35 above), at 184.

[110] See Mancini, "The European Court of Justice Trade in Services and Trade Related Aspects of the Protection of Industrial and Intellectual Property Rights", in Davies, Lyon Caen, Sciarra and Simitis (eds.), *Principles and Perspectives on European Community Law* (Oxford, Oxford University Press, 1996).

2

The Classical Readings of Article 30 and the European Economic Constitution

This chapter is intended to highlight the need to introduce constitutional and institutional choice analyses in the traditional debates on Article 30. The main section will consist of a description and critical analysis of the different readings that have been made of Article 30 and the case law of the European Court of Justice on free movement of goods. These readings will be divided into three categories according to the tests advanced by different authors to guide the application of Article 30 in the review of State measures: (a) discrimination tests; (b) typological tests; (c) balance or cost/benefit tests.

In the second section, it will be argued that underlying the debate on Article 30 are different concepts of the European Economic Constitution and mainly a dilemma between economic liberalism and anti-protectionism. It will be argued that decisions on the review of State measures under Article 30 imply both choices with regard to the limits to State and public intervention in the market and the division of competencies between the European Union and the Member States. The discussion will highlight the constitutional dimension and institutional choices inherent in the application of Article 30.

THE CLASSICAL READINGS OF ARTICLE 30: DISCRIMINATION VERSUS BALANCING

Different theories have been put forward regarding Article 30 and the case law of the European Court of Justice with regard to the concept of "measures having equivalent effect to quantitative restrictions" enshrined in Article 30. These different theories can be divided into three categories on the basis of the tests proposed to guide the application of Article 30 in the review of State measures: (a) discrimination tests; (b) typological tests; and (c) balance or cost/benefit tests. As the analysis of these different tests will show, the discussion is centered around the concepts of discrimination and balancing and the degree of discretion that those concepts warrant to the courts and the States. Discrimination tests limit the review of national measures under Article 30 to cases of discrimination while balance tests argue for a broader judicial activism in the review of measures with an effect on trade, in this way restricting State discretion in regulating the market. Typological tests define different types of measures to be subject either to discrimination or balance tests.

These tests have normally been put forward from both a normative and a positive standpoint. In other words, they refer to what the Court ought to do and to what it is actually doing. They are normally assumed to be not just normatively correct but also descriptively true. Even though these different tests can be connected to different conceptions of the scope to be given by the Court to Article 30 in controlling national regulations (the discrimination tests would correspond to a narrow approach, the typological tests to a gradualist approach, and the balance tests to a wide approach) they all, with few and limited exceptions, sanction the degree of intervention the Court has had until now. The narrow, gradual or wide character differentiating them from a normative standpoint is diluted, from a descriptive perspective, by their agreement with the degree of intervention corresponding to the Court's case law.

This first section will review these three groups of tests focusing on their value in explaining the case law of the Court with regard to Article 30 and the European Economic Constitution.

Discrimination tests

Under this heading are included all things from the notion of protectionism intent to that of protectionist effects, and from the concept of formal discrimination to material discrimination. The common concern here is all the protectionist practices that traditionally dominate commerce among States. Unlike the doctrinal disputes over the commerce clause in the USA, where many different discrimination tests have been put forward, the doctrinal disputes over the free movement of goods in the European Community have not led to a proliferation of different versions of this test. At present, the most comprehensive and powerful defence of the discrimination theory in the European context has been made by Giuliano Marenco.[1]

In his article Marenco argues that the decisions of the Court which concern the concept of "measures having an equivalent effect to quantitative restrictions" can be divided into three categories according to the character of the measures under review. All the categories are, however, linked to the idea of discrimination, be it in an express form or in one much more subtle.[2] These categories are: (1) cases of express or formal discrimination (Marenco includes here the cases where a rule either applies exclusively to foreign goods or where

[1] G. Marenco, "Pour une interprétation traditionelle de la notion de mesure d'effet equivalent à une restriction quantitative", (1984) CDE, 291. Another author who appears to defend a discrimination thesis, albeit with some doubts, is Burrows: see *Free Movement in European Community Law* (Oxford, Clarendon Press, 1987), mainly at 54.

[2] Ibid, see eg at 304.

its application gives rise to a distinction between national and imported goods);[3] (2) cases of material discrimination (these involves measures applicable without distinction to both national and foreign goods, but which are worded so as to favour national products and do not take into consideration the different situation of foreign products—in this way, they create *de facto* discrimination);[4] (3) cases of measures applicable without distinction which require changes to be made to the imported products, and which are either excessively rigid (since the imported product is substantially in conformity with the measures) or not proportional to the aims of the measures.[5] This last category is no doubt the most difficult to reconcile with a discrimination test as it coincides with the cases normally associated with the use of a balance test. This means that a further consideration of this aspect of Marenco's theory is required.

For Marenco the third category of cases mentioned is a very sophisticated refinement of the concept of discrimination.[6] In his view, measures applicable without distinction are in principle lawful even if they restrict trade; but the application of the mandatory requirements test may, in a second stage of the analysis, render some of them unlawful. "The mandatory requirements, unlike the reasons set out in Article 36, constitute a criterion, not of *legality* . . ., but of *illegality*, in the sense that their absence colours negatively measures which would otherwise be lawful (because they are non-discriminatory)".[7]

He starts by distinguishing two types of measures applicable without distinction: those that require changes to be made to products and those that do not. The latter had never been considered as contrary to Article 30 by the Court but the same is not true for the former.[8] Those measures that require changes to be made to products in the form of requirements on labelling, packaging, shape, composition or controls will normally impose costs on imported products that are not imposed on national products. This is so because imported products will have to conform to two sets of rules: those of

[3] Ibid, at 305–6.

[4] Ibid, at 306–8 and 312–13.

[5] Ibid, at 308–13. It is perhaps adequate to quote Marenco's own summary: "*les cas dans lesquels la Cour a estimé que l'article 30 était applicable peuvent être tous rangés en quatre catégories:*

— discrmination formelle;

— discrimination matérielle;

et, pour les mesures indistinctement applicables qui rendent nécessaire une manipulation des produits importés,

— rigidité excessive, alors que le produit importé se conforme substantiellement à la mesure;

— disproportion entre les moyens et les objectifs.

Dans tous ces cas la situation des importations est moins favorable que celle où se trouve la production interne", at 312. Here, these last two are taken as a single category.

[6] Ibid, at 308.

[7] Ibid, at 300, author's translation. In the original: "*C'est que les exigences impératives, contrairement aux raisons visées à l'article 36, constituent un critère, non de légalité . . ., mais d'illégalité, dans le sens que leur absence colore négativement des mesures autrement licites car non discriminatoires*". See also, for example, at 297, 299–301.

[8] Ibid. at 308–9.

their own market and those of the market into which they are imported. Thus, they will be submited to two sets of requirements over inspection, labelling, packaging, etc.[9] Even so, Marenco argues that these measures were only taken to be prohibited under Article 30 by the Court in the two types of cases mentioned above: cases where the measures were considered excessively rigid and cases where the measures were considered as being out of proportion to their aims. These could both be included in what legal authors normally analyse under the heading of "proportionality". It seems that, for Marenco, the first type of cases refers to measures where the national authorities did not take into consideration the fact that the imported products already conformed in substance with the aims of the national rules.[10] The second type of cases concerns measures where the aim of the national rules could be achieved at a lower cost to imported products.[11] These are the two tests to which, according to Marenco, measures applicable without distinction requiring changes to be made to imported products are submited by the Court in order to ascertain whether there is discrimination for the purposes of Article 30.[12] In general all measures requiring changes to be made to imported products discriminate against imports as they impose on them an extra cost to which national products are not submited.[13] However, Marenco prefers to speak of this as a case of a specific restrictive effect ("*effet restrictif spécifique*") on imports, which becomes discrimination only when such specific restrictive effect can be imputed to the Member State of import, and not to a lack of harmonisation. What allows the Court to lay the blame for the specific restrictive effect on the importing Member State is the test of mandatory requirements, the argument being that if the measure is not necessary under any mandatory requirement, then its specific restrictive effect on imports is the fault of that Member State, and the measure is thus discriminatory.[14] This also allows Marenco to reconcile his theory with *Dassonville*[15] and *Cassis de Dijon*:[16] they deal with specific restrictive effects on imports and the way in which these can be imputed to a Member State.[17]

In sum, Marenco's theory is that: "the idea of discrimination, in the largest sense of the word, must always be present: either the measure itself contains formal or material discrimination, or the choice that it represents is based on

[9] *Free Movement in European Community Law* (Oxford, Clarendon Press, 1987), at 308–9, 312, 320.

[10] For example, if they had been already submitted in their country of origin to controls identical to those that were now required from them in the country of import or if the information provided for in the labels of origin fulfil the same aims intended by a special requirement of national measures. See, ibid, at 309–10.

[11] Ibid, at 310–12.

[12] Ibid, for example, at 312–13, 330 and 349.

[13] Ibid, see at 320.

[14] See, ibid, especially, at 318.

[15] Case 8/74, *Dassonville* [1974] ECR 1974.

[16] Case 120/78, *Rewe-Zentral AG* v. *Bundesmonopolverwaltung für Branntwein* [1979] ECR 649.

[17] Ibid, eg, at 327 ff.

a discriminatory attitude, albeit not deliberate, where the Legislator fails to take account of imported products".[18]

Marenco makes a good case for a discrimination test and there was also some case law support for it. If *Dassonville* adopted a rule covering non-discriminatory measures, the case law that followed it—until *Cassis de Dijon*—brought together the *Dassonville* doctrine and the Commission Directive on measures having an equivalent effect to quantitative restrictions[19] under a broad concept of discrimination: a comparison between the situation in which national and imported products are placed is always present.[20] Even after *Cassis de Dijon*, discrimination arguments are often used by the Court either as the basis for a decision or as a supporting argument. In spite of this, Marenco's thesis is difficult to hold as a faithful description of the Court's approach to Article 30 in face of the progressive tendency in the Court's case law to have less and less recourse to discrimination arguments in the justification of decisions concerning measures having equivalent effect to quantitative restrictions.[21] A tendency reversed, however, in part, in *Keck*.[22]

There are many decisions in the Court case law where no reference is made to discrimination criteria. These decisions are better explained by different analysis, as will be seen below. It must be stressed that Marenco's article dates from 1984, and thus pre-dates the most controversial decisions which made use of the *Dassonville* and *Cassis de Dijon* doctrines in reviewing measures indistinctly applicable to foreign and national products.[23] Also, since that date

[18] Ibid, at 349. In the original: "*L'idée de discrimination, dans le sens plus large de l'expression, doit être toujours présent: soit que la mesure contient en elle-même une discrimination formelle ou matérielle, soit que le choix qu'elle représente relève d'une attitude discriminatoire tout au moins par négligence, consistant dans une absence de sollicitude du législateur à l'égard des importations*".

[19] Commission Directive 70/50/EEC, JO L 13, 1970, 29.

[20] See, for example: Case 65/75, *Ricardo Tasca*, [1976] ECR 291, para 13; Joined Cases 88 to 90/75, *Societa Sadam* [1976] ECR 323; Case 74/76, *Iannelli* v. *Meroni* [1977] ECR 557; Case 13/77, *GB-INNO* v. *ATAB* [1977] ECR 2115, see paras 47, 48, 52–6; Case 82/77, *Van Tiggele* [1978] ECR 25 (on material discrimination or protectionist effects, though in this case, they are already considerably flexible and extensive — see paras 14, 16 and 18, mainly the reference in para 16 to "effects detrimental to the marketing of imported products alone"); Case 13/78, *Eggers Sohn* [1978] ECR 1935, see para 23.

[21] The author's review of the Court case law reveals that although it is still possible to find many expressions of concern over discrimination in the ECJ analysis of Article 30, the relevance and importance of such expressions has diminished with time until very recently. For some examples following *Cassis de Dijon* see: Case 152/78, *Commission* v. *France* [1980] ECR 2299 (especially paras 11, 13, 14, 17 and 18); Case 155/80, *Oebel* [1981] ECR 1993 (especially para 20); Case 193/80, *Vinegar* [1981] ECR 3019 (especially para 20); Case 75/81, *Thomas Blesgen* [1982] ECR 1211 (especially paras 9 and 11); Joined Cases 314 to 316/81 and 83/82, *Waterkeyn* [1982] ECR 4337 (especially para 9); Case 72/82, *Commission* v. *Italy* (Tobacco monopoly) [1983] ECR 1955 (especially para 12); Case 176/84, *Commission* v. *Greece* (Greek Beer Purity Law) [1987] ECR 1193 (especially para 44); Case 298/87, *Smanor* [1988] ECR 4489 (especially para 13); Case 45/87, *Commission* v. *Ireland* [1988] ECR 4929 (especially paras 19 and 20); Case C–23/89, *Quietlynn* [1990] ECR 4695 (especially paras 9 and 10).

[22] Joined Cases C–267 and C–268/91, *Keck and Mithouard* [1993] ECR I–6097. For an analysis of this judgment see below.

[23] See, for example, Joined Cases 80 and 159/85, *Edah* [1986] ECR 3359; Case 179/84, *Commission* v. *Germany* (Petillant de Raisin) [1986] ECR 3879; Beer Purity Law cases: Case

the Court has applied the test of mandatory requirements to measures that do not require changes to be made to imported products (at least in in the sense the latter are described by Marenco).[24] Answering to these developments, Defalque has extended Marenco's theory to cover those cases as well (mainly cases on measures regulating market circumstances).[25] However, more than supporting the theory this highlights the loose character of the distinction and its distance from a true discrimination test.

In order to fit the Court's case law into an antidiscrimination reading, Marenco and Defalque lose from sight the normative underpinning of a discrimination test: the prevention of protectionism in the form of discrimination against products or nationals from nationals of other Member States. Discrimination becomes any sort of burden incurred by foreign products, including the cost involved in adapting to a different national legislation. The difference between discrimination and lack of harmonisation is thus trivial or, even, non-existent. It is not clear what is the added value of a discrimination test in this case or the role it is supposed to play in face of the constitutional conflicts underlying Article 30: the balances between regulation and deregulation and Member States and European Union competencies. This also stresses one of the problems involved in adopting a discrimination test: discrimination is now a word with too many different meanings and the tests are either too easy to evade or so broad that virtually any state regulation is brought under review. If for example, formal discrimination is the adopted criterion it is obvious that many protectionist State measures will be able to evade it. If one widens the definition to cover discriminatory effects, it is still not certain that protectionism will be prevented, and one has also to face the difficulties involved in identifying those effects. If, as is the case with Marenco and Defalque, one broadens the discrimination criterion even further, cost/benefit analysis will become predominant in the assessment of discrimination; the form will be kept without the substance. The only requirement coming from the Marenco test that adds to the requirements of the wide approaches to Article 30 is that, in order to come under Article 30, measures not formally

176/84, *Commission* v. *Greece* [1987] ECR 1193; Case 178/84, *Commssion* v. *Germany* [1987] ECR 1227; Case 298/87, Smanor [1988] ECR 4489; Case 407/85, *3 Glocken* v. *USL* (Pasta case) [1988] ECR 4233; Case 302/86, *Commission* v. *Denmark* (Danish Bottles) [1988] ECR 4489. In some of these cases, however, it is possible to argue that protectionism was at the base of the State regulations, and this was relevant in the Courts' final decision. This was notable in the Beer cases: see, eg, in the German case, paras 32 and 51.

[24] Among others, see: Case 229/83, *Leclerc* (Prix du libre) [1985] ECR 1 (concerning legislation imposing a minimum retail price for books); Case C–362/88, *GB-INNO* [1990] I–667; the Sunday Trading Cases (see discussion below); Joined Cases C–1/90 and C–176/90, *Aragonesa* [1991] ECR I–4151 (concerning Catalan legislation on the advertisement of alcoholic drinks); Case C–126/91, *Yves Rocher* [1993] ECR I–2361 (also concerning sales methods). There is a Court decision preceding Marenco's article that already advances such developments in the Court's approach to Article 30, but it probably came to late for Marenco to consider it—Case 286/81, *Oosthoek's* [1982] ECR 4575 (free gifts regulation).

[25] L. Defalque, 'Le concept de discrimination en matiere de libre circulation des marchandises', (1987) 23 CDE, 471, mainly at 481.

or materially discriminatory are required to impose changes to imported products. A requirement that appears to coincide with that introduced by the Court in the *Keck* decision[26] but both difficult to justify and easy to circumvent (almost any measure that has an effect on trade can be said to require changes to imported products, even if it is related to commercial strategy[27]). Excluding this requirement, Marenco theory coincides with the balance test approach to Article 30 to be discussed below. In fact, his view is that Article 30 forbids all *per se* discriminatory measures and those that are considered to be so as not being justified under the mandatory requirements test. There is no new proposal as to the way to interpret and apply the mandatory requirements test within the discrimination theory. Whenever there is a "specific restrictive effect" on imports (in the sense discussed above almost always) Marenco ends up close to the position of those arguing for balance as the best way to prevent protectionism.[28] The only difference is that while the latter argue that mandatory requirements can render legal something that would otherwise be illegal, Marenco argues that it is the absence of mandatory requirements that renders illegal an otherwise legal measure.[29] It is a difference of emphasis of little consequence in practice since neither theory really reaches any conclusion as to the circumstances and manner (including the burden of proof) in which the mandatory requirements test is to be applied.

From a descriptive point of view, even a broad test of discrimination, as the one advanced by Marenco and Defalque, is not supported in the Court's case law (at least until the *Keck* decision). That a measure does not need to be discriminatory to come under Article 30 was clearly stated by the Court in 1985 in *Cinéthèque*,[30] a case concerning French legislation which prohibited the commercial exploitation of cinematographic works in recorded form, mainly video-cassettes, before the end of a set time-limit:

> "it must be observed that such a system, if it applies without distinction to both video-cassettes manufactured in the national territory and to imported video-cassettes, does not have the purpose of regulating trade patterns; *its effect is not to favour national production as against the production of other Member States*, but to encourage cinematographic production as such.
>
> *Nevertheless, the application of such a system may create barriers to intra-Community trade* . . . In those circumstances a prohibition of exploitation laid down

[26] As will be discussed below there are good arguments to read the *Keck* decision in light of the test proposed by Marenco, though it seems preferable to identify the *Keck* criteria with those advanced by White (see below). There is, in substance, many similarities between the test of Marenco and that of White's and the Court (post-*Keck*).

[27] This parallel was at the basis of the Court extension of Article 30 to cover non-discriminatory measures other than those regulating product requirements or characteristics which regulate market circumstances in Case 286/81, *Oosthoek's* [1982] ECR 4575. See in Chapter 3 below, the analysis of the *Oosthoek's* line of cases.

[28] Though Marenco also appears to understand balance as dominated by a rationale of equivalence. See below the discussion on different types of balance.

[29] Marenco, "Pour une interpretation traditionelle" (n.1 above), 299.

[30] Cases 60 and 61/84, *Cinéthèque* [1985] ECR 2605.

by such system is not compatible with the principle of free movement of goods provided for in the Treaty unless any obstacle to intra-community trade thereby created does not exceed that which is necessary in order to ensure the attainment of the objective in view and unless that objective is justified with regard to Community law".[31]

The Court has also repeatedly stated that mandatory requirements do not apply to measures of discriminatory nature.[32] Furthermore, the broad concept of discrimination advocated by Marenco does not fit with the concept of discrimination used by the Court when interpreting Articles 7 and 34 for the purposes of free movement of goods. For example, in *Smit*[33] the Court interpreted the prohibition on discrimination on nationality as not covering "any disparity in the way in which undertakings of different Member States are treated as a result of differences between the legislation of the Member States".[34] The Court has generally interpreted Article 7 as covering discrimination over nationality, but not differences in treatment arising from legislative disparities. Nor has it developed any test similar to "mandatory requirements" to impute the costs imposed on some nationals by these legislative disparities to a specific Member State. As will be remembered such legislative disparities are precisely what determines the changes required of imported products which Marenco says are at the origins of the third type of discriminatory measures.[35]

[31] See paras 21 and 22, emphasis added. More recently, the Court had reaffirmed this interpretation in the first of the "Sunday Trading" cases: Case C–145/88, *Torfaen Borough Council* [1989] ECR 3851 (see paras 11 and 12).

[32] See, for example, Case 6/81, *Groep* v. *Beele* [1982] ECR 707 (para 7); Case 59/82, *Schutzverbaud gegen unwere in der Wirschaft* v. *Wienvertriebs* (Vermouth) [1983] ECR 1217 (para 11); Case C–2/90, *Commission* v. *Belgium* [1992] ECR 4471 (para 33—however, in spite of its statement the Court may indeed have applied mandatory requirements here). It could be argued that the Court is referring to formal discrimination as opposed to other forms of discrimination which are uncovered only by the absence of mandatory requirements (or the lack of proportionality). However, in Marenco's view, mandatory requirements apply to all measures requiring changes to imported products because this imposes on them a burden that is not placed on national products. Thus they apply to measures which have a different effect on national products than they do on imported ones ie discriminatory measures in a very broad sense. In this way an explanation of why mandatory requirements apply to some "discriminatory" measures (in the latter sense) and not to others would be required. Moreover, other measures that do not require changes to be made on imports (and, thus, are not covered by Marenco's test) may, nevertheless, also impose a cost on imports that is not imposed on national products: as mentioned before, compliance with a different set of national rules always does so. Are not these measures having a specific restrictive effect on imports equal to that imposed by measures requiring changes to be made on imports? Why shouldn't this be considered discrimination as well, in the broad sense mentioned?; or, why is the mandatory requirements test not triggered in the case of those measures that, although they do not require changes to be made to imports, do have the same specific restrictive effect highlighted by Marenco?

[33] Case 126/82, *Smit* [1983] ECR 73.

[34] At the end of para 27.

[35] Note, however, that Marenco distinguishes between a specific restrictive effect on free movement that can be attributed to a specific measure (this being discriminatory) and a specific restrictive effect which can be attributed to a disparity among national legislations (this being non-discriminatory). The mandatory requirements test serves to identify whether we are in the presence of one or the other. There is not much support in the case law of the Court for this distinction.

With regard to Article 34, in *Jongeneel Kaas*, a measure determining a loss of export opportunities and higher costs to national products was *prima facie* declared as non-discriminatory and thus not covered by Article 34.[36] If the concept of discrimination invoked by Marenco was applied here, such a measure should at least have been submitted to a mandatory requirements test.

Discrimination has become a word with too many meanings and without a clear normative foundation in the Community context. It is certainly possible to argue that whenever there is a double burden imposed on imports from the lack of harmonisation of national regulations there is discrimination against those imports. The relevant questions are: what does this tell us?; is such a concept of discrimination in any way related to the traditional concerns underlying antidiscrimination discourse?; is it of any help in addressing the constitutional balance of competences between States and the EU and the choice between regulation and deregulation? A discrimination test is of little value without a normative theory of protectionism or other constitutional construction supporting it. At the same time, discrimination can either be too broad or too narrow and it is always a preliminary test: it only tells us which measures are going to be subject to stricter review including a balance of costs and benefits. In this sense, it is, above all, an institutional choice: it determines when the Court is to balance the costs and benefits of national measures. A discrimination test must face and depart from the constitutional questions and institutional choices involved in its application. The ideas of discrimination and protectionism as essential elements in this area should, however, be preserved, in particular the concern to avoid costs being transferred to foreign nationals by national rules, and a concern for the representation of their interests in the framing of those rules. It is in view of these ideas, and of the entire body of political and economic values present in the process of European integration that we should, at the present stage of the European Union development, reassess what we mean by protectionism and decide how we should fight it. This is part of the normative task of the interpretation of Article 30 and its role in the European Economic Constitution.

Typological tests

Under this heading are included all theories that attempt to limit the scope of Article 30 by defining only measures of a certain nature or with certain effects as measures having equivalent effect to a quantitative restriction. The most well known is perhaps White's theory, that excludes from Article 30 measures relating to market circumstances.[37] This theory was later argued by him, in the Commission's submission, in the first of the "Sunday Trading" cases.[38]

[36] Case 237/82, *Jongeneel Kaas* [1984] ECR 483 (see paras 21 to 23).
[37] "In Search of the Limits to Article 30 of the EEC Treaty", (1989) 26 *CMLRev.*, 235.
[38] Case C–145/88, *Torfaen Borough Council* [1989] ECR 3851.

Also in this case, Advocate-General Van Gerven argued for a different theory: that only measures resulting in a partitioning (or compartmentalisation) of the market should be considered as measures having an effect equivalent to quantitative restrictions. Another theory, that can be considered as a refinement of White's theory, is Mortelmans proposal to exclude from Article 30 only those rules concerning market circumstances which have a territorial element.[39] Since then Steiner has argued for a limitation of the scope of Article 30 by looking at the effects of the measures and the degree of threat to the Single Market.[40]

For White, "the philosophy of the Court appears to be that Article 30 be interpreted in the light of its objective which is the creation of a unified market . . . Accordingly, goods should be manufactured wherever the conditions are most favourable".[41] It is with this aim in mind that the *Cassis de Dijon* case law on measures having an equivalent effect to quantitative restrictions can be understood as (*prima facie*) forbidding "the application by a Member State to products legally produced and marketed in another Member State of its national rules relating to the characteristics required of such products on its territory (which therefore prevents this product from benefiting in the importing Member State from the advantages arising out of its production in the different legal and economic environment prevailing in the other Member State)".[42] The same concern does not exist in the case of the application to imported products of national rules relating to the circumstances in which products can be sold or used, provided the products enjoy equal access to the market.[43] The important distinction is then between rules relating to the characteristics of goods (such as composition, size, shape, weight, presentation, denomination and labelling), which would fall under Article 30; and rules regulating the circumstances under which all goods of the same kind should be sold or used, which would not fall under Article 30. There are two exceptions: rules of the latter kind would fall under Article 30 if they were discriminatory or if they restricted imports so severely that they could be considered as amounting to a quantitative restriction. The attraction of White's theory lies in its (apparently) clear-cut, easy-to-use definition, which provides an efficient tool for dealing with the high number of cases on market circumstances which were and still are overloading the Court.[44] It can also reduce the use of Article

[39] "Article 30 of the EC Treaty and Legislation Relating to Market Circumstances: Time to Consider a New Definition", 28 (1991) *CMLRev.*, 115.

[40] "Drawing the Line: Uses and Abuses of Article 30 EEC", 26 (1992) *CMLRev.*, 749.

[41] E. L. White, "In Search of the Limits to Article 30" (n.37 above), at 245.

[42] Ibid, at 247.

[43] Ibid, at 246. White adds that any restrictions arising in these cases are not due to disparities between national rules, but rather to the existence of the rules in the importing Member State, at 246. For the sake of simplicity, these type of rules will be referred to here as rules on market circumstances, in order to distinguish them from rules on product requirements or product characteristics.

[44] For a list of cases on market circumstances pending before the Court at the end of 1990 see Mortelmans, "Article 30 of the EC Treaty" (n.39 above), footnotes 6–9.

30 in challenges to national regulatory policies irrespective of any intention to regulate intra-state trade, which has been particularly clear in cases concerning rules on market circumstances.[45] This is certainly part of the explanation that can be provided for the adoption of White's test by the Court in *Keck*.[46] However, the distinction between rules on product requirements and rules on market circumstances does not appear to be sufficiently clear or soundly-based to stand for long, nor does there seem to be any normative basis for making such distinction. White's theory appears to be a formal criterion intended to solve problems of "dock-control".[47]

The same can be said of the test proposed by Mortelmans, a refinement of White's theory.[48] He also makes a distinction between "rules concerning the composition, characteristics and presentation of *products*, and rules concerning the *market circumstances* surrounding the sale of products".[49] However, he introduces a new distinction within the latter category: "legislation with a territorial element, i.e. relating to activities situated in a fixed location . . . and legislation without such an element".[50] For Mortelmans there are two categories of rules governing market circumstances *prima facie* prohibited by Article 30: (1) rules which apply differently to national and imported products; and (2) rules applicable without distinction without a territorial element.[51] These last rules "could pose a real threat to the completion of the internal market because they actually assume free circulation of persons and/or goods",[52] the same not being true for rules with a territorial element. However, this reasoning is not developed so as to explain why this should be so. Similarly, the definition of a territorial element is not entirely clear. In my view, Mortelman's new conceptualisation may bring more confusion into the already unstable distinction between rules on product requirements and rules on market circumstances. According to Mortelman's theory, it appears that if a State makes regulations applicable without distinction on the retail sales of national and imported products in shops, it is not bound to justify this by reference to a mandatory requirement. The same will not be the case if it regulates without distinction the selling of national and imported goods through door-to-door sales. Such a distinction is not very convincing and can even be considered paradoxical as it imposes a higher burden of justification on the regulation of a method of selling goods (door-to-door) which *prima facie* requires more attention than sales in shops.

In the same "Sunday Trading" case[53] where White proposed to the Court

[45] See Chapter 3 below.

[46] See, also, Chapter 3 below.

[47] Again more developed critique of this test is left to the analysis of the *Keck* decision, in Chapter 3 below.

[48] See Mortelmans, "Article 30 of the EC Treaty" (n.39 above).

[49] Ibid, at 115.

[50] Ibid, at 116.

[51] Ibid, at 130.

[52] Ibid.

[53] *Torfaen Borough Council* (n.38 above).

the adoption of his test distinguishing between rules on product requirements and rules on market circumstances, Advocate General Van Gerven, who was also hoping to limit the scope of Article 30,[54] made a new analysis of the Court's case law and reached the conclusion that the essential factor in determining whether a measure would fall under Article 30 should be its contribution to the partitioning of the Community market into national markets. According to Van Gerven, the Court's application of the prohibition laid down in Article 30 should extend beyond discriminatory measures to cover rules that "either on their own or as part of an entire legal and economic context, can lead to a national market being screened off, or access to that market being unacceptably difficult or less attractive for economic operators from other Member States".[55] In the case of rules that themselves *screen off* a national market,[56] Article 30 would apply automatically. Instead, where "the national rule at issue merely increases the difficulty in penetrating the national market, the prohibition in Article 30 is applicable only if it appears from the entire legal and economic context that the interweaving of national markets sought by the Treaty is thereby threatened".[57] The underlying constitutional goal, that should guide the application of both free movement and competition rules is the unity and integrity of the common market.

In its judgment, however, the Court did not adopt the Advocate General's proposal. Van Gerven, like White, wanted to limit the number of cases flooding to the Court as a consequence of the broad interpretation given to Article 30. However, while White attempts to reach certainty by proposing a test based on the nature of the measure (rules on product requirements and rules on market circumstances), Van Gerven bases his test on economic criteria[58] (partitioning of the market). The alternative foreseen and rejected by Van Gerven is also largely dependent on an economic analysis: the reasonableness of policy decisions.[59] Van Gerven's test appears to have two advantages over this economic analysis: first, there are less legitimacy problems in having the Court assess the partitioning of the market (understood to be a factual analysis of economic data) than the reasonableness of State policy choices (understood to be policy-making). Secondly, it appears easier and more certain to determine the partitioning of the market than to decide the reasonableness of a policy choice. In spite of all this, the advantages of Van Gerven's test are more illusory than real when we examine them more closely. Mortelmans is

[54] "The question in point is therefore whether, and if so which, national rules found to have a certain restrictive effect on imports may still fall outside the scope of Article 30 of EEC Treaty": Opinion of Advocate General Van Gerven, in *Torfaen Borough Council* (n.38 above), at 3869.

[55] Ibid, 3874.

[56] "That is the case with national rules which . . . establish a straightforward ban of the market (or a ban limited in time) on marketing . . .", ibid, 3878.

[57] Ibid, footnote omitted.

[58] For Mortelmans, "Article 30 of the EEC Treaty" (n.39 above), at 126. Van Gerven's argument is economic, while that of White and the Commission legal.

[59] See at 3879–80 of his Opinion.

right in noting that what the Advocate General is really applying is a *de minimus* rule.[60] This *de minimus* rule will apply in the case of rules that do not *screen off* a national market, but merely increase the difficulty in penetrating it. These rules would only be prohibited by Article 30 if it is made "sufficiently probable by a number of quantitative factors . . . that the application of the rule makes it more difficult to penetrate the market, thereby rendering the market so inaccessible (expensive, unprofitable) that it must be feared that the majority of imported products will disappear from the market".[61] This may even show Van Gerven's test to be but another reformulation of the discrimination test. The test appears too vague for Van Gerven's purpose of achieving a substantial reduction in the number of cases going before the Court.[62] Furthermore, an assessment of market partitioning may easily lead the Court, in effect, to perform either a protectionist effects test, or a cost/benefit analysis of national regulatory policies, something Van Gerven wanted the Court to avoid.[63]

Another author attempting to reduce the uncertainty surrounding Article 30 and the consequent "uses and abuses" of it, is Steiner.[64] She also intends to limit the use of Article 30 to measures which pose a real threat to the single market.[65] Steiner stresses that the important element of analysis in Article 30 is whether a national measure is capable of *hindering* trade (the test given in *Dassonville*) and not, as in Article 85, whether it has an *effect* on trade. According to Steiner, trade between Member States is likely to be hindered in two situations:

> "Firstly, when traders, whether as producers, exporters, importers or dealers who seek to sell goods in a Member State outside their State of origin are forced to adapt their production or marketing methods to meet the demands of the importing State, in the form of production, packaging, advertising, registration or other requirements, positive or negative in that State.[66]
>
> Secondly, where conditions of sale or marketing in the importing State, whilst not imposing extra burdens on exporters or importers, or resulting in loss of advantages, either preclude imports or restrict marketing opportunities, in the importing State to such an extent as to render the importation of the product in question unattractive, or simply not worthwhile".[67]

This dual classification corresponds, to some degree, with the distinction made by White and now also by the Court between rules on product

[60] Mortelmans, "Article 30 of the EEC Treaty" (n. 39 above), 128.

[61] Van Gerven, Advocate-General Opinion in *Torfaen Borough Council* (n.38 above), 3878.

[62] According to Mortelmans, the dependence on economic criteria will also lead to a lack of uniformity in the application of Community law by the national courts. Mortelmans cites a study on this by Colinet and Maresceau: Mortelmans, "Article 30 of the EEC Treaty" (n.38 above), 127 and 130.

[63] See, also, the discussion on anti-protectionism in Chapter 5 below.

[64] Steiner, "Drawing the Line" (n.40 above), at 749.

[65] Ibid, 767.

[66] Ibid, 769.

[67] Ibid, 770.

requirements and rules on marketing circumstances.[68] The difference lies in the test used to identify measures governing marketing circumstances that fall under Article 30. Whilst for White and the Court, measures relating to market circumstances are only *prima facie* prohibited by Article 30 if they discriminate in law or in fact against imported products, for Steiner those measures are *prima facie* prohibited by Article 30 if they preclude imports or marketing opportunities "to such an extent as to render the importation of the product in question unattractive, or simply not worthwhile".[69] This does not cover measures which only "limit marketing opportunities to a small extent".[70] However, what is a "small extent" is (to a "large extent") unclear and to define it Steiner has no option but to rely on a *de minimus* rule concerning the effects of the measure on imports. In her own words: "A measure which is minimal in its effects on imports . . . will not deter imports. Even if it causes some reduction in imports, it will not be a hindrance to inter-state trade".[71] Interestingly, although Steiner has stressed so much the need to distinguish *effects on trade* from *hindrances to trade*, it appears that the latter is determined by the former: there is *hindrance to trade* whenever a certain degree of *effect on trade* occurs.

It appears that Steiner's theory brings few advantages. It addresses none of the problems with the theory put forward by White and the Court theory while, at the same time, it increases its uncertainty, by replacing the discrimination test with a *de minimus* rule for the test applying to the second category of rules. With regard to the case law on Article 30, it is true that a *de minimus* rule has also found its way into some Court decisions,[72] but the few cases in which it is mentioned or in which it may have been taken into consideration are insignificant in view of the progressive broadening of the scope of Article 30 by the Court in giving full effect to the *Dassonville*[73] statement that "all trading rules enacted by Member States which are capable of hindering, directly or indirectly, actually or potentially, intra-Community trade are to be considered as measures having an effect equivalent to quantitative restrictions".[74]

[68] Not completely so because she includes in the first group rules which regulate marketing methods, such as advertising.

[69] Ibid, 770.

[70] Ibid, at 771–3.

[71] Ibid, 773.

[72] In this sense, see: Case 155/80, *Oebel* [1981] ECR 1993, para 20 and Case C–169/91, *Stoke-on-Trent* (another "Sunday Trading" case) [1992] ECR I–6635, para 15. At same time, also the uncertainty regarding the "measurement of effects" is visible in the case law of the Court. In *Yves Rocher* (Case C–126/91, *Yves Rocher* [1993] ECR I–2361), the Court starts by saying that the Article 30 test has nothing to do with the intensity of the effects. However, it goes on to exclude rules with hypothetical effects only, but not those which do not have effects but may come to have them.

[73] Case 8/74, *Dassonville* [1974] ECR 731, para 5. The expression "trading rules" was subsequently abandoned, increasing even more the scope of this statement.

[74] This includes, for example, the mere affecting of marketing prospects for imports from other Member States. See Case 152/78, *Commission* v. *France* [1980] ECR 2299, para 11 and Case

Balance or cost/benefit tests

Balance theories maintain that the correct test to be used in the application of the rules on the free movement of goods is one that promotes a balance between the costs of national measures and their benefits, taking into account the interests involved in the free movement of goods and the interests protected by the national measure. The first step in this test is a wide interpretation of Article 30, bringing within its scope almost any national regulatory measure. The second step is the review of those measures under Article 36 and the mandatory requirements tests. Unlike the previous theories, there will be no national measures *prima facie* permitted by Article 30. This is because any regulation of the market is bound to have some effects on trade, which is considered the "triggering" factor in the application of Article 30. The limits to the free movement of goods lie exclusively in Article 36 and in the "mandatory requirements" test put forward by the Court in *Cassis de Dijon*. If a national measure is not justified under any of those headings it is prohibited by the Treaty. However, different concerns may underlie "balancing" and these may produce different outcomes, depending on who does the balancing of the costs and the benefits of national regulations and how it is done.

This theory was predominant in the interpretation of the case law of the Court of Justice regarding the free movement of goods until *Keck*. It was argued both in terms of what the Court was doing and in terms of what the Court should do.[75] The use of a balance test in the application of the rules on the free movement of goods became possible from the moment the *Dassonville* decision gave a wide interpretation of Article 30. The fact that it was sufficient for a measure to be "captured" by Article 30 for it to be "capable of hindering directly or indirectly, actually or potentially, intra-community trade", in effect subjected all market regulations to a balance test review under Article 30, since they all have by their very nature an impact on trade. The reference to "intra-Community trade" might authorise a restriction on the scope of the *Dassonville* statement by distinguishing between impact on trade and impact on intra-Community trade. In other words, it could be argued that the

75/81, *Thomas Blesgen* [1982] ECR 1211, para 7. In Joined Cases 177 and 178/82, *Van de Haar and Kaveka de Meern* [1984] ECR 1797, the Court stated that a measure was covered by Article 30 even though the hindrance was slight (para 13.).

[75] See, for example: A. Mattera, "Le Marché Unique Européen", *Jupiter*, 1988, mainly at 191–2; L.W. Gormley, *Prohibiting Restrictions on Trade Within the EEC* (Amsterdam, Elsevier Science Publishers), mainly at 14–19, 71, 264–5; G. Celona, *La Libera Circolazione Delle Merci E Il Mercato Unico Europeo Nella Giurisprudenza* (Milano, Giuffré, 1991), mainly at 165; E. Cortese Pinto, *Ostacolli Non Tariffari Agli Scambi Nel Diritto Communitario* (Milano, Franco Angeli, 1985), mainly at 74–6; P. Oliver, *Free Movement of Goods in the EEC*, 2nd edn., (London, European Law Center, 1988), mainly at 87–9. In the latest edition of his book (*Free Movement of Goods in the European Community*, 3rd edn., (London, Sweet and Maxwell, 1996)), Oliver, however, praises the Court's decision in *Keck* which limits balance to a more restricted scope of Article 30. See at 114.

Dassonville formula should only apply where there is a discriminatory impact between national trade and intra-Community trade. Such "discrimination dressing" of the *Dassonville* formula would be similar to the interpretation of "burden on trade" in the United States Supreme Court[76] and has in part occurred with the *Keck* decision.[77] In fact, the first decisions following *Dassonville* gave a discrimination-based reading of its formula.[78] It is normally thought that it was in *Cassis de Dijon* that the Court moved away from discrimination to balancing as the controlling rationale in the application of Article 30. It can be argued that prior to *Cassis de Dijon* the Court had already reviewed State measures on a cost/benefit basis,[79] however, it is with the *Cassis de Dijon* decision that it took its most important step towards a balance test approach. The Court stated:

> "Obstacles to movement within the Community resulting from disparities between the national laws relating to the marketing of the products in question must be accepted in so far as those provisions may be recognized as being necessary in order to satisfy mandatory requirements relating in particular to the effectiveness of fiscal supervision, the protection of public health, the fairness of commercial transactions and the defence of the consumer".[80]

[76] See in Chapter 3 below, the analysis of the Supreme Court case law on the commerce clause.

[77] See Chapter 3 below.

[78] See: Case 65/75, *Tasca* [1976] ECR 291, para 13 and Cases 88 to 90/75, *Sadam* [1976] ECR 323, para 15. In Case 82/77, *Van Tiggele* [1978] ECR 25, para 16 this line of reasoning appears to follow but in fact, this decision extends the concept of discrimination beyond its normal boundaries (see below). Some doubts can be raised regarding Case 13/77, *GB-INNO* v. *ATAB* [1977] ECR 2115, paras 47, 52–4 and 56. In para 53 the Court appears even to advance as the relevant factor whether the measure has internal or external effects, but this test has not been developed since. In Case 74/76, *Iannelli* v. *Meroni* [1977] ECR 557, the Court actually ignored *Dassonville* and presented a "discrimination version" of Article 30 and Commission Directive 70/50/EEC. It stated: "The prohibition in Article 30 of all quantitative restrictions on imports or measures having equivalent effect is aimed, on the one hand, at those measures prohibiting imports in whole or in part and, on the other hand, as mentioned by Commission Directive No 70/50/EEC . . . at 'measures other than those applicable equally to domestic or imported products', which hinder imports which could otherwise take place, including measures which make importation 'more difficult or costly than the disposal of domestic production'" (para 8). See Commission Directive 70/50/EEC from 22/12/1969 on the abolition of measures which have an effect equivalent to quantitative restrictions on import [1970] OJ L13/29 and the difference between Article 2, applying to formal discriminatory measures, and Article 3, applying to equally applicable measures (that the Court appears to ignore).

[79] See Case 82/77, *Van Tiggele* [1978] ECR 25, para 14 and in particular Case 13/78, *Eggers Sohn* [1978] ECR 1935 paras 24 and 25. In the first case, the relevant development consists in expanding the concept of discrimination ("imported products are placed at a disadvantage in relation to identical domestic products") to cover the loss of competitive advantage (this case is one of the leading cases in the case law of the Court on price regulation to be discussed below). In the second case concerns over protectionism and discrimination are present: but the same could be said of *Cassis de Dijon*. What is new is the importance given, in assessing the regulation, to its policy aim, and the way in which the regulation aims to achieve it. Arguing that, contrary to "the widespread but erroneous impression", balance ("rule of reason") precedes *Cassis de Dijon*, see Gormley, "Reasoning Renounced? The Remarkable Judgment in Keck & Mithouard", (1994) *European Business Law Review*, 63, at 64.

[80] Case 120/78, *Rewe-Zentral AG* v. *Bundesmonopolverwaltung für Branntwein* [1979] ECR 649, para 8.

In *Dassonville*, the Court of Justice made no distinction between discriminatory and non-discriminatory measures with an impact on intra-Community trade, but in *Cassis de Dijon* it made it clear that all such measures were to be assessed in the light of objectives recognised as legitimate by the Community, such as those already set out in Article 36.[81] Moreover, *Cassis de Dijon* introduced what came to be known as the "principle of mutual recognition" of national regulations. According to this principle, a State has to accept the marketing in its own territory of products lawfully produced and marketed in other Member States. In the words of the Court:

> "There is therefore no valid reason why, provided that they have been lawfully produced and marketed in one of the Member States, alcoholic beverages should not be introduced to another Member State".[82]

This further enhanced the *Dassonville* formula, in permitting the challenge of any national legislation stricter than that valid in the Member State of origin. At the same time, as it definitively extended the balance test to non-discriminatory measures, the decision also added new grounds of justification, which were defined as mandatory requirements.

The exclusive reference to the words used in *Cassis de Dijon* might lead those less familiar with the rules on the free movement of goods to think that non-discriminatory measures could only be justified by the mandatory requirements there mentioned. In reality, it would not be possible for reasons of public security to justify a discriminatory measure under Article 36, but not a non-discriminatory one. The mandatory requirements test is, from a more formal point of view, part of the assessment of whether a measure is to be considered as having equivalent effect to a quantitative restriction for the purposes of Article 30. If that is the case, then Article 36 can always be applied.[83] In practical terms, what determines whether a measure is considered as having equivalent effect to a quantitative restriction is whether or not it hinders trade, as ascertained in accordance with the *Dassonville* formula. If this is the case, then the measure must be necessary and proportional, and have as its aim some of the objectives listed in Article 36 or included under the mandatory requirements statement.

One object of controversy is the opposite proposition: the possibility of justifying formal discriminatory measures on one or more of the grounds for mandatory requirements, as put forward in *Cassis de Dijon*. In other words, are mandatory requirements an extension of Article 36? Can any of the mandatory requirements justify a discriminatory measure? The traditional

[81] For Masclet, *Cassis de Dijon* confirms the requirements of permissibility enshrined in Article 36 (the direct link with one of the protected objectives and the necessity to that objective), the only new thing in the decision being the extension of the number of aims protected. See J.C. Masclet, "Les articles 30, 36, et 100 du traité à la lumière de l'arrêt 'Cassis de Dijon'", (1980) 16 *RTDE*, 611, at 619–26.

[82] See para 14.

[83] See, for example, Joined Cases C–1/90 and C–176/90, *Aragonesa* [1991] ECR I–4151.

understanding of Article 36—as an exception to the general rule which should be submitted to restrictive interpretation—is in opposition to this possibility, and, accordingly, the Court has always stated that the mandatory requirements cannot justify measures discriminating between national and imported products.[84] The Court of Justice rewrote the *Cassis de Dijon* statement in subsequent decisions so as to make it clear that mandatory requirements only apply to measures applicable without distinction to imported and national products.[85] Thus in *Groep* v. *Beele* it stated:

> "In the absence of common rules relating to the production and marketing of products, obstacles to movement within the Community resulting from disparities between national legislation must be accepted in so far as such legislation, *applying without discrimination to both domestic and imported products*, may be justified as being necessary in order to satisfy mandatory requirements".[86]

However, "things not always are what they seem": subsequent decisions of the Court have *de facto* applied mandatory requirements to measures formally discriminating between national and imported products, while at the same time, reaffirming that they do not apply. This approach started with Case 113/80, *Commission* v. *Ireland*,[87] where the Court, while explicitly denying that any of the grounds of justification put forward in the *Cassis de Dijon* mandatory requirements test applied to the formally discriminatory measure at stake, accepted the need to take those grounds into consideration to decide whether the measure was in substance non-discriminatory.[88] According to Oliver, "the idea that a distinctly applicable measure may be justified on grounds of consumer protection has been put out of the door and let in through the window".[89] Thus, in fact, mandatory requirements can already be considered as an extension to Article 36, albeit applied in a more restrictive manner to formally discriminatory measures.

Dassonville and *Cassis de Dijon* can thus be seen as establishing the foundations of a cost/benefit analysis (a balance test) under Article 30: the costs of the measures are to be assessed according to their effect on trade under the *Dassonville* formula and the *Cassis de Dijon* mutual recognition principle; the benefits of the measures are to be assessed under the mandatory requirements and Article 36 tests.

A balance test may take many forms. In particular, it may vary as to the interests to balance and over the way in which balancing is structured (includ-

[84] See Weatherill, "Consumer Safety Legislation in the United Kingdom and Article 30 EEC", (1988) ELR, 87, at 91.

[85] The hypothetical interpretation of Article 36 as non-exhaustive list in *Cassis de Dijon* was eg criticised by Masclet. See Masclet, "Les articles 30, 36 et 100" (n.81 above), at 623–6.

[86] Case 6/81, *Groep* v. *Beele* [1982] ECR 707, para 7, emphasis added.

[87] [1982] ECR 1625.

[88] Which was not the case: see paras 9 *et seq*.

[89] Oliver, *Free Movement of Goods*, 2nd edn., (London, European Law Centre, 1988), at 94 and references at footnote 94. For a more recent decision confirming this view, see Case C–2/90, *Commission* v. *Belgium* [1992] ECR I–4433, at paras 29–36, mainly 34–36.

ing the definition and measurement of those interests). In an article on the American "commerce clause", Regan[90] cites two different types of balancing: "open-ended private interest balancing" and "national-interest balancing" (the national has to be replaced by Community in our context). In the first, the costs imposed on a private person may not suffice to strike down the State measure but have to be taken into account.[91] In the second, the interests to be put in opposition to State interests could be interests in economic union, interests in the free movement of goods, interests in access to markets, interests in the uniform regulation of commerce, interest in efficiency, and finally interests in avoiding State protectionism.[92] Such discussion is absent from Community debates: authors arguing for balance normally avoid detailed discussion of the possible interests involved in that balance; and the Court, in its dealings with proportionality, has not really addressed the issue.

A kind of "open-ended private interest balancing" is what would result from the conception of Article 30 as a fundamental economic right to market access. At the other end of the spectrum is the conception of the balance test as an efficient way of avoiding State protectionism.[93] In this case, discrimination or protectionist effects tests are seen as inefficient in fighting protectionism because they allow too many protectionist measures to escape judicial consideration. A balance test would allow the Court to review almost any State measure from an anti-protectionist perspective. Other commentators, perhaps the majority, focus on balancing the State's interest in the regulation with the interference it causes with trade.[94] This is closely linked with approaches which emphasise the importance of achieving the common market.[95] Neither of these concerns (free trade and common market) can, however, be assessed in isolation, as they are not final goals but only instrumental in the achievement of other goals (such as economies of scale, lower prices,

[90] D.H. Regan, "The Supreme Court and State Protectionism: Making Sense of the Dormant Commerce Clause", (1986) 84 *Michigan Law Review*, 1091.

[91] Ibid, at 1102–3.

[92] Ibid, at 1103–4.

[93] See: Mattera, "Le Marche Unique" (n.75 above), at 191–2 (but he also appears to ascribe a broader role to *Cassis de Dijon* in the construction and functioning of the internal market: see, "De l'arrêt 'Dassonville' à l'arrêt 'Keck': l'obscure clarté d'une jurisprudence riche en principes novateurs et en contradictions", (1994) *Revue du Marché Unique Européen*, 117, at 134); Masclet "Les articles 30, 36 et 100", (n.81 above) at 612. This emphasis in avoiding protectionism is associated with the creation of a common market, that, in itself, may demand more than preventing protectionism.

[94] See: J.L. Buendia Sierra, "Las Secuelas del caso 'Cassis de Dijon'. Libre circulacion de productos alimenticios y reglementaciones nacionales", (1989) 16 *Revista de Instituciones Europeas*, 135, at the end; E. Cortese Pinto, *Ostacolli Non Tariffari Agli Scambi Nel Diritto Communitario* (Milano, Franco Angeli, 1985), at 80; Gormley, *Prohibiting Restrictions on Trade* (n.75 above), at 14.

[95] Celona, *La Libera Circolazione* (n.75 above).In his opinion, the interpretation given by the Commission and the Court to Article 30 made it into a basic norm that "*racchiude la* ratio *dell'intero Trattato*". It would even be possible to consider Article 30 as unnecessary in view of the general obligation upon Member States to favour the establishment of a common market; see at 165.

new products, and consumer freedom of choice). Although it may thus be possible to measure the degree of hindrance to trade, it is not easy to compare this with the social value of regulatory measures (assuming that this is possible to measure at all). Thus, imagine the following balance: "x" protection of the environment against "y" hindrance of trade. We need a different metric to tell us how much benefit corresponds to "x" protection of the environment and how much cost corresponds to y hindrance of trade. For example, we have to identify the values protected by free trade and assess how much are they affected by "y" hindrance to trade. Thus, we are faced again with constitutional questions regarding the nature and content of the European Economic Constitution which have normally been ignored in the debate on Article 30.

The Court has never clearly addressed the issue of which interests should be balanced. The notion of "Community interests" is either used on a case by case basis to assess the benefits of the measures from a Community perspective[96] or related to the free movement of goods and the aim of creating a common market. Interests affected and costs are included under these general headings and not specified. In reality these headings cover several other goals the interest of which cannot be defined as private or Community interests. In general terms, a burden on trade corresponds to a less-effective resource allocation in terms of producers (eg loss of economies of scale, companies not able to locate in the optimal place of production) and consumers (higher prices, less choice). However, such costs imposed by a regulation are not necessarily dependent on a cross-frontier element, but are more the "natural" result of State regulations limiting access to the market. The assessment of the Community interest, defined as the interest in free trade, thus becomes closely associated with private-interest balancing. This result is well reflected in Wils' definition:

> "The borderline between legitimate and illegitimate national regulation under Article 30 should reflect the *balance between the desire for integration, that is, the desire to limit the influence of national governments on people's activities* throughout the Community, *and the desire for government intervention*, translated—for practical reasons or reasons of principle—into a desire for national regulation".[97]

In this case, balance would be guided by a certain understanding of the right degree of public intervention in the market. One alternative and possible way of limiting balance would be to accept without reserves the specific goal established by the State and to assess literally the "necessity" of the measure with regard to that goal as defined by the State. The underlying idea is that the State's definition of policy is left intact while it remains possible to control measures that, though presented as "necessary" for such policies, are in fact

[96] See, in Chapter 3 below, the analysis of majoritarian activism in the Court's case law.

[97] Wils, "The Search for the Rule in Article 30 EEC: much ado about nothing?", (1993) ELR, 475, at 478 (emphasis added).

not so and in consequence can be understood as intended or unintended protectionism. Thus, it would be for the States themselves to define adequate policies and the right degree of protection for the purposes of the aims recognised as legitimate under Article 36 and the mandatory requirements. Nonetheless formal non-conformity of the foreign products with national rules might not be sufficient to prevent them from entering the national market, as long as they substantially complied with the national policies which set the standards of protection. This is still strictly linked with a conception of the exceptions to free movement as an area reserved for state powers controlled through a kind of "abus de droit" doctrine.[98] This conception could find support in a restrictive reading of *Cassis de Dijon*. In effect, the Court in that decision stated that obstacles to the free movement of goods resulting from disparities between national laws are acceptable "in so far as those provisions may be recognised as necessary in order to satisfy mandatory requirements". Unlike the Commission and the Advocate-General, the Court of Justice did not require an assessment of the proportionality of the measures. Balancing under proportionality can be seen as broader and more discretionary than balancing under necessity. Literally, proportionality implies that the policy objective pursued by a measure can be reconstructed or even abandoned, in part or completely, depending on the costs imposed by the measure. On the other hand, an assessment of the necessity of a measure will leave the definition of the policy objective untouched and will concentrate exclusively on determining whether the measure could be achieved in a manner which imposes a lesser burden on trade. The wording of *Cassis de Dijon,* in referring exclusively to an assessment of whether measures are "necessary in order to satisfy mandatory requirements", could lead to the conclusion that the Court was expressing its preference for a balance of the latter kind, which would in effect be close to a "principle of equivalence" such as that which for long was in place over the free movement of persons.[99] This interpretation of the *Cassis de Dijon* test and mutual recognition principle can be found, in part, in the Communication of the Commission on *Cassis de Dijon*.[100] Such application of the balance test would be aimed at preventing protectionism and not to controlling the degree of public intervention in the market.

Cost/benefit or balance tests can vary deeply, depending on the aims pursued that guide the exercise of the broad discretionary powers they entail. If,

[98] "Abus de droit" doctrine is also how Waelbrook qualifies the approach of the Commission in Directive 70/50; D. Waelbrook, "La compatibilité des legislations nationales indistinctement applicables au produits nationaux et importés avec les regles européennes de libre circulation des merchandises", (1983) CDE, 241, at 243.

[99] See, for example, P. Watson, "Freedom of Establishment and Freedom to Provide Services: Some Recent Developments", (1983) *CMLRev*, 767.

[100] OJ 1980 NC256, 2. The Commission stated: "where a product 'suitably and satisfactorily' fulfils the legitimate objective of a Member State's own rules . . . the importing country cannot justify prohibiting its sale in its territory by claiming that the way it fulfils the objective is different from that imposed on domestic products".

in general terms, balancing can be identified as B versus C, in which B stands for benefits and C for costs, the particular form of "equivalence balance" could be represented in the following way: B1 versus C1 v. C2 v. C3 etc. Here the definition of B is for the State to set. In other words, it is the State that sets the adequate degree of protection for any of the mandatory requirements. Balancing is restricted to assessing whether a measure with lesser costs could attain the *same degree of protection*. In this case balance is used as a test of equivalence between the regulations to which domestic and imported products are submitted. The issue is not a balance between the degree of protection of the legitimate interests safeguarded by the regulations of the recipient-State and the burden imposed upon free trade; rather it is whether the different national regulations, in spite of their formal differences, protect those interests in the same way. As Weatherill stated: "Member States are in principle obliged to permit the import of products lawfully produced and marketed in another Member State, even if goods infringe their domestic specifications, provided the goods meet the overall objective, if not the precise detail, of the national law".[101] Naturally much depends on the choice between "the overall objective" or "the precise detail" To assess whether the exporting State regulation achieves the "overall objective" of consumer protection as well as the importing State regulation is one thing. To require the regulations in the exporting State regulation to guarantee exactly the same consumer protection which is required by the regulations of the importing State is quite another. While replacing labelling requirements for rules on the composition of foodstuffs may be a normal outcome under the first type of balance, it can only be argued with difficulty that such outcome meets the "precise detail" of the recipient-State regulation.

Equivalence balance is, to a great extent, a refinement of a discrimination test, similar to the refinement which occurred in the construction of the principle of equivalence over the free movement of persons. To extend the Court's discretion by using the "overall objective" notion immediately requires policy judgements regarding the best way to pursue aims such as consumer or environmental protection, which depend upon different risk assessments and cultural traditions. This is becoming a kind of balance which could be described as net balance (B1 versus C1). Here the benefits are submitted to balance. The State may have to lower the degree of protection if the benefits arising from it are less than the costs. From the moment the standard of protection is itself submitted to review this area can no longer be seen as an area for reserved powers for the States. Net balance implies that the degree of protection set by the State is balanced against the burden imposed on trade, and if the costs of that burden outweigh the benefits of that degree of protection, this degree has

[101] S. Weatherill, "Consumer Safety Legislation in the United Kingdom and Article 30 EEC", (1988) *ELR*, 87, at 91. See also, Olivier, The Free Movement of Goods, 2nd. edn., (n.89 above), pp 95 *et seq*.

to be changed. However, in net balance as long as the benefits outweigh the costs no comparison can be made with other possible measures.[102]

As with equivalence balance, net balance has never been systematically defined and followed by the Court. There is no basis in the Court case law to construct any notion of balance which is limited. If we are to accept that the Court is really balancing the costs and the benefits of State measures under Article 30, then a kind of pure balance appears as predominant. It can be described in the following way: B1 versus C1; B2 versus C2 etc. Here it is not sufficient for the benefits to outweigh the costs if another measure produces a higher net outcome between costs and benefits. Again, there is no clear definition of such balance test in the Court's case law, but it appears to be the outcome of the developments therein under the proportionality rationale. Already in *Commission* v. *Belgium (Certificates of Authenticity)*, which was heard soon after *Cassis de Dijon*, the Court moved from assessing whether measures are necessary for a legitimate objective of the State to an assessment of whether they "are unreasonable in that they are disproportionate in relation to that objective".[103] Proportionality has become the name by which balancing is known in the Community context, even though the *Cassis de Dijon* heading of "necessity" is still often the one to which the Court exclusively refers to.[104] Necessity and proportionality have been interpreted by the Court as requiring the State to choose the means that least hinders the free movement of goods,[105] or in other words, as requiring them not to impose unnecessary burdens on trade.[106] Clearly, it is not sufficient merely that the benefits of a measure outweigh its costs in order for it to be upheld under the proportionality test. Moreover, when it assesses whether the State's goal, recognised as legitimate by Community law, is attained, the Court does not refer

102 An example of this type of balancing can be seen in Case 2/78, *Commission* v. *Belgium* (Certificates of authenticity) [1979] ECR 1761. The case concerned alternative systems to ensure the authenticity of origin of spirits. The Court refused to compare the system proposed by the Commission with that of the Belgian Government, considering that the benefits arising from the new Belgium system were sufficient to validate it, even though the Commission argued that the protection of the designation of origin could be assured just as well by a system of sealing and labelling which would raise fewer obstacles to trade.

103 See para 38. Though, as first mentioned, the Court performed a kind of net balance (not pure balance) in this case.

104 See, as examples of balancing under the necessity clause of *Cassis de Dijon* (and not proportionality): Case 286/81, *Oosthoek's* [1982] ECR 4575; Case 94/82, *De Kikvorsch* [1983] ECR 947; Joined Cases 60 and 61/84, *Cinéthèque* [1985] ECR 2605; Case 216/84, *Commission* v. *France* (Milk powder) [1988] ECR 809; Case C–362/88, *GB-INNO* [1990] ECR 683.

105 See, for example, Case 176/84, *Commission* v. *Greece* (Beer Purity Law) [1987] ECR 1193, at para 29; Case 216/84, *Commission* v. *France* (Milk powder) [1988] ECR 809, at para 4; Case 76/86, *Commission* v. *Germany* [1989] ECR 1021, at para 13; Case 382/87, *Buet* (Canvassing) [1989] ECR 1235, at para 11; Case C–241/89, *SARPP* [1990] ECR I–4695, at para 31.

106 See Case 178/84, *Commission* v. *Germany* (Beer Purity Law) [1987] ECR 1227 para 25. Note, that there is a difference between requiring the application of the measure on imported products to be *necessary* because imported products do not have to comply with equivalent requirements in their State of origin (which corresponds to the principle of equivalence) and requiring the burden on trade to be *necessary* in attaining a legitimate goal (which is pure balance).

to a specified degree of protection but simply to general aims such as consumer or environmental protection; it has also expressly recognised that a State may be forced to lower its degree of protection.[107] Thus we must conclude that both the benefits and the costs of the measures are to be assessed and that, even if a State measure produces a net benefit, it is to be subject to comparison with alternative measures that, in the opinion of the Court, produce an higher net benefit. In other words, pure balance is the predominant interpretation of the *Cassis de Dijon* test. In *RTT (Telephone Equipment)* the Court brought together the different balancing tests following from *Cassis de Dijon* in a single statement:

> "disparities between national provisions must be accepted in so far as those provisions, which are applicable without distinction to national products and to imported products, can be justified as being necessary in order to satisfy imperative requirements of Community law. The Court has, however, held that such rules must be proportionate to the object to be achieved and that, where a Member State has a choice between a number of measures suited to achieving the same purpose, it must choose the means that least hinders the free movement of goods".[108]

However, the evidence of a broad balance test to review national measures under Article 30 may be contradicted by the substantive application of such test and the outcomes of the judicial decisions. Does such a balance test correspond (or did it correspond until *Keck*) to a true cost/benefit analysis of national regulations or is it guided by a different concern?; is it directed to control the degree of public regulation of the market or the degree of State regulation of the market? As I will argue in more detail in the following chapter, the balance test adopted by the Court is a true balance test only in the discretion it grants to the Court in the review of national measures. The argument will be advanced below that what drives the assessment of national regulations by the Court is not a real cost/benefit analysis but, simply, whether such regulations correspond to the European majority policy on the issue under review.

THE UNDERLYING CONFLICT: ECONOMIC LIBERALISM VERSUS ANTI-PROTECTIONISM

When reviewing national measures with an effect on trade under Article 30, the Court of Justice must both decide whether there should be regulation and—if so—who will have the power to regulate. Thus, the Court has, through Article 30, defined many of the essential foundations of the European Economic Constitution. The extent of regulatory powers left to Member States will depend much on the scope given to Article 30. In the same way,

[107] See Case 76/86, *Commission* v. *Germany* [1989] ECR 1021, at para 16.
[108] Case C–18/88, *RTT* [1991] ECR I–5941, para 30.

the criteria followed in upholding or striking down national measures brought under review through Article 30 will reflect the level of market regulation. The decision to review national regulations, and if so according to which criteria, implies choices regarding the division of competences between the Member States and the Union. It also presupposes choices regarding the constitutional limits to State or public intervention in the market.

In the case law and literature on Article 30, deepening and broadening progressed together. As mentioned, even discrimination tests have tended to rubber stamp the broad scope granted to Article 30 in the review of national regulations. As a result, almost any State measure could be submitted to judicial review under the *Dassonville* test. With few exceptions commentators have long stressed the inability of restrictive tests (such as discrimination) to control State activities which affect the free movement of goods and argued in favour of greater judicial control over national regulations. In so doing, they have often neglected the institutional choices which are inherent in that view. They underline the need to balance free movement with regulatory aims and examine the problems involved in leaving it to States to define that balance; they do not, however, analyse the problems involved in allowing the Court to define the balance. To have the Court balance the costs and benefits of a certain provision under a test of proportionality means, to a great extent, making it responsible for defining the appropriate regulatory policy. The institutional choice involved should compare the merits and demerits of both the States and the Court. As Komesar puts it: "an institution is inefficient only when it functions less perfectly than an alternative available institution".[109] The capacity of courts is limited by their structure (measures brought to court are supposed to be exceptional events and not part of an everyday participation in the regulatory process). Moreover, they often lack expertise and have high administrative costs, are subject to information problems (information is closely dependent on those who are sufficiently organised to participate in the judicial process), and may decide issues without hearing some of the affected interests (some interested parties are unable to participate for lack of standing). Above all, they face questions of legitimacy, which have consequences for the acceptance of their decisions and their authority.

To decide when the Court should balance between the costs and benefits of a measure and when this should be left to the Member States depends largely on the position one takes regarding the European Economic Constitution and its relation to the rules of free movement. There are basically two general alternative concepts behind the control of the application of Article 30. They reflect different conceptions of the Economic Constitution of the Community

109 Komesar, "In Search of a General Approach to Legal Analysis: A Comparative Institutional Alternative", (1981) 79 *Michigan Law Review*, 1350, at 1359. Institutional choices and comparative institutional analysis are coherently and thoroughly discussed in his book: *Imperfect Alternatives—Choosing Institutions in Law, Economics and Public Policy* (Chicago and London, The University of Chicago Press, 1994).

or the European Union. Commentators, however, have often neglected the conflict between these two economic constitutional conceptions of the Community and the dilemma, reflecting them, facing the case law of the Court. In *Hünermund*, Advocate-General Thesauro has, finally, clearly assumed this constitutional dilemma:

> "Is Article 30 of the Treaty a provision intended to liberalize intra-Community trade or is it intended more generally to encourage the unhindered pursuit of commerce in individual Member States?"[110]

The first concept can be summed up with the idea that the aim of Article 30 is to prevent State protectionism. Such protectionism assumes subtle forms which require constant refinement of the criteria used to review national measures. The second concept leads to the transformation of Article 30 into a kind of "economic due process" clause. It is based on a conception of the Economic Constitution of the Community built on the free market, open competition, and a particular view of the kinds of regulation that are acceptable. According to this concept, judicial review of national rules under Article 30 should assess State intervention in the market.

These concepts are not necessarily reflected in the different interpretations being put forward for Article 30. Balance tests, for example, have been argued on grounds ranging from anti-protectionism to "economic due process". However, these two concepts encapsulate the normative dilemma underlying this area of the law and its relation with the European Economic Constitution. In the following chapter, the case law of the Court of Justice will be analysed in the context of the constitutional dilemmas and institutional choices highlighted. In Chapters 4 and 5, these issues will be addressed from a normative standpoint, reviewing different alternative models of the European Economic Constitution and proposing a new approach to Article 30 and its role in the European Constitution.

[110] Opinion of Advocate General Thesauro delivered on 27 October 1993 in Case C–292/92, *Hünermund* [1993] ECR I–6787.

3

The Judicial Model of the European Economic Constitution and Article 30: Majoritarian Activism

THE EXPANSION OF ARTICLE 30 AND THE LIMITS TO STATE REGULATION OF THE MARKET

Until the recent decision in *Keck*[1] the Court's approach to Article 30 was characterised by a progressive extension of its scope, building on the *Dassonville* decision.[2] As repeatedly stated, the Court held that :

> "All trading rules enacted by Member States which are capable of hindering, directly or indirectly, actually or potentially, intra-Community trade are to be considered as measures having an effect equivalent to quantitative restrictions".[3]

In spite of the broad character of this *ratio decidendi*, especially after the abandonment of the "trading rules" words, subsequent decisions kept a close link with a discrimination test. With *Cassis de Dijon*, the *Dassonville* doctrine was given new life and Article 30 began its progressive extension which allows it to catch any State measure capable of interfering with the market in respect of the trade in goods, even if (as we have seen) other, more restrictive, criteria can still be found in the case law of the Court.[4] *Cassis de Dijon* dealt with a national regulation that was probably protectionist and materially discriminatory, but the impulse given to the broad *Dassonville* statement and the introduction of what came to be know as the principle of mutual recognition among national laws, led to an extension of the range of action of Article 30 that was taken up and developed in following decisions. Such development can be seen in many decisions on national measures applicable without distinction where the objective of the State was not regulate trade with other States but to regulate the market in the pursuit of public goals other than economic protectionism.

[1] Joined Cases C–267/91 and C–268/91, *Keck and Mithouard* [1993] ECR I–6097.

[2] Case 8/74, *Dassonville* [1974] ECR 837.

[3] See para 5.

[4] See the analysis of the different interpretations of Article 30 and the Court's case law in the previous chapter.

Soon after *Cassis de Dijon*, in *Fietje*,[5] the Court was faced with a Dutch law imposing an obligation to use the word "*likeur*" to describe certain beverages defined therein. Though such legislation could not be said to be discriminatory, it could, nevertheless, make the marketing of imports more difficult[6] since it made it "impossible to market the imported product without altering the label under which the beverage is lawfully marketed in the exporting Member State".[7] In consequence, it had to be determined whether such a requirement was really necessary. The Court found that the obligation to use the word "*likeur*" was not necessary when "the details given on the original label of the imported product have as their content information on the nature of the product and that content included at least the same information, and is just as capable of being understood by consumers in the importing State, as the description prescribed by the rules of that State".[8] This was in fact the start of a policy giving preference to labelling over mandatory requirements regarding the designation, composition or other characteristics of imported products. In a series of cases, the Court has redefined many national regulatory policies on the characteristics and designations of goods. Those national regulations prevented (in absolute terms or under certain constraints) the marketing of goods not complying with certain national requirements, designed to protect consumers, health, fair trading etc. These different national regulations created obstacles to trade that the Court generally considered excessive in view of their aim and of the alternative policy available. This alternative policy is a consumer information policy. Already in *Cassis de Dijon* the Court had stated that "it is a simple matter to ensure that suitable information is conveyed to the purchaser by requiring the display of an indication of origin and of the alcohol content on the packaging of products".[9] According to the Court, labelling legislation does not restrict the importation of goods while generally safeguarding consumer protection and fair trading in providing the consumer with the information necessary to make his/her choice in full knowledge of the facts.[10] This labelling argument has been pushed forward in many other decisions. In some cases, the Court was dealing with traditional national characteristics or designations, such as that regarding the designation of "vinegar";[11] the shape of wine bottles;[12] beer purity laws;[13]

[5] Case 27/80, *Fietje* [1980] ECR 3839. See also, shortly before, Case 788/79, *Gilli and Andres* (Vinegar I) [1980] ECR 2071.

[6] See para 10.

[7] See para 8.

[8] See para 12.

[9] See para 13.

[10] Case 193/80, *Commission* v. *Italy* (Vinegar II) [1981] ECR 3019, para 27.

[11] Ibid and also *Commission* v. *Italy* (Vinegar I) n.5.

[12] Case 176/84, *Commission* v. *Germany* (Petillant de Raisin) [1986] ECR 3879.

[13] Beer Purity Law cases: Case 176/84, *Commission* v. *Greece* [1987] ECR 1193 and Case 178/84, *Commission* v. *Germany* [1987] ECR 1227.

pasta requirements;[14] and the names of cheeses.[15] In other cases it faced measures of a more technical and nationally neutral nature, such as those requiring a specific amount of dry matter in loaves;[16] specific packages for margarine;[17] use of the words "deep-frozen fermented milk" or "yogurt";[18] and references to "sugar".[19]

Whereas the extension of Article 30 in the review of national regulations of the market is visible from the cases cited above and has been criticised for being deregulatory,[20] it is with another type of case that the deregulatory use of Article 30 as an "economic due process" clause protecting market freedom from public intervention is more associated: cases whose impact on imports appear as a consequence of the more general restrictions imposed by national rules on trade and access to the market. This is confirmed by the fact that many of these national measures and regulations are challenged in the Court by nationals of the State in question, not other EU nationals or importers.[21] It suffices to recall the cases on Sunday trading and the litigation strategies of companies like GB-INNO-BM and Leclerc, referred to above,[22] to see that the interests underlying many such cases had nothing to do with imports, but with regulatory burdens imposed on national companies. What is normally at stake in these cases is the general restriction imposed on access to the market and competition therein. Under the balance test developed by the Court following *Dassonville* and *Cassis de Dijon*, many measures of this kind have been subjected to the balance test, even where they did not discriminate against foreign products. Examples of legislation of this kind being submitted to cost/benefit analysis include: rules on advertising and sales methods;[23] national health-system rules on subsidies on medical products and on pharmaceutical monopolies;[24] price regulations;[25] national recycling systems;[26]

[14] Case 407/85, *3 Gloken and another* v. *USL Centro-Sud and another* (Pasta) [1988] ECR 4233.

[15] Case 286/86, *Deserbais* [1988] ECR 4907.

[16] Case 130/80, *Kelderman* [1981] ECR 527.

[17] Case 261/81, *Walter Rau* (Margarine) [1982] ECR 3961.

[18] Case 298/87, *Smanor* [1988] ECR 4489.

[19] Case C–241/89, *SARPP* [1990] ECR 4695.

[20] See, H.-C. von Heydebrand ud. Lasa, "Free Movement of Foodstuffs, Consumer Protection and Food Standards in the European Community: Has the Court of Justice Got It Wrong?", (1991) 16 *ELR*, 391.

[21] See, among the many cases representing different types of measures challenged: Case 286/81, *Oosthoek's* [1982] ECR 4575; Case 126/82, *Smit* [1983] ECR 73; Case 237/82, *Jongeneel Kaas* [1984] ECR 483; Joined Cases 80 and 159/85, *Edah* [1986] ECR 3359; *Smanor* n.18; and Case C–241/89, *SARPP* [1990] ECR I–4695.

[22] See Chapter 1.

[23] See: *Oosthoek's* (n.21 above); Case C–362/88, *GB-INNO* [1990] ECR I–667; Case 382/87, *Buet* (Canvassing) [1989] ECR 1235; Joined Cases C–1/90 and C–176/90, *Aragonesa* [1991] ECR I–4151; and Case C–126/91, *Yves Rocher.* [1993] ECR I–2361.

[24] See Case 238/82, *Duphar* [1984] ECR 523 and Case C–369/88, *Delattre* [1991] ECR I–1487.

[25] See, for example, Case 29/83, *Leclerc* (Prix du Libre) [1985] ECR 1. There are other cases on price regulations. Since there is a complex interplay between cost/benefit analyses, competition rules, loss of competitive advantage and non-discrimination they will be discussed in more detail below.

[26] See Case 302/86, *Commission* v. *Denmark* [1988] ECR 4607.

prohibition on Sunday trading or on employing workers on Sundays;[27] public law monopolies on the approval of equipment;[28] and the organisation of dock work.[29]

The process by which the scope of action of Article 30 was extended to include virtually any national regulatory measure can be seen in three important groups of decisions.

Expanding the concept of discrimination: loss of a competitive advantage and price regulations case law

The first group of decisions, through which the Court has extended the scope of Article 30, has to do with the progressive extension of the concept of discrimination itself. This occurred with the introduction into the concept of discrimination of the notion of the "loss of a competitive advantage" by foreign products, in parallel with the introduction of competition rules into the legal discourse on the free movement of goods. This is the basis of the Court's approach to price regulations. In two initial cases the Court clearly developed an approach to price regulation based on concerns over protectionism and discrimination. In *Tasca* and *Sadam*, the Court stated that price regulations applicable without distinction which impose maximum prices were acceptable unless they were fixed at such a level that would make the sale of imported products impossible or more difficult than that of national products.[30] Thus, it was not sufficient simply for imports to lose any advantages acquired due to their State of origin: the regulations had to place imports in a disadvantaged position *vis-à-vis* national products in order for them to be considered measures having equivalent effect to a quantitative restriction within the meaning of Article 30. However, soon after these two decisions, the Court took two steps which eroded the powers of Member States to make price regulations valid under Article 30. The first was the introduction of competition values into the discourse on the review of State measures under the fundamental rules governing free movement in the common market. Inspired by a question from a national court, the Court of Justice, adopted the idea that the competition rules of the Treaty, designed to apply to private actors, can also be applied through Article 5 EC to Member States, whenever a State regulation requires, favours or reinforces private behaviour contrary to those rules.[31]

[27] See Case C–145/88, *Torfaen Borough Council* [1989] ECR 3851; Case C–312/89, *Conforama* [1991] ECR I–991; Case C–332/89, *Marchandise* [1991] ECR I–1027; Case C–169/91, *Stoke-on-Trent* [1992] ECR I–6635.

[28] Case C–18/8, *RTT* (Telephone Equipment) [1991] ECR I–5941.

[29] Case C–179/90, *Merci Convenzionali Porto di Genova* [1991] ECR I–5889.

[30] For example, if the maximum price were fixed at such a low level that imports could only be made at a loss: Case 65/75, *Tasca* [1976] ECR 291, para 13; Joined Cases 88 to 90/75, *Sadam* [1976] ECR 323.

[31] Case 13/77, *GB-INNO* v. *ATAB* [1977] ECR 2115.

The second step was taken soon after this, in *Van Tiggele*,[32] where the Court conceptualised the loss of a competitive advantage enjoyed by imports as a form of discrimination.[33] This was the case where a minimum price did not allow the lower cost price of imports to be reflected in the retail selling price.[34] However, the loss of a competitive advantage is a natural effect of laws aimed at restricting competition such as those regulating prices. A minimum price also "discriminates" among different national producers of the same product, some of whom are able to produce goods for sale at a lower price than the regulation allows. There is only true discrimination between national and imported products where the regulated prices are set in view of national production costs; but the Court did not require this to be part of its test. It considered as sufficient the loss of a competitive advantage, thus in effect submitting a broad range of price regulations to cost/benefit analysis under Article 30.[35]

The broadening of the scope of Article 30 and the introduction of competition rules in the review of State measures come together in the *Leclerc* cases, where the Court struck down two French laws which imposed fixed prices.[36] In this case, the Court suggested a co-ordinated use of free movement and competition rules that opened other national regulations to challenge under intents of deregulation and not anti-protectionism.[37] This led to an initial discussion on the "economic due process" use of both Article 30 and (mainly) competition rules to review state regulations.[38]

[32] Case 82/77, *Van Tiggele* [1978] ECR 25.

[33] On the one hand, the Court says that provisions fixing prices in such a way that they cannot produce effects detrimental to imports alone are not measures having an equivalent effect to quantitative restrictions (para 16). On the other, it says that they are such if the provision "is capable of having an adverse effect on the marketing of the latter in so far as it prevents their lower cost from being reflected in the retail selling price" (para 18).

[34] Ibid.

[35] Thus, contrary, to what it is normally stated, it is not clear that price regulations constitute a separate body of case law, subject to a discrimination test even before *Keck*. See, in favour of a discrimination reading of price regulations cases: Gormley, "Actually or Potentially, Directly or Indirectly? Obstacles to Free Movement of Goods", (1990) *Yearbook of European Law* 197, and P. Oliver, *Free Movement of Goods*, 3rd edn. (London, Sweet and Maxwell, 1996), at 171.

[36] Case 229/83, *Leclerc* (Prix du libre) [1985] ECR 1 and Case 231/83, *Leclerc* (Prix de l'essence) [1985] ECR 305, followed by similar cases. See the analysis by Galmot, and Biancarelli, in "Les réglementations nationales en matière de prix au regard du droit communautaire", (1985) *RTDE*, 268. They argue that these decisions integrate community competition rules in the review of national prices regulations (at 273 and 291 *et seq*). Shortly before these cases the Court had, however, distinguished the objectives of Article 30 and competition rules. The former aimed at promoting free trade while the later at promoting effective competition: see Joined Cases 177 and 178/82, *Van de Haar and Kaveka de Meern* [1984] ECR 1797, paras 11–12.

[37] See, for example, Case C–332/89, *Marchandise* [1991] ECR I–1027; Case C–179/90, *Merci Convenzionale Porto di Genova* [1991] ECR I–5889; Case C–260/89, *ERT* [1991] ECR 2951 and Case C–18/88, *RTT* (Telephone Equipment) [1991] ECR I–5973. For an example involving a different area of Community law, see Case C–41/90, *Höfner* [1991] ECR 2010. The Court is still deciding cases where a regulation was challenged on those arguments: see Case C–379/92, *Matteo Peralta* [1994] ECR I–3453; Case C–412/93, *Leclerc* v. *TF 1 Publicite* [1995] ECR I–179.

[38] See the debate between Marenco and Pescatore: Pescatore, "Public and Private Aspects of European Competition Law", (1987) 10 *Fordham International Law Journal*, 373 and his rejoinder at 444; Marenco, "Competition Between National Economies and Competition Between Business—A Response to Judge Pescatore", (1987) 10 *Fordham International Law Journal*, 420.

Non-discriminatory rules on marketing circumstances: the Oosthoek's case law

A second important group of decisions in the expansion of Article 30 is identified with the *Oosthoek's*[39] case, in which the Court extended[40] the scope of the *Dassonville* doctrine to include measures applicable without distinction that do not even require any changes to be made to imported products (in the form of different production methods or labelling for example) but simply a change in their marketing methods, thereby affecting their marketing opportunities.[41] The Court argued that "to compel a producer either to adopt advertising or sales promotion schemes which differ from one Member State to another or to discontinue a scheme he considers particularly effective may constitute an obstacle to imports even if the legislation in question applies to domestic and imported products without distinction".[42] In a latter case, in which the Court repeated this approach, it made it particularly clear that there were no concerns over protectionism in this reasoning, and what counted was the proportionality of the measure *vis-à-vis* its goals. The Court, with reference to the legislation under review, stated that "it is common ground that the French legislature adopted the prohibition of canvassing in question out of concern to protect consumers against the risk of ill-considered purchases".[43] However, that is not sufficient and "such rules must be proportionate to the goals pursued, and if a Member State has at its disposal less restrictive means of obtaining the same goals, it is under an obligation to make use of them".[44] The reason to include such type of rules under the concept of measures having equivalent effect to a quantitative restriction is identical to that commanding the inclusion of rules requiring changes to be made to imported products (rules on product requirements): the double burden that foreign producers have to face by being forced to change the strategies and methods of marketing their products (as when they have to change the characteristics of these products).[45]

[39] Case 286/81, *Oosthoek's* [1982] ECR 4575.

[40] See para 15.

[41] However, such an approach was already anticipated in Case 152/78, *Commission* v. *France* [1980] ECR 2299, at para 11.

[42] *Oosthoek's* (n.39 above) para 15. Restated, for example, in *GB-INNO* (n.23 above), para 7; *SARPP* (n.21 above), at para 29; *Delattre* (n.24 above), para 50, and *Yves Rocher* (n.23 above), para 10.

[43] Case 382/87, *Buet and another* [1989] ECR 1235, para 11.

[44] Ibid.

[45] See, for example, *Oosthoek's*, (n.39 above), para 15, and *Yves Rocher* (n.23 above), para 10. Though the Court also refers to the single obligation to "discontinue a scheme he considers particularly effective", which does not require a double burden to be imposed on imports.

The explicit abandonment of discrimination: Cinéthèque

The last important element in the expansion of Article 30 as a tool to review state regulatory measures comes in *Cinéthèque* where the Court expressly declared that Article 30 also covered non-discriminatory national measures:

> "it must be observed that such a system, if it applies without distinction to both video-cassettes manufactured in the national territory and to imported video-cassettes, does not have the purpose of regulating trade patterns; its effect is not to favour national production as against production of other Member States, but to encourage cinematographic production as such.
>
> Nevertheless, the application of such system may create barriers to intra-Community trade because of the disparities between the systems operated in different Member States and between the conditions for release of cinematographic works in the cinemas of those States. In those circumstances a prohibition of exploitation laid down by such a system is not compatible with the principle of the free movement of goods provided for in the Treaty unless any obstacle to intra-Community trade thereby created does not exceed that which is necessary in order to ensure the attainment of the objective in view and unless that objective is justified with regard to Community law".[46]

The outcome of these developments in the Court's case law was that almost any national regulatory measure became susceptible to review under Article 30. The proportionality test meant that a balance had to be struck between their costs and their benefits. This gave the Court a leading role in defining the adequate regulatory level of the common market and transformed Article 30 into a potential "economic due process" clause reviewing the degree of public intervention in the market.

In comparing the costs and benefits of national regulatory policies, the Court does more than simply ensure free trade among the Member States: it determines the acceptable degree of public regulation, balancing public intervention against free market values. This may reinforce the view that Article 30 has in effect been transformed into an "economic due process" clause through which the Court of Justice will be able to review the reasonableness of public intervention in the market.

However, the fact that a balance test involves a judgement of the reasonableness of national regulatory measures does not mean that such assessments are governed by a rationale of the constitutional limits to *public* intervention in the market. The broad scope given to Article 30 by the Court when reviewing State intervention in the market cannot be seen exclusively from the perspective of the regulation/deregulation debate; account must also be taken of the centralisation/decentralisation debate. We cannot deduce from the case law of the Court that it has a certain "free market" conception of the economic constitution of the European Union which is to be protected as a constitutional right and which the Court considers legitimate to impose on public authorities. In fact, the mar-

[46] Joined Cases 60 and 61/84, *Cinéthèque* [1985] ECR 2605, paras 21–22.

ket conception advanced by the Court in free movement of goods cases is not a neo-liberal one; nor is it presented as a fundamental economic right to be upheld by the Court against *public* intervention. Instead, limits are imposed on *State* intervention and such case law is more understandable as the product of a "*legislateur de substituition*",[47] which does not intend to impose a constitutional conception of the market and of economic organisation, but which aims to transfer economic decisions affecting the internal market from State level to Community level, in the pursuance of the judicial harmonisation of State rules the diversity of which is capable of restricting free trade and the optimal gains offered by the common market. It is argued below that the criterion guiding the Court in balancing the costs and benefits of national regulations has not been a specific (de)regulatory ideology but an attempt to identify the majoritarian view on that issue, taking the European Union as the relevant polity.

THE EUROPEAN COURT OF JUSTICE: MAJORITARIAN ACTIVISM

Article 30: a process of Europeanisation

The first element which contradicts an economic due process reading of the case law on Article 30 is that, even after *Cassis de Dijon,* many decisions present a discrimination test as the *ratio decidendio* to be followed in reviewing national measures restricting free trade.[48] The mixture of different tests and the presence of elements of anti-protectionism and economic due process in the case law of the Court is best understood in light of concerns over harmonisation and market integration. The Court itself, takes up the role of harmonising national laws, as far as it is able, pending Community legislation.[49] The lack of harmonisation of national rules places a burden on economic agents in the extra costs of having to comply with more than one set of rules. This impedes the achievement of some of the essential aims of an integrated market, such as economies of scale and lower prices. The problem is not the burden which the regulation imposes *per se* on economic agents, it is the burden which derives from the existence of more than one regulation.[50] In the

[47] This expression is taken from M. Bettati, "Le 'Law-Making Power' de la Cour", 48 (1989) *Pouvoirs*, 57, at 62.

[48] See, for example: Case 155/80, *Oebel* [1981] ECR 1993; Case 75/81, *Blesgen* [1982] ECR 1211; Case 72/82, *Commission* v. *Italy (Tobacco monopoly)* [1983] ECR 1955; Case 298/87, *Smanor* [1988] ECR 4489; Case C–23/89, *Quietlynn* [1990] ECR 4695. See also the discussion on discrimination tests in Chapter 2 above.

[49] It is in this light that: "both Article 36 and the 'rule of reason' can be seen as provisional exceptions, pending action at the Community level for harmonisation of divergent national laws": Forwood and Clough, "The Single European Act and Free Movement of Goods—Legal Implications for the Completion of the Internal Market", (1986) 11 *ELR*, 383, at 386.

[50] The Court made it clear in *Cinétheque* (n.46 above): "the application of such system may create barriers to intra-Community trade because of the disparities between the systems operated in different Member States and between the conditions for release of cinematographic works in the cinemas of those States": para 29.

cases dealing with measures applicable without distinction in which the Court does not identify discrimination or protectionism[51] it is such a burden, arising from non-harmonised national rules, that triggers the application of a balance test. As the Court argued in *RTT*, having to comply with different national requirements, even though this does not exclude imports, makes their sale more difficult or more onerous since the producer has to take into account several different requirements when manufacturing the product.[52] This is clearly the logic behind the case law on product requirements and the alternative labelling policy. But, as mentioned, the Court also stresses the burden coming from different national rules in having to change marketing methods, such as advertising or other forms of promotion. Already in *Oosthoek's* the Court stressed that a restriction on imports could be found in compelling the producer to adopt different advertising or sales promotion schemes in different Member States.[53] This was the basis for reviewing many of the national regulations discussed above, the effects on trade of which were incidental or a reflection of market regulation.

The cases reviewing States' price control systems can also be read in this light albeit in a more limited manner: the cost of having to comply with two different rules lies in not being able to programme production and marketing strategies in advance, as choices regarding production costs made under a certain regulatory system may be invalidated by the necessity of complying with a different set of rules in a different system. There is a duplication of price controls without taking into consideration the cost price in the State of origin.[54] It is true, however, that in the these cases (and a few other cases, mainly those on Sunday trading[55]) the burden coming from the lack of harmonisation is not so clear. These cases may be understood as a side-effect of the broad test necessary to capture all other national measures whose lack of harmonisation might reduce the gains arising from a common market. The broad scope given to Article 30, designed to push for the Europeanisation of regulatory law and so to reduce the costs of non-harmonised regulations, catches in its net any national regulatory measures even those where extra costs are irrelevant or do not exist at all. In reality it would be difficult for the Court to sustain a broad interpretation of Article 30 without ending up by having to review all State intervention in the market even where there was no particular burden arising from the existence of different national rules (as in the

[51] Such an extra burden is naturally present in all cases in which a discrimination or protectionist test is used by the Court. There, however, not only are imports subject to more than a set of rules, they are also subject to a more stringent set of rules than national products.

[52] Case C–18/88, *RTT* [1991] ECR I–5973.

[53] Case 286/81, *Oosthoek's* [1982] ECR 4575, para 15. As stated, however, it appeared to go even further, saying that it could be sufficient to compel the producer to abandon a scheme it considers particularly efficient.

[54] See *Leclerc* (Prix du libre) (n.37 above), para 25.

[55] Case C–145/88, *Torfaen Borough Council* [1989] ECR 3851; Case C–312/89, *Conforama* [1991] ECR I–997; Case C–332/89, *Marchandise* [1991] ECR I–1027; Case C–169/91, *Stoke-on-Trent* [1992] ECR I–6655.

Sunday trading cases). Moreover, in cases such as those on national price controls there are, as mentioned above, elements of anti-discrimination[56] as well as a close relation to competition rules.

If all this explains the broad scope given to Article 30 in the case law of the European Court of Justice it also requires a further investigation into this role of judicial harmonisation undertaken by the Court. There are two other important aspects in explaining the case law of the Court with regard to Article 30 and the European Economic Constitution: a democratic concern and a majoritarian approach. They have to do with the way balancing takes place: what guides the Court in reviewing the costs and benefits of a national measure caught in the "net" of Article 30, or, in other words, what guides the Court in its judicial harmonisation of national rules.

The democratic concern

The Court is not simply concerned with the absence of harmonisation and the obstacles which that poses to the integration of the market. It is also concerned with leaving the regulation of products from all over the common market to a Member State. National regulations are biased by the national market in which they were developed. Habits of consumption and production, regulatory traditions and the monopoly of information enjoyed by national interest groups sometimes make national political processes unlikely institutions to enact regulations affecting interests of nationals of other Member States in the same manner as they affect the interests of home nationals. In the view of the Court, the establishment of a common market means that the requirements imposed on goods and their marketing should take into account the traditions and interests of all Member States. This is made particularly clear in the well known "German Beer Purity Law" decision. The Court stated:

> "First, consumers' conceptions which vary from one Member State to the other are also likely to evolve in the course of time within a Member State. The establishment of a common market is, it should be added, one of the factors that may play a major contributory role in that development. . . . As the Court has already held in another context (judgment of 27 February 1980 in Case 170/78 *Commission* v. *United Kingdom* [1980] ECR 417), the legislation of a Member State must not 'crystallise' given consumer habits so as to consolidate an advantage acquired by national industries concerned to comply with them.
>
> Secondly, in the other Member States of the Community the designations corresponding to the German designation 'Bier' are generic designations for a fermented

[56] This is the basis put forward by the Court to the different approach towards fixed trading margins when compared with that taken with regard to fixed prices. The former are generally acceptable since national products are also prevented from granting market premiums or the fixed margins fall equally on all products and are not intended to support national fixed prices. In these cases, the costs of production of imported products can still be reflected in their retail price and it is this the Court aims to protect. See Case 72/82, *Commission* v. *Italy* (Tobacco monopoly) [1983] ECR 1995, paras 13 and 14, and Joined Cases 80 and 159/85, *Edah* [1986] ECR 3359, paras 13–15. However, as argued above, the test applied in price controls cases goes beyond discrimination.

beverage manufactured from malted barley, whether malted barley on its own or with the addition of rice or maize. The same approach is taken in Community law . . .

The German designation 'Bier' and its equivalents in the languages of the other Member States of the Community may therefore not be restricted to beers manufactured in accordance with the rules in force in the Federal Republic of Germany".[57]

This also explains why the Court generally accepts reverse discrimination (States discrimination against their own nationals). For example, the German government could still continue to impose the "German Beer Purity Law" requirements to German producers. The Court does not feel necessary to correct national democratic processes with regard to the treatment they grant to home nationals. Article 30 only applies to imported products, and not to national products. Since, according to the Court the purpose of Article 30 "is to eliminate obstacles to the importation of goods and not to ensure that goods of national origin always enjoy the same treatment as imported goods",[58] cases of reverse discrimination over the free movement of goods are outside the scope of Community law. The only exception is for re-imported goods.[59] Although the Court has been asked several times to extend the protection granted by Article 30 to home nationals and national products, it has consistently refused to do so.[60] This means that, according to the Court, Article 30 does not regulate access to the market, but rather protects imported products from other Member States.

In the same manner, it has interpreted Community secondary legislation, in cases of doubt, as not preventing Member States from regulating *with regard to their own nationals*.[61] In *Jongeneel Kaas* the Court, in the absence of a express statement in a Council Regulation, interpreted Article 30 as regulating not freedom of access to the market, but free movement between Member States.[62] This confirms that the case law of the Court of Justice with regards

[57] See paras 31–4.

[58] Case 98/86, *Mathot* [1987] ECR 809, para 7. See also para 10 of Case 355/85, *Cognet* [1986] ECR 3232 and para 18 of Joined Cases 80 and 159/85, *Edah* [1986] ECR 3359.

[59] See Case 229/83, *Leclerc* (Prix du Libre) [1985] ECR 1, para 26, and *Cognet* (n.58 above), para 10.

[60] For example, see Joined Cases 314 to 316/81 and 83/82, *Waterkein* [1982] ECR 4337, where it expressly stated that "contrary to the contention advanced by the accused, the judgment of 10 July 1980 only affects the treatment of products imported from other Member States": para 11.

[61] See: Case 126/82, *Smit* [1983] ECR 73, paras 17–24; Joined Cases C–251/90 and C–252/90, *Gordon Wood* [1992] ECR I–2873, paras 17–19; and Case C–11/92, *Gallaher* [1993] ECR I–3545, para 20.

[62] "However, the fact that the legislation in question makes no mention of the designation and quality of cheese does not mean that the Community has consciously and of necessity decided to impose on the Member States in the sector an obligation to adhere to a system of absolute freedom of production. In the absence of any rule of Community law on the quality of cheese products the Court considers that the Member States retain the power to apply rules of that kind to cheese producers established within the territory. That power extends not only to rules considered necessary for the protection of the consumer or public health but also to rules which a Member State may wish to enact for the purpose of promoting the quality of domestic

to the European Economic Constitution does not correspond to a economic due process model of judicial review. However, deregulation may occur as a consequence of Article 30 even with regard to home nationals due to two factors: first, States may not want to continue to subject their own nationals to stricter rules or they may not be authorised to do so according to national law (eg national constitutional principles of equality); secondly, in some cases it is impossible to distinguish between the effects of the judicial decision on imported and domestic products since the striking down of national rules with regard to imported products automatically covers domestic products (for example, the Sunday trading legislation).

The Court does not, however, limit itself to a "democratic" review of national legislation; it does not restrict itself to a finding of whether the interests of nationals of other Member States are represented in national policy choices but requires those policies to be harmonised in accordance with a Community constructed policy process in the Court. At the same time, the kind of cost/benefit analysis taking place in the Court is not driven by a review of efficiency of the national measure according to a particular view of free market values, but is more interested in its "normality", that is to say, in assessing whether it is a regulatory choice divergent from the "canons" common to the different Member States' regulations. The push towards harmonisation, coupled with a distrust of national regulatory processes, is the driving force behind the majoritarian approach of the Court.

The majoritarian approach

For the Court, the common market could not support the costs of non-harmonised national rules. This means that State regulations can no longer diverge on the basis of different traditions and policy choices. Different national regulations are to be assessed in view of Community-designed values and concepts. In Case 193/80, *Commission* v. *Italy*, the Court assessed the need to restrict the use of the designation "vinegar", to prevent consumers from being misled. In doing so, it did not, however, consider the concept of "vinegar" which was traditionally used in the Italian market, but instead it looked at the concepts used in all Member States and the concept inferred from Community legislation.[63] This case is representative of a bulk of cases in which the majoritarian approach is particularly evident. These are cases regarding State regulation of traditional national products, or of specific national traditions concerning the composition or presentation of products. Here, we see a minoritarian interest—one State's tradition—as opposed to the majoritarian interest, which takes the form of the interests of all other

production. Such rules cannot however discriminate against imported products or hinder the importation of products from other Member States": Case 237/82, *Jongeneel Kaas* [1984] ECR 483, para 13. See also paras 10–12.

[63] Case 193/80, *Commission* v. *Italy* (Vinegar II) [1981] ECR 3019, para 26.

Member States not sharing or conforming to that tradition. In all the cases found by the author in this area, the Court struck down the national regulation.[64]

A second category of cases, more difficult to analyse, are concerned with measures imposing certain requirements which do not correspond to national traditional products, but to more technical issues or risk assessments: matters such as animal feeding-stuffs,[65] additives to foodstuffs[66] and substitutes for milk and dairy products.[67] Here the Court is no longer so ready to strike down national measures, since the majoritarian view is sometimes difficult to ascertain. The different national regulations are not always mentioned either in the decision, the proceedings or the opinion of the Advocate-General, making it more difficult to analyse this part of the case law with regard to the thesis advanced here. Nonetheless, in all the cases analysed where the different national rules on the issue at stake were referred to, the Court clearly adopted a majoritarian perspective. Thus, it upheld national measures protecting from a risk which was recognised by the uncertainties prevailing in different Member States legislation.[68] On the other hand, it struck down national rules whenever their policy was not shared by the majority of Member States.[69] In the cases where no overview of national legislation is given, it is still possible to find other elements of a majoritarian approach. For example, in *Sandoz* the Court founds its decision on what it reconstructs as being the Community Legislature's policy.[70] Case law references to the Labelling Directive[71] can also be read in this light. The Court, in co-ordinating its approach with that of the

[64] *Cassis de Dijon* is the first one. Then follows: Case 788/79, *Gilli and Andres* (Vinegar I) [1980] ECR 2071; Case 27/80, *Fietje* [1980] ECR 3839; Case 94/82, *Kikvorsch Groothandel* [1983] ECR 947; Case 16/83, *Prantl* [1984] ECR 1299; Case 176/84, *Petillant de Raisin* [1986] ECR 3879; Case 176/84, *Commission* v. *Greece* (Bee Purity Law) [1987] ECR 1193; Case 178/84, *Commission* v. *Germany* [1987] ECR 1227; Case 407/85, *3 Glocken and another* v. *USL Centro-sud and another* (Pasta) [1988] ECR 4233; Case 90/86, *Zoni* (Pasta) [1988] ECR 4285; Case 247/87, *Commission* v. *Germany* [1989] ECR 229.

[65] See Case 251/78, *Denkavit* [1979] ECR 3369.

[66] See, eg Case 53/80, *Kaasfabriek Eyssen* [1981] ECR 409.

[67] See, eg Case 76/86, *Commission* v. *Germany* [1989] ECR 1021.

[68] See Case 53/80, *Kaasfabriek Eyssen* [1981] ECR 409, para 16 and Case 97/83, *Melkunie* [1984] ECR 2367, para 18 and para 17 stressing the parallel with other Member States' legislation. In *Denkavit* the Court upheld and struck down different parts of the measure in question, in accordance with the prevailing practices in the Member States, see Case 251/78, *Denkavit* [1979] ECR 3369. Not referring to Member States' legislation but following the Commission and stressing international scientific sources, see Case C–42/90, *Bellon* [1990] ECR I–4863.

[69] *Smanor* (n.48 above), paras 16 *et seq*; Case 286/86, *Deserbais* [1988] ECR 4907 (in this case the measure was supported by an international convention but only four Member States were parties to it and the Court stated that the decisive element must be "how are the products generally known by that name in the Community", para 13); Case 21/84, *Commission* v. *France* [1985] ECR 1355 (in the observations it is noted that the postal franking machines refused by France were approved by most Member States and Community institutions).

[70] Case 174/82, *Sandoz* [1983] ECR 2445, paras 13, 14 and, mainly, 15. In the same sense, see Case 227/82, *Van Bennekom* [1983] ECR 3883.

[71] Council Directive 79/112/EEC (of 18 December 1978) relating to the labelling, presentation and advertising for foodstuffs for sale to the ultimate consumer (OJ 08.02.79 L33/1).

Commission, appeared to interpret the Labelling Directive as involving a Community judgment on mandatory requirements.[72] In *SARPP*[73] we can clearly see the different types of review to which national measures will be subjected, depending on whether or not the Directive applies; and the importance given to the Community majority opinion, as deduced from the different national rules.[74] The importance of Community legislation in determining the majority opinion is also seen in cases where the Court applies Community legislation by analogy to free movement of goods cases[75] or where it respects powers given therein to Member States to restrict free movement.[76]

The confirmation of this majoritarian activism can be found in the most controversial cases, such as those on "market circumstances", where the Court's case law was seen as following an "economic due process" model and playing a deregulatory role. However, if such deregulation takes place, it does so only at national level. There is no deregulation from an European perspective. In other words, the policy which results from the outcome of the cost/benefit analysis of those measures in the Court corresponds to the policy in the majority of States in the Europe Union. That is the case, for instance, in two of the most-discussed Court decisions such as *GB-INNO*[77] and *Yves Rocher*.[78] These two decisions, seen as deregulatory in the national context, are not so from a Community point of view, since, according to the Court, their outcomes lead to situations which correspond to the legislation of almost all Member States.[79] This outcome is not the exception but the rule. Most measures of this kind were in fact upheld as they were identical to the legislation in many Member States or they represented a policy uncertainty reflected in different Member States' market regulations.[80]

[72] Case 130/80, *Kelderman* [1981] ECR 527; Case 216/84, *Commission* v. *France* (Milk Powder) [1988] ECR 793; Case 76/86, *Commission* v. *Germany* [1989] ECR 1021. The argument drawn from the Directive is also present in many of the other decisions already mentioned. For an analysis of the parallelism between the Labelling Directive and the Court's policy, see: C. Lister, "The naming of foods: the European Community's rules for non-brand food product names", (1993) ELR, 179, mainly at 200.

[73] Case C–241/89, *SARPP* [1990] ECR 4695, paras 14 and 30.

[74] An exception to the majoritarian interpretation can, perhaps, be seen in the decision taken in Case 261/81, *Rau* [1983] ECR 3961, which concerned a Belgian regulation imposing a certain shape for margarine packages. Though Member States regulations varied as to the shape required, almost all States shared such policy.

[75] See: Case 94/82, *De Kikvoorsch* [1983] ECR 947, para 11; Case 45/87, *Commission* v. *Ireland* [1988] ECR 4929, para 22; and Case 247/87, *Commission* v. *Germany* [1989] ECR 947, para 14.

[76] Case 53/80, *Kaasfabriek Eyssen* [1981] ECR 409, para 15. The other side of this is that Member States can no longer make recourse to Article 36 when the level of necessary protection has already been established by Community legislation. See, in this respect, Masclet, "Les artcles 30, 36, et 100 du traité à la lumiere de l'arret 'Cassis de Dijon'", (1980) 16 *RTDE*, 611.

[77] See n.23 above.

[78] See n.23 above.

[79] See para 12 of *GB-INNO* and para 18 of *Yves Rocher*.

[80] Case 155/80, *Oebel* [1981] ECR 1993, paras 13 and 18 (this case involves a measure of the type discussed, which was not, however, subject to balance review by the Court); Case 75/81, *Blesgen* [1982] ECR 1211 (see the information given by the Commission, on the legislation of the different Member States); Case 286/81, *Oosthoek's* [1982] ECR 4575 (according to the

The absence of a neo-liberal reading of Treaty rules by the Court is furthermore confirmed by the approach followed by the Court when it is called on to judge the validity of State regulations directly with regard to competition values, as with its case law on Articles 85, 86, 90 and 92. It, according to one author, "is very cautious in censuring a state regulation".[81]

The European Court has consistently held that Articles 85 and 86 cannot be directly applied to Member States' measures.[82] Nevertheless, since *GB-INNO* v. *ATAB* in 1977,[83] the ECJ has also consistently held that Member States cannot adopt measures that will remove the effectiveness ("*effet utile*") of articles 85 and 86,[84] which is open to different interpretations. However, the Court has limited the application of Articles 85 and 86 to State measures to cases where the State either reinforces or supports private behaviour contrary to those Articles or delegates to private actors the responsibility for the adoption of the measure. The Court has generally applied these concepts in a restrictive manner.[85] In *Meng*, the Court has removed any doubts regarding any extension of its control of State measures affecting competition under Articles 85 and 86 and confirmed the intention to limit that control to measures having a link with private behaviour contrary to Articles 85 and

Commission legislation on the issue varied among Member States and it is extremely complex; also, several Member States intervened to defend the legislation; but, see also para 20 of the decision that may oppose this reading); Case 238/82, *Duphar* [1984] ECR 523, para 15; Joined Cases 60 and 61/84, *Cinéthèque* [1985] ECR 3879; Case C–23/89, *Quietlynn* [1990] ECR 3061; Case C–369/88, *Delattre* [1991] ECR 1487, para 54; Joined Cases C–1/90 and C–176/90, *Aragonesa* [1991] ECR I–4151 (such legislation exists in many States, as Belgium and the UK reminded the Court; the measure could be held to be discriminatory but even the Commission contests this); and, finally, the Sunday trading cases: Case C–145/88, *Torfaen Borough Council* [1989] ECR 3851; Case C–169/91, *Stoke on Trent* [1992] ECR I–6635; Case C–312/89, *Conforama* [1991] I–997; Case C–332/89, *Marchandise* [1991] ECR I–1027 (such type of regulation exists, albeit with some differences, in many Member States).

[81] In the original: "*se montre trés reticente pour censurer une réglementation étatique*". D. Triantafyllou, "Les règles de la concurrence et l'activité étatique y compris les marchés publics", (1996) *RTDE*, 32, at 68. See, also, P. Mengozzi, "Il Principio dell'Investitore in una Economia di Mercato e i Valori del Diritto Comunitario", (1995) *Rivista di Diritto Europeo*, 19, mainly the conclusions at 24.

[82] See Case 78/70, *Deutsche Grammophon* [1971] ECR 487. For a more recent confirmation of this statement see Case C–153/93, *Delta Schiffahrts-Und Speditionsgesselschaft* [1994] ECR I–2157, at para 14.

[83] Case 13/77, GB-*INNO* v. *ATAB* [1977] ECR 2115.

[84] In the case *GB-INNO* v. *ATAB*, the Court set up the principle but did not apply it, giving priority to the application of Article 30. For some examples of the application of this principle, striking down State measures: Joined Cases 209 to 213/84, *Asjes (Nouvelles Frontières)* [1986] ECR 1425; Case 66/86, *Ahmed Saeed* [1989] ECR 803; Case 311/85, *Vlaamse Reisbureaus* [1987] ECR 3801.

[85] It seems that it will only restrict State intervention in very clear cases: where the regulation tries to impose to the undertakings a conduct contrary to EC competition rules or gives a recommendation in that sense, or when the State delegates completely to private operators the task of regulating without maintaining the possibility of rejecting the private operators' decision and imposing its own decision. For the first type of measures, see cases cited in the previous note. For examples of the second type of cases see: Case 267/86, *Van Eycke* [1988] ECR 4769, para 14 and *Delta* (n.82 above).

86.[86] Since the initial steps undertaken towards the review of public regulation under a co-ordinated application of Articles 85 and 86 (the competition rules applicable to undertakings) with Articles 3g and 5 of the EC Treaty it was visible that the Court activism in this area was subject to the application of free movement rules.[87] What has occurred is that the scope granted to Article 30 was so wide that it is this one that has controlled the eventual application of competition values to challenge national regulations.

The policy followed by the Court towards State aids is one more element which fits well with the majoritarian approach for Article 30 highlighted above. As one author stated, the Court "has generally upheld the Commission's interpretation of the scope of Article 92(1)"[88] (concept of aid). And, as the same author notes, this is followed by substantial discretion being granted to the Commission also in the application of Article 92(3), to decide whether those aids can benefit from any exception.[89] The form of judicial review of Commission decisions accepting or prohibiting State aid is a sort of weak administrative review, focusing on procedural questions, and does not take into account any constitutional notion of the Treaties protecting economic freedom or free competition. The Commission judgments on the balance between such values and those protected by state aid is upheld and supported by the Court, confirming in this area the majoritarian activism detected in regard to the free movement of goods.

Community intervention in the market

Community legislation was also called upon to play a leading role in ascertaining the majoritarian policy and guiding judicial harmonisation[90] but was not itself subject to scrutiny under free movement of goods. In *Bodin*, it appears clear that when there is a Directive intended to approximate national laws establishing a certain policy, it is not possible to question this Directive under

[86] Case C–2/91, *Meng* [1993] ECR I–5752. See N. Reich, "The 'November Revolution' of the European Court of Justice: Keck, Meng and Audi Revisited", (1994) 31 *CMLRev*, 459, and Maillo and Poiares Maduro, "Regulatory Reform in the European Union—A View From the European Court of Justice", CD-Rom from the Fourth Biennial International Conference of the European Community Studies Association, 11–14 May (Charleston, South Carolina, 1995).

[87] See *GB-INNO* v. *ATAB*, (n.83 above). See, also Leclerc (Prix du Liberal) (n. 37 above), Case C–179/90, *Merci Convenzionale Porto di Genova* [1991] ECR I–5889 and Case C–41/90, *Höfner* [1991] ECR I–1979.

[88] L. Hancher, "State Aids and Judicial Control in the European Community", (1994) *ECLR* 134.

[89] Ibid. See also the references therein and in Yves Jenny, "Competition and State Aid Policy in the European Community", (1994) *Fordham International Law Journal*, 525, mainly at 553.

[90] See Case 382/87, *Buet* (Canvassing) [1989] ECR 1235, para 16 and references given, in n.72 above. A decision more difficult to interpret is that on the Belgium Wallonia Region law on waste (Case C–2/90, *Commission* v. *Belgium* [1992] ECR 4471). In this case, the Court imposed the free movement of dangerous waste because a Directive so required, but at the same time admitted that the restriction to the free movement of non-dangerous waste was acceptable. The reason may lie in the fact that the Directive on dangerous waste established a complete system that the Court could not provide for non-dangerous waste through Article 30.

Article 30, even if it restricts trade;[91] and this even though the Court has stated, on other occasions, the principle that Community secondary legislation has to respect the free movement of goods (part of Community primary or constitutional law).[92] In effect, the latter appears to be the general principle proclaimed by the Court in its case law. Recently the Court has restated that:

> "It is settled law that the prohibition of quantitative restrictions and of all measures having equivalent effect applies not only to national measures but also to measures adopted by the Community institutions".[93]

However, in this same decision the Court maintain its consistent line of cases upholding Community legislation in this area.[94] Although, as mentioned, rules on free movement, being primary law, are applicable to Community secondary legislation, the standard of review of Community legislation under these rules and under the principle of non-discrimination is much less strict and respectful towards the Community legislator discretion than the standard of review used with regard to national legislation.[95] To the author's knowledge the Court only once invalidated Community legislation because of a conflict with the principle of free movement, and that was where the violation of Treaty rules was striking since the legislation purported to allow the introduction of tariffs among Member States.[96] This confirms that there is not an "economic due process" approach to Article 30 or the European Economic Constitution, but a majoritarian construction of regulatory law in a European perspective. This explains the deference of the Court with regard to Community legislation. If the Court agreed with a notion of the European Economic Constitution as protecting the market from *public* intervention, that notion would be as valid towards State legislation as towards Community legislation but we find no such approach with regard to Community legislation. Instead, Community legislation is

[91] Case 241/86, *Bodin and Minguet* [1987] ECR 2573.

[92] See, for example, Joined Cases 80 and 81/77, *Commissionnaires Reunis* [1978] ECR 927; Case 37/83, *Firma Rewe-Zentrale AG* [1984] ECR 1229; Case 15/83, *Denkavit* [1984] ECR 2171; and Case C–51/93, *Meyhui* [1994] ECR I–3879.

[93] Case C–114/96, *Kieffer and Thill* (judgment of the Court of 25 June 1997, not yet reported), para 27. Moreover, it even appears that the concept of measures of equivalent effect applying to Community legislation is broader than that applicable to national legislation after *Keck* (see para 28).

[94] Ibid, para 37.

[95] See: Case 337/82, *St. Nikolaus Brennerei* [1984] ECR 1051, para 15; Case 37/83, *Firma Rewe-Zentrale AG* [1984] ECR 1229, paras 17–21; Case 15/83, *Denkavit* [1984] ECR 2171; Case 240/83, *ADBHU* [1985] ECR 0531, paras 16–21; Case 46/86, *Albert Romkes* [1987] ECR 267, paras 21–24; Joined Cases 181/88, 182/88 and 218/88, *Jean-Francois Deschamps* [1989] ECR 438; Joined Cases C–251/90 and C–252/90, *Gordon Wood* [1992] ECR I–2873, para 19; and Case C–11/92, *Gallaher* [1993] ECR I–2545, para 18. A striking example of the same sort of legislation being struck down as national legislation but upheld as Community legislation comes from comparing Case C–369/89, *Piageme* [1991] ECR I–2971 with Case C–51/93, *Meyhui* [1994] ECR I–3879 (*Keck* will not justify a different outcome since that case deals with product requirements). Another example, less clear-cut because pre-emption is involved in the answer of the Court, is Case 150/88, *Parfumerie Fabrik* [1989] ECR 3891, as compared with Case C–39/90, *Denkavit* (Compound feedingstuffs) [1991] ECR I–3069.

[96] Joined Cases 80 and 81–77, *Commissionnaires Reunis* [1978] ECR 927.

normally upheld. The Court is generous towards the general interests pursued by the Community which restrict the exercise of economic activities.[97]

Conclusion

What the Court does when it considers Article 30 is not to impose a certain constitutional conception of public intervention in the market, but to compensate for the lack of Community harmonisation. This is why the regulatory balance set by the Court normally corresponds to the view of the Commission, and to the legislation in the majority of Member States. On the one hand, the Court is not imposing its own particular economic model of regulation. On the other hand, the Court does not accept States' different economic models, even if non-protectionist. Its yardstick is what the Court identifies as the European Union majority policy, in this way subjecting States regulations to harmonisation in the Court.

The conclusion to be drawn is that what is taking place in the Court is a kind of Community legislative process, with the Court trying to harmonise national rules in accordance with an "ideally drafted" representation of all States' interests.

To sum up, the Court has always been more concerned with *State* intervention than with *public* intervention in the market. This is confirmed by a "double standard" regarding the review of State measures and Community measures under the European Economic Constitution. The broad reading given to the provisions on free movement of goods has brought many national provisions under review. Nevertheless, this must be interpreted as intended to widen Community control over national regulation in the common market, and not as intended to widen the Court's control over the degree of regulation in the market. We have been witnessing a process of Europeanisation of regulation in the common market through the judicial process, which may have to be reassessed in light of the most novel decisions of the Court.

AFTER *KECK*

Keck: revolution or reform?

The *Keck* decision[98] brought the concept of discrimination back to the heart of Article 30. The case concerned the compatibility with Community law of

[97] See: Case 240/83, *ADBHU* [1985] ECR 0531; Case 234/85, *Keller* [1986] ECR 2897, para 8 and Case C–370/88, *Marshall* [1990] ECR I–4071, paras 27–28.

[98] Joined Cases C–267 and C–268/91, *Keck and Mithouard* [1993] ECR I–6097. Confirmed, soon after, in Case C–292/92, *Hünermund* [1993] ECR I–6787, followed by other cases (see below).

a provision of French law prohibiting resale at a loss.[99] Mr Keck and Mr Mithouard were prosecuted because the two "*hypermarchés*" managed by them were found selling products in an unaltered state at prices lower than their actual purchase price. In their defence they contended that the French law was incompatible with several provisions of Community law namely Articles 7 and 30 of the EC Treaty, the free movement of persons, services and capital, and free competition. The Court dismissed all arguments, with the exception of that based upon Article 30. The rules on the free movement of persons, services and capital do not apply to legislation concerned with the marketing of goods.[100] Article 7 of the EC Treaty is not violated once the legislation applies regardless of nationality.[101] Finally, the anti-competitive effects of the rules in question cannot be appreciated only by reference to Article 3 of the EC Treaty which is not directly applicable.[102] The Court proceeded to analyse the prohibition of a resale at a loss from the perspective of free movement of goods and, whilst the answers given by the Court to the other questions may raise some interesting issues,[103] it is on the new approach to Article 30 upon which this case turns.

Keck can be seen as an answer to calls from legal commentators to increase certainty and to reduce the overload of cases in the Court, but it can also be seen in the context of a broader change in the philosophy behind the Court's case law.[104] However, *Keck* is more of a reform than a revolution.[105] The Court did not reverse *Dassonville* or *Cassis de Dijon*. Instead, it restricted *Cassis de Dijon* to measures relating to product-requirements and reinterpreted *Dassonville* but only with reference to measures restricting or prohibiting "selling arrangements", such as those at issue in *Keck*. In the previous cases concerning such measures, the Court's approach, in line with its general approach to Article 30, was that from the moment a measure could affect trade it would have to be submitted to the "mandatory requirements" or Article 36 tests.[106]

In *Keck,* the Court renewed its approach to Article 30. Its main concern is to discourage "the increasing tendency of traders to invoke Article 30 of the

[99] Article 1 of French Law No 63–628 of 2 July 1963, as amended by Article 32 of Order No 86–1243 of 1 December 1986.

[100] See para 6.

[101] See paras 7 and 8.

[102] See para 9.

[103] In particular, a definite retreat from an interconnected use of the free movement of goods and competition rules. See, confirming this: Case C–379/92, *Matteo Peralta* [1994] ECR I–3453, paras 19–22; Case C–412/93, *Leclerc* v. *TF 1 Publicité* [1995] ECR I–179, paras 25–27; and Case C–387/93, *Domingo Banchero* [1995] ECR I–4663.

[104] See below.

[105] Pierre le Mire describes it as an "*exemple remarquable du 'toilettage' de sa jurisprudence*" by the Court: "Note—Keck", AJDA, *L'Actualité Juridique, Droit Administratif*, 20 January 1994, 57, at 58; while Reich speaks of a revolution, placing this decision in the context of other important changes in the Court's jurisprudence: see "The 'November Revolution' of the European Court of Justice: Keck, Meng and Audi Revisited", 31 (1994) *CMLRev*, 459.

[106] See, above, the analysis of the Court's case law.

Treaty as a means of challenging any rules whose effect is to limit their commercial freedom even where such rules are not aimed at products from other Member States".[107] To this end the Court starts by reinterpreting *Cassis de Dijon* in a way that restricts its application to product requirements:

> "In '*Cassis de Dijon*' it was held that, in the absence of harmonisation of legislation, measures of equivalent effect prohibited by *Article 30 include obstacles to the free movement of goods where they are the consequence of applying rules that lay down requirements to be met by such goods* (such as requirements as to designation, form, size, weight, composition, presentation, labelling, packaging) *to goods from other Member States where they are lawfully manufactured and marketed*, even if those rules apply without distinction to all products unless their application can be justified by a public-interest objective taking precedence over the free movement of goods".[108]

Thus, measures laying down product requirements are submitted to a balance test: the benefits to the public-interest objective must be superior to the costs that flow from the restriction imposed on free movement of goods. However, the same is not the case with regard to "national provisions restricting or prohibiting certain selling arrangements".[109] In the case of such measures the Court decided to reverse, not *Dassonville*, but the interpretation given to *Dassonville* in subsequent decisions concerning national measures governing "selling arrangements". It held:

> "contrary to what has previously been decided, the application to products from other Member States of national provisions restricting or prohibiting certain selling arrangements is not such as to hinder directly or indirectly, actually or potentially, trade between Member States within the meaning of the *Dassonville* judgment, provided that those provisions apply to all affected traders operating within the national territory and *provided that they affect in the same manner, in law and in fact*, the marketing of domestic products and of those from other Member States".[110]

In the case of measures prohibiting or restricting certain selling arrangements it is therefore not sufficient that they may constitute an obstacle to free movement of goods to fall under Article 30. Such measures must now discriminate "in law or in fact" against imported products.[111]

[107] See para 14.

[108] See para 15, citation omitted and emphasis added.

[109] See para 16.

[110] See para 16, citation omitted and emphasis added.

[111] It is not clear upon whom the important burden of proof lies: on the affected interests to show that the provision discriminates in law or in fact against imports, or for the State to show that the measure is non-discriminatory? In reality, it will probably happen that there will be no clear allocation of the burden of proof, the Court deciding the issue on the balance of the evidence adduced by both parties.

Interpreting *Keck*

Under a restrictive view the decision can be understood in light of an article by a former *référedaire* at the Court.[112] In his article (subtitled "Much ado about nothing") Wils defends a balance test as the optimal test[113] but at the same time recognises that "the limitations of judicial administration may require more simplified tests". Interestingly, there is no assessment of legitimacy problems. Instead, he emphasises the trade-off between administrative costs and error costs. In his own words:

> "In general a full test, which takes all relevant factors into account, has the advantage of being more difficult to apply, thus imposing high administrative costs on the courts and parties involved. On the other hand a simplified test, as it does not take into account all relevant factors, engenders errors".[114]

Wils proposes that the Court continues to apply, as a general rule, a balance test[115] but at the same time to use more simplified tests ("rule-like test") in certain categories of cases or measures were there can be no doubt as to the superiority of the regulatory value over the integration interest.[116] Wils considers this to be already established in the Court's case law.[117] If one follows this argument, *Keck* could be seen as creating a simplified standard or rule-like test for measures restricting or prohibiting certain selling arrangements. Though such an interpretation fits well with the Court's exclusive reference to provisions concerning selling arrangements it seems too modest for the aim the Court appears to give to *Keck*. The arguments given by the Court and its reinterpretation of both *Cassis de Dijon* and *Dassonville* have to be understood as a wish to send a more ambitious sign as regards its general case law on free movement of goods[118]—otherwise it would be "much ado about nothing". Furthermore such a restrictive interpretation would do little to reduce the overload of the Court.

Another possibility is to interpret *Keck* more extensively as signifying a return to a discrimination test as the main criterion in the application of Article 30. The main objection to this overall reinterpretation of Article 30 is that the Court has left untouched in *Keck* its *Cassis de Dijon* case law on product requirements which is normally understood as based on a balance test, not

[112] Wils, "The Search for the rule in Article 30 EEC: much ado about nothing?", (1993) *ELR*, 475.

[113] Ibid, mainly at 478–9.

[114] Ibid, at 486.

[115] Ibid, mainly at 489–91.

[116] "In such non-borderline cases, there is no real trade-off between administrative costs and error costs, and simplification of the test is unambiguously preferable. Moreover, the simplified tests applied by the Court remained standard-like, as they were derived from the specificity of each case": ibid at 488.

[117] Ibid, eg at 483.

[118] This is confirmed by further signs of restraint given by the Court (see below).

requiring discrimination. However, it may now be possible to revive the argument put forward by Marenco in 1984.[119] As will be remembered, according to this author national measures applicable without distinction could be classified as one of two types: measures that require products to be manipulated and those that do not require such manipulation. Briefly restated, the argument was that measures that require changes to products such as labelling, packaging, composition or controls normally impose costs on imported products (in the form of double controls, relabelling etc) which are not imposed on similar national products.[120] One could say that such measures are *prima facie* discriminatory and correspond to the notion of product-requirements adopted by the Court. The same would not be the case for measures relating to market circumstances. A discrimination thesis finds other support in *Keck*. For example, in paragraph 14 the Court expresses its intention to limit the use of Article 30 to challenge rules the effect of which is to limit the commercial freedom of traders "even where such rules are not aimed at products from other Member States". Furthermore, the reason given for accepting provisions restricting or prohibiting selling arrangements, once the conditions set forward in paragraph 16 are fulfilled, is that in their application to imported products they are "not by nature such as to prevent their access to the market or to impede access any more than it impedes the access of domestic products. Such rules therefore fall outside the scope of Article 30 of the Treaty".[121] It could be argued that this is a *rationale* of discrimination that from now on dominates the interpretation of Article 30.[122] This is a viable interpretation but some problems can be raised: first, it seems difficult to accept that the Court will in fact make such a shift in its case law; secondly, as argued above, a concept of discrimination such as this proposed by Marenco, would be so flexible as to deprive discrimination of a true normative value; thirdly, it cannot sufficiently justify the difference established by the Court between the test to be applied to product requirements and the test to be applied to measures on selling arrangements (as the latter may also involve a double-cost); finally, such an undetermined concept of discrimination will not reduce the overload of cases before the Court.

In my view *Keck* is best understood in light of the test proposed by White, first in his article in the *Common Market Law Review*[123] and later, in name of the Commission in the first "Sunday trading case"[124] (although in practice

[119] "Pour une interprétation traditionelle de la mesure d'effet equivalent a une restriction quantitative", (1984) *CDE*, 291. See Chapter 2 above.

[120] Ibid at 308–9, 312, 320.

[121] See para 17.

[122] This is the interpretation given to *Keck* in an article by Nicolas Bernard: "Discrimination and Free Movement in EC Law", (1996) 45 *International and Comparative Law Quarterly*, 82, at 92.

[123] White, "In Search of the Limits to Article 30 of the EEC Treaty", (1989) *CMLRev*, 235.

[124] Case C–145/88, *Torfaen Borough Council* [1989] ECR 3851.

this test in quite similar to that of Marenco). As will be recalled, White distinguishes between rules relating to the characteristics of goods, such as their composition, size, shape, weight, presentation, denomination and labelling, which would fall under Article 30, and rules regulating the circumstances under which all goods of the same kind should be sold or used, which would not fall under Article 30. With two exceptions: rules of the latter kind would fall under Article 30 if they are discriminatory or if they restrict imports so severely that they could be considered as amounting to a quantitative restriction on imports. This kind of test is also developed by Advocate-General Tesauro in his observations in *Hünermund*,[125] which apparently influenced the Court in its *Keck* decision. Although the Court has refused to apply such a test in the first Sunday trading case the argument in *Keck* seems to accept White's distinction between rules relating to product characteristics[126] and rules relating to market circumstances, as is the case for provisions concerning selling arrangements.[127] Moreover, the decisions following *Keck* have showed that *Keck* covers measures well beyond a strict conception of selling arrangements, involving all measures relating to rules on products other than product requirements.[128] At the same time, the Court has also manifested its self-restraint on measures not covered by *Keck*, restricting the application of Article 30 on the grounds that the effect of the measures on free movement were too uncertain and indirect.[129]

A critique

At this point two questions must be raised: first, is the new approach capable of attaining the aims it sets out to achieve? Secondly, does it answer the questions raised by the previous approach of the Court and the conflicting values at play in the rules governing free movement of goods? In my view both these questions are to be answered in the negative.

Keck will not considerably increase certainty in this area of the law, nor will it help much in reducing the overload of cases before the Court. The distinction between rules which relate to the characteristics of products and rules

[125] Case C–292/92, *Hünermund* [1993] ECR I–6787.

[126] See para 15.

[127] See para 16.

[128] The Court has made a very elastic interpretation of "selling arrangements", covering, in effect, all measures on market circumstances. See Case C–391/92, *Commission* v. *Greece* [1995] ECR I–1621; *Leclerc* v. *TF 1 Publicité* (n.103 above); *Domingo Banchero* (n.103 above). For decisions on product requirements that appear to maintain the majoritarian approach, see Case C–315/92, *Clinique* [1994] ECR I–317 (see in particular para 11) and Case C–51/94, *Commission* v. *Germany* [1995] ECR I–3599.

[129] See Case C–379, *Peralta* [1994] ECR I–3453 and Case C–134/94, *Esso Spañola* [1995] ECR I–4223. See also Case C–93/92, *CMC Motorradcenter* [1993] ECR I–5009, that in effect presaged the *Keck* changes.

applicable to market circumstances is not clear cut[130] and the application to these types of rules of two different tests lacks a normative justification.[131] Thus, although price controls govern market circumstances, according to White they fall under Article 30 because "it is clear that price regulatory measures can prevent imports from benefiting from the advantages (whether lower price or higher quality or simply different characteristics) arising out of the legal and economic environment of the Member State of origin". In this way both rules on the characteristics of products and rules on market circumstances would be controlled by the same rationale. The real criterion is the loss of a competitive advantage by imported products or the gain of a competitive advantage by domestic products. The reason why rules relating to the characteristics of products are always caught by Article 30 is that they automatically confer a competitive advantage on domestic products or remove a competitive advantage from imported products. Instead, rules relating to market circumstances are assessed by searching for a discriminatory element. If one examines this more closely, any obstacle to imports, including rules on market circumstances, will always prevent imports from enjoying some competitive advantage. At the very least they are restricted in profiting from their competitive advantages (if their role is, in any way, limited, so is their profit from the competitive advantage). In my view, what lays behind the different tests proposed for rules which relate to the characteristics of products and rules applicable to market circumstances is the conviction that in the case of market circumstances, domestic products will in many instances also be prevented from enjoying their competitive advantages whilst the same would not be true in the case of rules relating to product characteristics. This in fact amounts to a discrimination criterion such as the one mentioned above in which rules relating to product characteristics will be *prima facie* discriminatory while rules relating to market circumstances will be *prima facie* non-discriminatory. Such a distinction is quite arbitrary and will further enhance the inherent uncertainty of the concepts and tests used.

If one does not agree with the statement that all rules on product characteristics are *prima facie* discriminatory, in the sense mentioned, and should

[130] See Case C–470/93, *Mars* [1995] ECR I–1923 relating to an advertising campaign that involved the promotion of the campaign in the label of the product. The Court included the prohibition of such advertising in the category of rules which relate to the characteristics of products.

[131] A possible reason underlying the decision is that, in many cases relating to rules on market circumstances, it is not possible to restrict the effects of the decisions to imports, the consequence being that, more than a mutual recognition of other States' legislation, the State is obliged to repeal its own legislation (think what would happen if Sunday trading legislation was found to violate Article 30). See M. Todino, and T. Lüder, "La jurisprudence 'Keck' en matière de publicité: vers un marché unique inachevé ?", (1995) *Revue du Marche Unique Européen*, 171, at 175. However, not all cases on market circumstances will lead to such a result, and it can also be argued that decisions on product requirements may also result in the repeal of national regulations (to avoid reverse discrimination against domestic products).

automatically fall under Article 30, it becomes even more difficult to explain the distinction between rules governing product characteristics and those applicable to market circumstances leading to a discrimination test which applies only to rules relating to market circumstances. The logical consequence to be drawn from the rationale proposed by White and adopted by the Court is that rules relating to market circumstances should be subject to a case by case analysis to see if the imported product is prevented "from benefiting in the importing Member State from the advantages arising out of its production in the different legal and economic environment prevailing in the other Member State",[132] and not to a discrimination test.

Furthermore, many of the examples given by White (and now, it seems, by the Court) regarding rules on product characteristics do not really concern the loss of an advantage arising to the product by reason of its production in a particular Member State. When rules impose a certain shape or size on a product, for instance, what is really at stake is not that the production in a certain legal and economic environment confers to products produced therein an advantage that is taken away by the rule of the importing Member State, but that the divergence between the rules of importing and exporting Member States imposes an extra cost on producers. Such an additional cost may, and normally will, also apply to domestic products since they too, if exported, may have to comply with two sets of rules and will, to that extent, be prevented from enjoying a competitive advantage. What is relevant here, as with rules on market circumstances, is that the extra cost to domestic and imported products of having to comply with two sets of rules to enter into two national markets will be reflected in their cost in either of those markets.[133] Many of these extra costs, which White takes as a loss of a competitive advantage, are also present in many non-discriminatory rules relating to market circumstances. As we have seen, it is on that basis that since *Oosthoek's* the Court has made a uniform interpretation of rules on product requirements and other market circumstances.[134] Thus, for example, in *Yves Rocher,* not long before *Keck,* the Court considered the cost imposed on an economic agent by having to comply with two different sets of rules on market circumstances as relevant in ascertaining whether there was an obstacle to free movement of goods.[135] Whether we call this discrimination (applying Marenco's theory) or a loss of a competitive advantage (applying White's theory), the truth is that the burden coming from double regulation (identified in product requirements

[132] White, "In Search of the Limits to Article 30" (n.123 above), at 247.

[133] This shows that the problem in these cases is not the competitive advantages arising out of production in a specific legal or economic environment but the costs for products from the lack of co-ordination of national regulations—aproblem that does not exist only in the case of rules relating to characteristics of products (such as size, shape and weight) but also in the case of rules relating to market circumstances.

[134] See above the analysis of the *Osthoek´s* line of cases.

[135] See para 5.

rules) is as well present in rules on market circumstances. As Advocate-General Jacobs said in his observations in *Leclerc* v. *TF 1 Publicité*, recalling the previous case law of the Court, "if traders had to modify their publicity brochures in accordance with the legislation of each Member State, they would incur the same sort of additional burden that is imposed when the goods themselves have to be modified".[136] Will such an extra cost be represented as discrimination?[137] When those measures are challenged before the Court, why should a different outcome occur in rules relating to market circumstances and not in rules relating to the characteristics of products where, as mentioned above, the issue is not always a competitive advantage but the extra cost of having to comply with two different rules?

Keck does not completely clarify the Court's case law with respect to free movement, but the emphasis is now put on the fight against State protectionism. The different arguments put forward by the Court to support the national regulation in *Keck* show the reluctance of the Court of Justice to maintain its involvement in the analysis of the propriety of national regulatory policies. Thus, in paragraph 12 the Court states that it is not the purpose of the national provision "to regulate trade in goods between Member States". In paragraph 14 it makes explicit its intention to limit the use of Article 30 as an instrument to challenge rules affecting commercial freedom. Finally, the conception of Article 30 as a refined anti-protectionism rule can be seen again in paragraph 17 of the judgment. The Court intends, "not to interfere with neutral and general legislation, applicable without distinction to imported and national products, and to reserve these regulations to the sphere of Member States".[138] However, the distinction between rules on product characteristics and rules on market circumstances is contradictory both in itself and with an

[136] See n.103 above.

[137] The difficulties in applying the discrimination test of Keck can already be seen in joined Cases C–418/93, C–419/93 to C–421/93, C–460/93 to C–462/93, C–464/93, C–9/94 to C–11/94, C–14/94, C–14/94, C–23/94, C–24/94 and C–332/94, *Semeraro* (judgment of 20 June 1996). These cases concerned Italian legislation prohibiting trading on Sunday and public holidays and followed an initial decision of the Court excluding the application of Article 30, on the basis of *Keck*, in Joined Cases C–69/93 and C–258/93, *Punto Casa and PPV* [1994] ECR I–2355. In *Semeraro*, the national court considered that *Punto Casa* did not sufficiently answer its questions because the prohibition of Sunday trading could be considered as discriminating indirectly against imports. This was so, in its opinion, because shops that would normally open on Sunday are normally large shopping centres that offer much more foreign products than the small businesses to which trade is diverted with the prohibition of Sunday trading (thus indirectly diverting trade from foreign to national products). However, the Court did not share this view, placing the accent in the lack of evidence that the aim of the rules at issue was to regulate trade in goods (see para 24). This demonstrates how difficult it is to avoid the expansion of a discrimination criterion without remaining prisoner of protectionism intent.

[138] M. van Huffel, "Le champ d'application de l'article 30 du Traité de Rome et les arrêts Keck et Mithouard, Hünermund et Clinique: la nouvelle liberté de la libre circulation des marchandises ou 'l'enfer c'est les autres'?", (1994) *Revue Europeenne de Droit de la Consommation*, 95, at 110. Author's translation; in the original: "*L'attitude de la Cour s'explique, on l'a dit, par son désir de ne plus s'immiscer dans des législations neutres et générales, indistinctement applicables aux produits importés et nationaux, et de réserver ces réglementations à la compétence des Etats membres*".

anti-protectionist reading of Article 30. Whilst according to White,[139] the *prima facie* prohibition of rules on product characteristics is justified to allow producers to be able to choose the best legal and economic environment in which to manufacture their products, the same is not true for rules on market circumstances where the emphasis for their *prima facie* justification is placed on their neutrality *vis-à-vis* products from other Member States.[140] The question one may ask is why should Article 30 favour regulatory competition over rules on product characteristics while not accepting regulatory competition over rules on market circumstances? If one follows White's analysis of Article 30, the *Keck* doctrine might lead to a dual conception of Article 30 as an economic due process clause with regard to measures on product requirements and an anti-protectionism clause with regard to rules governing market circumstances. Even if, as it is case, one does not accept an economic due process reading (promoting regulatory competition) of the product requirements case law, the paradox of the dual conception of Article 30 is maintained: why should Article 30 favour judicial harmonisation of rules on product characteristics while not promoting such harmonisation with regard to rules on market circumstances?

The conclusion to be drawn from *Keck* is that the Court has faced some of the problems and contradictions of its case law in this area, but that it has not yet made up its mind as to a definite course of action to follow. The distinction between product characteristics and market circumstances may even prove itself useful in reducing the workload of the Court in the short term but lacks the normative foundation necessary to stand in the long term. A more stable solution must be based upon the institutional and value choices which will be discussed in the following chapters.

Explaining *Keck*

Keck is bound to suffer many criticisms, on different bases but with a focus on its main consequence: the retreat from balancing and the greater margin of discretion left to Member State regulations.[141] The ostensible reasons for

[139] White, "In Search of the Limits to Article 30" (n.123 above), at 246.

[140] Ibid at 247.

[141] Two examples are the review articles by Mattera, "De l'arrêt 'Dassonville' a l'arrêt Keck: l'obscure clarté d'une jurisprudence riche en principes novateurs et en contradictions", (1994) *Revue du Marché Unique Européen*, 117 and Gormley, "Reasoning Renounced?" The Remarkable Judgment in Keck and Mithouard", (1994) European Business Law Review, 63. For a limited critique, aiming mainly at a refinement of *Keck* (applying Article 30 also in cases on measures equally applicable that impose a direct and substantial hindrance on the access of goods) and at harmonising it with the recent case law on services and persons see: Weatherhill, "After *Keck*: Some Thoughts on How to Clarify the Clarification", (1996) *CMLRev*, 885, mainly at 896–8, and also his annotation to *Bosman* in (1996) *CMLRev*, 991, at 1003–4. In a similar sense, arguing that the non-discrimination principle has to be complemented by a preventive principle (where access to the market is prevented) see: D. Chalmers, "Repackaging the Internal Market—The

this change were probably the increase in the number of cases before the Court, following the extensive scope given to Article 30; the general political atmosphere; and the increasing academic and even judicial[142] criticism of the activism and the functional approach of the Court. All of this led to a desire for greater prudence and more certainty. Judges of the Court have themselves recognised that these reasons have been quite influential in forming the new approach of the Court.[143] However, if one places the developments in the Court's case law within the context of the broader institutional alternatives in the regulation of the internal market, these developments can be seen in a new dimension, and one can perhaps argue that the Court is setting up a new kind of approach to the common market with reflections in the European Economic Constitution. Moreover, to greater self-restraint in free movement of goods may correspond greater activism in other areas of market integration. The next section will introduce the concepts of market maintenance and market building to help explain *Keck* and the different levels of activism in the case law of the Court on market integration and the European Economic Constitution.

MARKET MAINTENANCE AND MARKET BUILDING

This section will advance a "simple" thesis regarding the role of the judiciary in the construction of federal markets. It identifies two different styles of judicial activism: market building and market maintenance. In the case of market building the main attention of courts is devoted to national legislation and the need to harmonise the different national regulatory frameworks so as to create the foundations of the integrated market. Market building focuses on promoting the new set of rights brought by the larger integrated area and to break the path-dependence of actors from national systems. In a nutshell, it shifts the rationality of market agents and political actors from the national to the integrated space. Market maintenance assumes that the dominant rationality of both market agents and the national political systems has been shifted to the larger economic and political space. The focus is on reducing uncertainty within the new system and in regulating the competition between States and between these and the federal level that arises from the different economic and political forums that now exist.

To enable better identification of what these two approaches consist in and how they may be explained, a brief analysis follows of the case law of the

Ramifications of the *Keck* Judgement", (1994) *ELR*, 385, mainly at 401–2. In favour of the *Keck* policy of restraint see: M. Lopez Escudero, "La jurisprudencia Keck y Mithouard: Una Revision del Concepto de Medida de Efecto Equivalente", (1994) Revista de Instituciones Europeas, 379, at 412 *et seq.* and N. Bernard, "Discrimination and Free Movement in EC Law", (1996) *International and Comparative Quarterly*, 82, at 108.

[142] For example, the German Constitutional Court "Maastricht" decision; see Chapter 1 above.

[143] See Chapter 1 above.

United States Supreme Court on the American commerce clause;[144] this is then compared with the approach that has been taken by the European Court of Justice with regard to the free movement goods. This analysis will allow us to see that the Supreme Court has been taking an anti-protectionism-based approach to State regulation affecting free trade. That case law will be described as "market maintenance", in contrast with the more activist approach of the European Court, defined as "market building". The different approaches will be explained here on the basis of the institutional alternatives[145] which are available in the American system to the Supreme Court; and in this light, the new steps undertaken by the European Court of Justice may be interpreted as a possible move towards a market maintenance approach in view of the institutional changes in the European system.

There is nothing new in identifying the USA as an integrated market and Europe as a market in the process of integration. What it is hoped to do here is to demonstrate the way in which the concepts of market building and market maintenance are related to the different approaches followed by the Supreme Court and the European Court of Justice. It may help to identify the priorities courts should have during different moments in the market integration process and the interplay between the case law and different institutional environments. This will hopefully provide a better understanding of the case law of the Court of Justice following *Keck*.

It will be argued that the reason for the different degrees of activism of the Court of Justice and the Supreme Court lie in the institutional alternatives to those courts. Both the market and the political process can be seen as decision-making systems that generate, interfere with, and adapt to, free trade. The level of integration of the American market and the internalising of a long experience by American market participants allowed that market to develop its own mechanisms capable of resolving many obstacles to trade. This, together with the capacity for intervention of the American political process, and the broader demands on the judicial process beyond market integration, led the Supreme Court to adopt a lower profile towards the review of State regulations under the commerce clause, than that which is adopted by the Court of Justice in reviewing State measures under the rules on the free movement of goods. The European Court, with its understanding of the institutional malfunctions in the European political process, the path-dependence of economic actors from national markets, and the incapacity of the different national markets for self-integration, considered itself "authorised" to promote integration if necessary through the judicial harmonisation of States'

[144] In its negative reading (that is, in reviewing states' measures) it broadly corresponds to the European Union rules on free movement.

[145] The concept of institutions adopted here is very broad including, eg, the market and the political process. See N. Komesar, *Imperfect Alternatives—Choosing Institutions in Law, Economics and Public Policy* (Chicago and London, The University of Chicago Press, 1995), at 9–10.

rules. The argument below will be that institutional developments in the European Union may explain and justify a change of priorities in the Court's case law.

Market maintenance and market building: the Supreme Court Commerce Clause case law compared with the European Court's Article 30 case law

In 1982, Sandalow and Stein discussed the view that the Court of Justice "adopted principles more restrictive of State power than those adopted by the Supreme Court".[146] In their opinion, support for this could be found in the case law of those Courts, but no definite conclusions could be drawn: "the cases [were] plainly too few in number to permit a judgement about the depth of the [Court of Justice] commitment to . . ."[147] the idea that "the Treaty provisions expressing the free-movement-of-goods principle not only proscribe protectionism, but embody a policy of integration which supersedes state legislation that would hinder the establishment of a single, unified market".[148] Today it is possible to argue that there are sufficient cases to support, and even to reinforce, that conclusion. As discussed above, from 1982 many State measures were struck down, or were at least subject to the strict scrutiny of the Court of Justice, on grounds other than anti-protectionism.

For the Supreme Court, the point of departure for its present jurisprudence is at first glance similar to that of the Court of Justice (at least in the pre-*Keck* period). The most important test in practice was given in the case of *Pike* v. *Church*, where the Supreme Court stated:

> "Where the state regulates evenhandedly to effectuate a legitimate local public interest and its effects on interstate commerce are only incidental, it will be upheld unless the burden imposed on such commerce is clearly excessive in relation to the putative local benefits".[149]

This formula is quite similar in its wording to that put forward by the Court of Justice in *Cassis de Dijon*:

> "Obstacles to movement within the Community resulting from disparities between the national laws . . . must be accepted in so far as those provisions may be recognised as being necessary in order to satisfy mandatory requirements relating in particular to the effectiveness of fiscal supervision, the protection of public health, the fairness of commercial transactions and the defence of the consumer".

[146] Stein and Sandalow, *Courts and Free Markets, Perspectives from the United States and Europe*, vol. 1 (Oxford, Clarendon Press, 1982), at 25.

[147] Ibid, at 27.

[148] Ibid, at 26.

[149] *Pike* v. *Bruce Church* 397 US 137, 90 S Ct 844, 25 L Ed 2d 174.

Both formulae attempt to set a balance between legitimate state interests and free trade.[150] Both formulae also require, at least as set out in subsequent cases, the non-existence of a less harmful means of achieving the state's goal. Nevertheless, there are important differences between the Supreme Court and the Court of Justice both in the development of those formulae and in the practical outcomes of their application.

As early as 1978, in *Philadelphia* v. *New Jersey*, the Supreme Court reproposed the *Pike* v. *Church* test as an anti-protectionism formula. After restating *Pike* v. *Church*, the Supreme Court concluded that "the crucial inquiry, therefore, must be directed to determining whether ch 363 is basically a protectionist measure, or whether it can fairly be viewed as a law directed to legitimate local concerns, with effects upon interstate commerce that are only incidental".[151] Later, in *Arkansas Electric Co-op*, the Supreme Court clearly stated that the most serious concern identified in *Pike* v. *Church* is economic protectionism.[152] The development of the *Pike* v. *Church* test by the Supreme Court highlights a major difference in the way that the notion of a "burden on trade" is conceived. Whereas the Court of Justice has taken, until *Keck*, a broad, literal definition of the notion of a "restriction on trade", the Supreme Court has introduced an element of discrimination into the concept of a "burden on trade". This is visible in *Philadelphia* v. *New Jersey* but also in the bulk of the decisions following *Pike* v. *Church*,[153] and can be said to be shown in the recurrent references to "discrimination against interstate commerce" in cases involving the commerce clause.[154] In *Bendix* v. *Midwesco*, the Supreme Court expounded the notion of burden on trade, giving it an indisputable discrimination colouring. It stated:

> "Where the burden of a state regulation falls on interstate commerce, restricting its flow in a manner not applicable to local business and trade, there may be either a discrimination that renders the regulation invalid without more, or cause to weigh and assess the State's putative interests against the interstate restraints to determine if the burden imposed is an unreasonable one".[155]

The assessment of the costs and benefits of state regulations is thus restricted to those regulations that restrict the flow of commerce "in a manner not

150 There is, however, a difference of degree in the wording of *Pike* v. *Church* that requires that the burden on commerce has to *clearly outweigh* the state interest for the legislation to be struck down.

151 *City of Philadelphia* v. *New Jersey* 437 US 617, 57 L Ed 2d 475, 98 S Ct 2531, at para 6.

152 *Arkansas Electric Co-op. Corp* 461 US 375, 103 S Ct 1905, 76, L Ed 2d 1.

153 See, for example, *Hughes* v. *Oklahoma* 441 US 322, 60 L Ed 2d 250, 99 S Ct 1727, at para 7; *Kassel* v. *Consolidated Freightways* 450 US 662, 67 L Ed 2d 580, 101 S Ct 1309, at para IV; *Bachus Imports* 468 US 263, 82 L Ed 2d 200, 104 S Ct 3049, at paras 6–8.

154 Collins stresses that discrimination against interstate or foreign commerce is not the same as discrimination against non-resident merchants and the former is actually more deferential towards state legislation. See R.B. Collins, "Economic Union as a Constitutional Value", (1988) 63 *New York University Law Review*, 43, at 78.

155 *Bendix* v. *Midwesco* 486 US 888, 100 L Ed 2d 896, 108 S Ct 2218, at para 1b, 2.

applicable to local business and trade". Only in this case is it possible to speak of a burden on interstate commerce.

The broader scope given by the Court of Justice to Article 30 is reflected in its workload in reviewing State measures with an impact on the free movement of goods. A comparison between the number of cases reviewed by the Court of Justice and the American Appeal and Supreme Courts, highlights strikingly different levels of judicial activism. It is not sufficient to compare the European Court of Justice with the Supreme Court, since the latter court case law is limited to very important, landmark, decisions, the bulk of the work being left in hands of the Courts of Appeal. From 1985 to 1992 the United States Courts of Appeal only four times struck down state legislation on grounds that it violated the *Pike* v. *Church* test. In the same period, state legislation submitted to the *Pike* v. *Church* test was upheld 20 times. In the European Community in 1990 alone the Court of Justice struck down seven State regulations and upheld three on the basis of the balance test given in *Cassis de Dijon*. A striking contrast. Pre-emption[156] is not a sufficient explanation, as there are still substantial policy areas in the hands of states in the USA. Moreover, in areas where standards of protection are being continuously reassessed (such as the protection of the environment) pre-emption has to be explicit. Thus, the possibility of conflict with the commerce clause is always present. Areas that have been at the centre of disputes under Article 30 in Europe (such as product requirements) are in many cases still governed by state law in the USA.[157] An analysis of the way in which the Supreme Court and the Court of Justice deal with similar issues, confirms that differences are not merely quantitative but also qualitative, and that they reflect different approaches regarding state regulation of free trade.

Many measures that are challenged in Europe on the grounds of the free movement of goods have been the object of state regulation in the USA without any commerce clause challenge being brought against them. Regulations on Sunday trading, which provoke so much discussion in Europe, have never been considered possible violations of the commerce clause in the USA. In areas such as trading or working hours, the Supreme Court has been particularly deferential to state regulations.[158] The commerce clause has not gone as far as the free movement rules in challenging state regulations of a general policy nature, such as those regulating canvassing, dock-work organisation and the advertising of prices.[159] When a state regulation on the advertising of

[156] As is well known, pre-emption is the American concept defining the occupation of a legislative area by federal legislation. In those area states can no longer legislate.

[157] See for an example of different state requirements which would probably be challenged under Article 30, the Mississipi and Wisconsin definitions of what can be sold as a dairy product: compare Miss. 75.31(1) and (8) with Wi 97.1(10) a) and c). Compare with the Court of Justice decision in *Deserbais*, (n.69 above).

[158] See *National League of Cities* v. *Usery* 426 US 833, 49 L Ed 2d 245, 96 S Ct 2465. There is, here, an interesting parallel with the choice of the Court of Justice in *Keck* to limit the use of Article 30 in challenging regulations regarding "selling arrangements".

[159] See, above, the references to these cases in the European Court of Justice.

sunglasses prices was brought before the Supreme Court on commerce clause arguments, it was upheld,[160] in contrast to the probable outcome of a similar case in the Court of Justice[161] if prior to *Keck*. Differences can also be found in the more controversial area of product requirements, such as the decisions on state regulation imposing requirements on the weight and composition of bread[162] and on the presentation of goods[163] for consumer protection.[164]

An interesting case for comparing the approaches of both Courts is the case law on price regulations. The Supreme Court authorises states to regulate prices so long as there are only limited extraterritorial effects. It has stated that the most important issue in determining the validity of such regulations is whether they "regulate out-of-state transactions".[165] It struck down state statutes which prohibited the sale of products imported from another state unless the price paid to the producer in the other state was up to the minimum prescribed by the first state for purchases from local producers, or which required producers to affirm that the prices which they charge to wholesalers within the importing state will be no higher than the lowest prices at which such sales *will be made* in other states.[166] But it upheld a statute requiring that sales made to wholesalers and retailers in the importing state be made at a price no higher than the lowest price at which sales were made anywhere in the USA during the *preceding month*.[167] The thin and very debatable line dividing these cases rules that a state may determine its prices on the basis of the prices that *were charged* in another state, but that it cannot set its prices so as to "determine" the prices *to be charged* in another state. In reality, such

[160] See *Head* v. *Board of Examiners* 374 US 424, 10 L Ed 2d 983, 83 S Ct 1759.

[161] See *GB-INNO* (n.23 above) and *Yves Rocher* (n.23 above). However, these decisions will not stand after *Keck*.

[162] Compare *Kelderman* (n.72 above) with *Schmidinger* v. *City of Chicago* 226 US 578, 57 L Ed 364, 33 S Ct 182; *Jay Burns Baking Company* 264 US 504, 68 L Ed 813, 44 S Ct 412, and *Petersen Baking Co.* 290 Us 570, 54 S Ct 277, 1934 US 456. Commerce clause arguments are not used in these Supreme Court cases. Instead, the Court stresses the extent of state and municipal policy power in this area. Only in *Jay Burns Baking Company* is the state law struck down, but this is done on the basis of the Fourteenth Amendment (this being a decision from the period of economic due process).

[163] Compare *Plumley* v. *Massachussets* 155 US 461, upholding a ban on yellow margarine for consumer protection with *Rau* (n.74 above), striking down the Belgian law imposing cube-shape packages on margarine, also in order to protect consumers.

[164] For more examples and references in comparing the Supreme Court and Court of Justice approaches in this area, see Heydebrand ud. Lasa, "Free Movement of Foodstuffs, Consumer Protection and Food Standards in the European Community: Has the Court of Justice Got It Wrong?", (1991) 16 *ELR*, 391, at 396.

[165] See *Baldwin* v. *GAF Seeling, Inc.* 294 US 511; 55 S Ct 497, 1935 US 54, 19 L Ed 1032, in particular at para 1; *Joseph E. Seagram & Sons* v. *Hostetter* 384 US 35, 16 L Ed 2d 336, 86 S Ct 1254, at paras 4, 5; *Brown-Forman Distillers* v. *New York* 476 US 573, 90 L Ed 2d 552, 106 S Ct 2080, in particular at paras 3,4. In *Baldwin* v. *Seeling*, the "extraterritorial effects" test is closely linked with arguments on the prevention of protectionism and the protection of different states' competitive advantages. In later cases it is made clear that the relevant criterion in assessing the constitutionality of price-control statutes under the commerce clause is whether they "regulate out-of-state transactions".

[166] See *Baldwin* v. *Seelig* and *Brown-Forman* (n.165 above).

[167] See *Seagram* (n.165 above).

a subtle distinction ignores the fact that commercial strategies are normally defined over a longer period of time (such as one year) and thus in both of the cases mentioned, state regulation will control prices to be charged throughout the year in the different states. In any case, the rationale of the Supreme Court appears to be that as long as the prices established by a state statute do not determine the prices to be made in another state ("do not regulate out-of-state transactions"), the statute is upheld. It is thus more limited than the test adopted by the Court of Justice, where the rationale appears to be that final prices of products should be able to reflect the prices paid or the costs of production in another state or that products should not be prevented from entering into the market by virtue of higher prices paid in other Member States. In both these cases, national legislation also has extraterritorial effects since it can affect both the competitive advantages gained by products in other states and the interests of home retailers or wholesalers in buying out-of-state products but there is no "regulation of out-of-state transactions". Thus a fixed final price would be subject to strict scrutiny by the Court of Justice, at least under its pre-*Keck* approach;[168] but the same would not happen in the Supreme Court.

The different approaches are well summarised in the Supreme Court's clear dismissal of the premise "that every action by a state that has the effect of reducing in some manner the flow of goods in interstate commerce is potentially an impermissible burden".[169] This is in obvious contrast with the full effect given by the Court of Justice (until *Keck*) to the *Dassonville* ruling that all State rules "which are capable of hindering, directly or indirectly, actually or potentially, intra-Community trade are to be considered as measures having an effect equivalent to quantitative restrictions".[170]

American authors have, as in Europe, argued for different interpretations of the commerce clause. The Supreme Court itself has balanced different criteria: it distinguished between national and state areas of regulation; ascertained the direct or indirect effect on intrastate commerce; balanced the legitimate interests of the state with the burden on intrastate commerce; and enquired into the protectionist purposes of state legislation.[171] As with its European counterpart, the American Supreme Court can be said not to give clear and precise rules regarding the interpretation of the commerce clause.[172]

[168] It is not clear what will be the global consequences of *Keck* on price controls regulations since this has been considered an area already dominated by a discrimination test; an understanding which is, however, discussed and challenged above.

[169] *Hughes* v. *Alexandria Scrap Corp* (n.153 above) at para B7a.

[170] Case 8/74, *Dassonville* [1974] ECR 837, para 5.

[171] For a summary of various classifications attempted by the Supreme Court, see E.M. Maltz, "How Much Regulation is Too Much—An Examination of Commerce Clause Jurisprudence", (1981–1982) 50 *George Washington Law Review*, 47, n.2 at 48.

[172] In this sense, R.B. Collins, "Economic Union as a Constitutional Value" (n.154 above), at 62 and Maltz, "How Much Regulation is Too Much" (n.171 above), at 85. Recourse to different rules may not necessarily be an element of conflict and uncertainty, but may be a result of the Courts's legal culture and learning process, and the integration of different legal visions into a

Nevertheless, the accent has clearly been placed on preventing protectionism. In one of the most comprehensive analyses of the commerce clause case law, Regan goes as far as to identify protectionism *purpose*, not simply protectionism effects, in the test adopted by the Supreme Court in the review of state regulations under the commerce clause. In his article, Regan[173] writes that: "in the central area of commerce clause jurisprudence comprising what I shall call 'movement of goods cases' (*Pike* v. *Bruce Church Inc.* may be taken as paradigmatic) the Court has been concerned exclusively with preventing states from engaging in purposed economic protectionism".[174]

Even if one does not agree with Regan, it is clear from the analysis made above that the Supreme Court shows more deference to the State's regulatory powers which may affect interstate trade than the European Court of Justice has shown in reviewing State intervention in the market capable of restricting trade in the common market. We must now look at why this is so and how it is reflected in the different approach which has already been designated as "market maintenance". The explanation for this may help in understanding the concept of market maintenance.

Market maintenance

Market integration has reached a "point of no return" in the USA. Furthermore, a common regulatory tradition has emerged in parallel with the degree of market and political integration. There is no risk of different regulatory traditions conflicting and creating obstacles to free movement. When differences arise they are mainly the expression of opposing ideological strategies or due to innovation and experimentation with new forms of regulation. There are less incentives for state protectionism as the core of economic policies changes from state to federal level. Even protectionism is, in market actors rationality, concentrated on federal protection against outside competitors. The dominant logic is that of the federal market. National political systems are not authorised to develop selfish policies but, at the same time,

legitimation process of a consensual result. One can speak of a turning-point, when a legal framework has reached such acceptance and stability in its operation, that different theories involved in legitimising it do not lead to conflicts but to sustenance. See Cass Sunstein, "Incompletely Theorized Agreements", (1995) 108 *Harvard Law Review*, 1733.

173 Regan continues in saying that: "not only is this what the Court has been doing, it is just what the Court should do. This and no more": D.H. Regan, "The Supreme Court and State Protectionism: Making Sense of the Dormant Commerce Clause", (1986) 84 *Michigan Law Review*6, 1091, at 1092. Protectionist effects will be significant (but not sufficient on their own) evidence of a protectionist purpose: ibid, at 1095. Arguing that a change in favour of more activism could occur in the court, see S. Kalen, "Reawakening the Dormant Commerce Clause in its First Century", (1987–88) 13 *University of Dayton Law Review*, 417, at 420. However, that does not appear to have been the case until now.

174 See, also, C.R. Sunstein, "Protectionism, the American Supreme Court, and Integrated Markets", in Bieber, Dehousse, Pinder, Weiler (eds.) *1992: One European Market?* (Baden-Baden, Nomos), 127, at 131.

are now an important element of innovation and experimentation in the American market. The dynamics of market integration and the time process in which it take place have taught market agents to operate within both federal and state rules and to incorporate its costs and advantages (such as the existence of diverse forums to push for more favourable policies). In the words of one author, "the American experience suggests that an integrated market is not incompatible with a wide variety of state and local regulatory standards".[175] According to Holmes the direct cost to firms of non-tariff barriers (including different standards and regulations) is actually quite modest and the full dynamic of market integration depends more on a change in corporate strategy and mentality.[176] In the American market, economic and political actors have acquired this new rationality and the focus is now on other elements of the system (not immunity from rules but a voice in their formulation)[177] and in securing certainty and stability. In the same way, path-dependence was created once agents became accustomed to operate in the present system.[178] Even if shortcuts exist, actors prefer to follow the path they know rather than try alternative investments in uncertain "direct trails". To try to push for legal harmonisation through the judicial process may be considered a too costly and uncertain alternative to the present system where access is in any case guaranteed and the costs of different regulations are known, as are the ways of pushing for harmonisation when desired through institutional alternatives to the courts. Instead, it may be preferable, even for economic actors, to try to focus the judicial system on consolidating the principles upon which the American market is found, reducing the risks of uncertainty, while pushing for new areas of judicial activism with regard to what is now the dominant element of economic regulation (the federal government).

A preference for a discrimination test in the USA can be related to the higher level of predictability such a test achieves, and to its conception as a test not intended to alter market structures and rules, but only to prevent deviant behaviour. In an integrated market, the focus shifts from access to stability. A test based on discrimination (or protectionism) instead of balancing reflects that priority. It is a choice in favour of more certainty at the expense of easier access. Economists have long stressed the importance of reducing uncertainty in the strategies of entrepreneurs and to promote trade exchanges. They have also emphasised the role that rules play in achieving that aim. As long as the operation of a free market is guaranteed it appears that the know-

[175] D. Vogel, "Protective Regulation and Protectionism in the European Community: The Creation of a Common Market for Food and Beverages", Paper prepared for the biennial conference of the European Community Studies Association (George Mason University, Virginia, May 1991), at 4.

[176] P. Holmes, "Non-Tariff Barriers", in G. McKenzie and A. Venables (eds.), *The Economics of the Single European Act* (London, MacMillan, 1991), 27.

[177] On exit and voice, see Chapter 4 below.

[178] On the concept of path-dependence see D. North, *Institutions, Institutional Change and Economic Performance* (Cambridge, Cambridge University Press, 1990).

ledge that market agents have of it and the existence of a level of stability and certainty sufficient for them to make decisions are more important than the substance of the regulatory model itself.[179] These factors are fundamental in planning economic strategies and feeling confident to enter into market transactions. Thus, obstacles to trade are not so much of a problem, as long as they can be overcome, and as long as market agents feel that the integrated market provides them sufficient levels of information, certainty and participation. Moreover, in the USA, challenges to trade restrictions are possible outside the legal basis of the "commerce clause". Both the political and the judicial system offer other opportunities to challenge or participate in regulation while the commerce clause can be focused in preserving the fundamentals of the American market (the prevention of state protectionism and selfish policies).

The preference for a discrimination test and the higher certainty it provides can also be associated to the different demands facing the United States Supreme Court. The jurisdiction of the Supreme Court is extremely large and it is asked to deal with many diverse subject areas. The adoption of a discrimination test in the application of the commerce clause reduces litigation in this area and is a form of administration of the workload of the Court and the federal judicial system in general. This allows the Supreme Court to focus its activism in other areas of the law.

The more limited scope of the commerce clause review of state measures is a consequence of the different priorities facing the integrated American market. The focus is in reducing transaction costs other than access and in maintaining a framework of rules capable of reducing uncertainty while permitting the development of different institutional alternatives. The structure of the American market, and the institutional setting supporting it, allow for a different function to be given to the commerce clause. Obstacles, not permissible at earlier stages of the creation of a common market can later be judicially acceptable, since the market itself, and the institutional system supporting it, have created their own mechanisms capable of solving these problems.[180] In

[179] In the USA, Roberta Romano has developed a theory of the "race for predictability and stability", according to which states success in competing with other states for investment and establishment of corporations depends, foremost, on the level of stability and predictability of their legal rules. See Roberta Romano, "The Political Economy of Takeover Statutes", (1987) *VA L Rev*, 114 and "The State Competition Debate in Corporate Law", (1987) *Cardozo Law Rev*, 709.

[180] This explains why matters over which pressure for harmonisation arose in earlier stages of market integration in the USA have later been devolved to different state treatment. An example of this can be seen in a comment of Roscoe Pound on the federal courts' case law on general and commercial law. In his words: "One of the first strokes against the rising cult of local law was the doctrine of the federal courts as to independent judgments upon questions of general and commercial law, making the law uniform for these courts, however diverse in the states in which they sat. In the present decade, despite the general shift to nationalize rather than localize, that doctrine has disappeared . . . it maintained itself for nearly a century, to the overthrown in the heydey of unification and nationalism": R. Pound, "Law and Federal Government", in *Federalism as a Democratic Process* (New Brunswick, Rutgers University Press, 1942), 3, at 17.

other words, the institution best able to deal with a particular issue changes with the degree of market integration and with the institutional developments taking place. The degree of activism of the Court varies according to its institutional alternatives and the different priorities in its judicial role. It can be said that both the choice of intervention under the commerce clause power of review, and the consequences of that intervention, depend upon and are reflected in different institutional choices. The Supreme Court decision for self-restraint is both a consequence of the different demands of its case law and of the operation of the other institutions playing a role in market integration. In this regard, of particular importance is the Supreme Court's view that in many cases Congress is a better institutional alternative to deal with the problems of interstate trade and state regulations;[181] while the Court of Justice, in view of the institutional malfunctions affecting Community institutions, decided to take the leading role in harmonising different national regulations.

THE EUROPEAN COURT'S MARKET BUILDING AND MARKET MAINTENANCE: DIFFERENT APPROACHES TO THE EUROPEAN ECONOMIC CONSTITUTION

Market agents in Europe are, by contrast to the American market, used to operating in a context of national markets. Their path-dependence has been linked to those: they know their way across national rules and national political processes; they have planned their strategies according to national markets (not necessarily only the domestic market); national political processes operate according to national accountability; and actors have constructed their networks around these national political and economic markets.[182] What the Court has done, in promoting a single market, is to break that path-dependence. At the same time, the institutional alternatives to the Court were, for a long period, dominated by a Community legislative process blocked by the use of unanimity in decision-making. This may explain why the Court has used Article 30 to supplement the Community process of harmonisation of national legislation.

The recent limits set in *Keck* to the *Cassis de Dijon* case law can be understood in the light of different factors. First, and as it is commonly argued, the previous approach of the Court had created an excessive workload and led to increased legal uncertainty, since any State measure could be argued to have

[181] In *Bendix* (n.155 above), Judge Scalia, concurring, defended the view that the Court should expressly abandon the "balancing" approach to the negative commerce clause, as it involves an essential legislative statement better left to Congress.

[182] Daniel Kiwit identifies "four criteria serving as clue to possible path dependence: (1) specific investments in material assets . . ., (2) specific investments in human capital . . ., (3) network effects . . ., (4) internalised institutions" (this includes rules): *Path-dependence in Technological and Institutional Change—Some Criticisms and Suggestions*, Diskussionsbreitrag 10/95: (Max-Planck-Institut zur Erforschung von Wirschaftssystemen Jena, 1995).

some effect on trade and thus automatically be submitted to a cost/benefit analysis. Secondly, the growing involvement of the Court in regulatory policy and the consequent increase in judicial activism was endangering the Court's legitimacy. This was already shaken by the post-Maastricht political debates in Europe; by the increased academic criticism; and even by judicial opposition at national level. Thirdly, the Court may be moving from a market building approach to a market maintenance approach in the area of free movement of goods, moving its resources to other, less integrated, areas of the common market. In these areas, we may be assisting a shift towards market building.

It must be stressed that the market maintenance approach that the Court is developing with regard to the free movement of goods not need to be (and, in fact, is not) identical to that of the Supreme Court with regard to the commerce clause. It is nonetheless an approach that recognises both the higher level of integration that the internal market has by now achieved (mainly in free movement of goods) and the institutional development of the European Union. In this area, "strengthening the internal market can mean consolidating rather than extending the principles upon which it is based".[183] The degree of integration already achieved in the free movement of goods, and the institutional changes in the Union (with the move from unanimity to majority voting in this area) may have led the Court to reduce its activism. This, in turn, allows it to be able to cope with an increased workload in other areas of the law and to face new demands for judicial activism: that can take place both with regard to other aspects of market integration and with regard to Community legislation.

There are elements indicating that less activism on the free movement of goods may correspond to more activism with regard to other free movement rules. The different developments in the institutional alternatives to the Court in regulating and integrating the common market may help in understanding the apparently contradictory expansion in the Court's case law regarding the freedom to provide services and the free movement of persons, when compared with the move to self-restraint in the area of free movement of goods.[184]

In the freedom to provide services there was a progressive tendency to uniformity with free movement of goods prior to *Keck*. The Court has since *Säger* adopted a test similar to the wide interpretation of *Cassis de Dijon*. It stated:

> "Article 59 of the Treaty requires not only the elimination of all discrimination against a person providing services on the ground of his nationality but also the abolition of any restriction, even if it applies without distinction to national providers

[183] Chalmers, "Repackaging the Internal Market" (n.141 above), at 403.

[184] Weatherhill makes an excellent attempt to make a global and common reading of the recent case law on the four freedoms. However, even this author appears to recognise that his reading is more a proposal to the Court (offering the possibility to construct a future single approach to the different freedoms) than an actual faithful interpretation of the decisions of the Court. See Weatherhill, "After Keck" (n.141 above).

of services and to those of other Member States, when it is liable to prohibit or otherwise impede the activities of a provider of services established in another Member State where he lawfully provides similar services. [Moreover. . .] as a fundamental principle of the Treaty, the freedom to provide services may be limited only by rules which are justified by imperative reasons relating to the public interest and which apply to all persons or undertakings pursuing an activity in the State of destination, in so far as that interest is not protected by the rules to which the person providing the services is subject in the Member State in which he is established. In particular, those requirements must be objectively necessary in order to ensure compliance with professional rules and to guarantee the protection of the recipient of services and they must not exceed what is necessary to attain those objectives".[185]

More striking than the developments in the freedom to provide services is the shift operated in the case law on the free movement of persons that has moved from a non-discrimination test to a balance test.[186] This is particularly striking in two decisions in the areas where the Court had long remained attached to a principle of non-discrimination or national treatment, in contrast to the free movement of goods and even services. In *Gebhard*, the Court interpreted the freedom of establishment as a fundamental freedom guaranteed by the Treaty and proceeded to state:

"that national measures liable to hinder or make less attractive the exercise of fundamental freedoms guaranteed by the Treaty must fulfil four conditions: they must be applied in a non-discriminatory manner; they must be justified by imperative requirements in the general interest; they must be suitable for securing the attainment of the objective which they pursue; and they must not go beyond what is necessary in order to attain it".[187]

In the famous *Bosman* case, the Court extends such criteria to the field of free movement of workers.[188] The Court is developing "a sort of "global

[185] Case C–76/90, *Säger* [1991] ECR I–4221, paras 12 and 15. See, confirming this decision: Case C–275/92, *Schindler* [1994] ECR I–1039; Case C–3/95, *Reisebüro Broede* [1996] ECR I–6511, and Case C–398/95, *Syndesmos ton en Elladi Touristikon kai Taxidiotikon Grafeion* (judgment of 5 June 1997, not yet reported).

[186] A concept of the rules on the free movement of persons as aiming to abolish all restrictions not necessary or proportional to their aims could be seen, at least in part, before the recent developments in the Court's case law, in the words of some authors. See Moutinho de Almeida, (presently judge at the ECJ) *Direito Comunitário—A Ordem Jurídica Comunitária—As Liberdades Fundamentais na CEE* (Lisboa, Centro de Publicações do Ministério da Justiça, 1985), at 447; F. Burrows, *Free Movement in European Community Law* (Oxford, Clarendon Press, 1987), at 125 (who presents 48(2) as distinct from 48(3), the latter referring also to non-discriminatory measures).

[187] Case C–55/94, *Gebhard* [1995] ECR I–4165, para 37.

[188] Case C–415/93, *Bosman* [1995] ECR I–4921, paras 102–4. This decision, however, comes in a sequence of progressive activism by the Court in this area of the law. According to Johnson and O'Keefe, writing in 1994, also in the area of free movement of workers, the Court has, "over the past five years, begun to demonstrate a more open hostility towards national measures which although not discriminatory, are capable of hindering the free movement of workers": E. Johnson, and D. O'Keefe, "From Discrimination to Obstacles to Free Movement: Recent Developments Concerning the Free Movement of Workers 1989–1994", (1994) 31 CMLR, 1313, at 1314.

approach" to the free movement of persons"[189] that requires national measures to satisfy four requirements in order to be valid under the Treaty rules on the free movement of persons:

"(a)—non discriminatory
(b)—justified by imperative requirements in the general interest
(c)—suitable for the attainment of their objective
(d)—necessary in order to attain this objective".[190]

The present line of case law in the realm of the European Economic Constitution appears to have two driving forces. One is the pressure for a uniform interpretation of free movement rules. In the later cases, as stated, the broad test given is presented as common to all fundamental freedoms of the EC Treaty. Moreover, the European Court, when confronted with its own ruling in *Keck* in cases regarding the other free movement rules, assumed that, in principle, the *Keck* ruling would also apply to the other freedoms but, in practice, it refused to apply *Keck* on the basis of a dubious distinction regarding the direct effect on access to the market in those cases. In *Alpine Investments* and *Bosman* the Court considered that both the prohibition of cold calling to offer financial services or the requirement of a transfer fee for the transfer of football players between European clubs directly prevented or affected the access to the market while that was not the case of the rules covered by the *Keck ratio decidendo*.[191] However, it is, by no means, clear how the rules reviewed in *Alpine Investments* and *Bosman* prevent access to the market in a different manner from that of the rules at stake in *Keck*. In this case, foreign producers are also prevented from accessing the market if they want to offer their products at a loss. This is the same as not being able to offer a service through cold calling or not being able to transfer a player without paying a transfer fee. In all these cases there is no absolute prevention of accessing the market. What happens is that market access is subject to certain conditions:[192] in *Alpine Investments*, Dutch companies could still provide financial services in other Member States though they could not offer such services through cold calling; in *Keck* products could still be imported to France though they could not be offered at prices lower than their purchase price.

The analysis made confirms the different approaches now present in the Court's case law on the free movement rules. The Court has shifted the focus of its activism from the free movement of goods to the other freedoms (notably the free movement of persons). This is the second driving force of

[189] L. Daniele, "Non-Discriminatory Restrictions to the Free Movement of Persons", (1997) ELR, 191, at 194.

[190] Ibid, at 194.

[191] Case C–384/93, *Alpine Investments* [1995] ECR I–1141, paras 37–38, and *Bosman*, (n.188 above), para 103.

[192] In the this sense see N. Bernard, "The Rights of Individuals in the Internal Market: Rights to Free Movement or Rights to Deregulation", paper presented at the SPTL Conference (Cambridge, September, 1996).

the present case law of the European Court: it favours self-restraint in the traditional areas of Court activism compensated by an enhanced role in the previously more "neglected" area of free movement of persons. This means that the Court will concentrate its market building efforts in those areas where market integration is less developed, and where the European Union decision-making process is still dominated by a unanimity rule and which have had less legislative attention (ie the free movement of persons).[193] The different developments in the institutional alternatives to the Court to integrate the market may well explain the recent developments in its case law.

[193] Again, acccording to Johnson and O'Keefe, free movement of workers is "an area of law which, in recent years at least, has received scant legislative attention from the Council": "From Discrimination to Obstacles to Free Movement" (n.188 above), at 1313.

4

The Alternative Models of the European Economic Constitution

THE DEBATE ON ARTICLE 30 AND EUROPEAN REGULATION: INSTITUTIONAL CHOICES, CONSTITUTIONAL MODELS AND THE LEGITIMACY OF EUROPEAN LAW

The *Keck*[1] decision represented one more step in the complex and difficult debate between anti-discrimination and cost/benefit analysis that has dominated both the case law of the Court and the legal writing on the review of State measures under Article 30. Both cost/benefit and discrimination tests on Article 30 have been unable, however, to provide a sound normative foundation for the Court's review of State regulation of the market and ignored the institutional choices and constitutional dilemmas involved. They have largely accepted the different levels of discretion that have been followed by the Court in its case law, while not addressing both the institutional choice inherent in the replacement of a State's assessment of a regulation by the Court's assessment of the same regulation, and the notion of the European Economic Constitution that should underlie any interpretation of Article 30 and its review of market regulation.

In a few words, one can say that discrimination tests limit the role of Article 30 to the review of State measures that discriminate against imports while cost/benefit tests argue for a wider use of Article 30, leading to the review of all measures with an effect on trade and balancing their costs and benefits. The debate between discrimination and cost/benefit analysis is mainly about the extent of discretion that courts and Member States should have in the realm of Article 30. At the same time, however, the debate between discrimination and cost/benefit analysis also leads to a discussion of the necessary degree of European regulation: once national regulation is no longer possible due to free movement rules, it is open to discussion whether or not national regulation should be replaced by European regulation; in other words, whether European market negative integration should be understood as an end in itself or as a step towards European market positive integration. The limits to national regulation (mainly by promoting cost/benefit tests) can be argued either to favour a European deregulated market or a European reregulated market. All these alternatives imply different conceptions of the European Economic Constitution and its source of legitimacy, as well as

[1] Joined Cases C–267 and C–268/91, *Keck and Mithouard* [1993] ECR I–6097.

different institutional choices regarding the allocation of regulatory powers over the European internal market.

The present chapter is devoted to assessing the institutional choices involved in this area and to reviewing the different alternative models of the European Economic Constitution. In this way, the analysis will review different types of institutional malfunction requiring a broader and more sophisticated approach of the European Court of Justice to the European Economic Constitution and the review of Community and national legislation. The different institutional alternatives to market regulation in Europe, arising from the debate on Article 30, are related to different economic constitutional models of the European Union. These models are mainly about allocating regulatory decisions to different institutions. This chapter will review these institutional alternatives, concentrating on problems of representation and accountability in a complex and multi-level system such as the European Union. The aim is to identify and review the different economic constitutional models underlying the debate on Article 30 and European regulation and to discuss the different institutional malfunctions present in the States, Community and market processes from which regulatory decisions arise in each of those models. In this regard, it will be stressed that the majoritarian approach followed by the Court in the review of State measures under Article 30 is insufficient and inadequate, since it focuses, exclusively, on problems with the States' regulatory process and ignores all other institutional malfunctions that may be present in the judicial, Community and market processes.

The approach followed in this chapter is essentially static, for heuristic purposes. Models are presented in their ideal form and taken separately. In the following chapter, this analysis will be related to a more dynamic approach in which institutional choices and constitutional goals are linked to comparative institutional analysis and a normative discussion of the role of Article 30 in the European Economic Constitution.

We begin by setting out the institutional choices involved in the interpretation of Article 30 through the example of the *Cassis de Dijon*[2] decision coupled with brief references to different stages in the legal and political approaches to Article 30 and market integration.

Institutional choices and the interpretation of Article 30

Different interpretations of Article 30 result in different institutions being made responsible for the regulation of the common market. This is true, not only for the Court of Justice decisions to review the regulatory choices of Member States under Article 30 but also for the regulatory choices the Court

[2] Case 120/78, *Rewe-Zentral AG* v. *Bundesmonopolverwaltung für Branntwein* [1979] ECR 649.

itself makes in balancing the costs and the benefits of such measures. To illustrate this we can take the example of *Cassis de Dijon*, the landmark decision of the European Court of Justice in the area of free movement of goods despite the "competition" of *Dassonville* and *Keck*.

As you may remember, the case concerned the importation into Germany of Cassis de Dijon, a French fruit liqueur the alcohol content of which (between 15 and 20 per cent) did not satisfy the 25 per cent minimum prescribed by German law. Although legally produced and marketed in France, Cassis de Dijon could not be sold in Germany in its original form. The French producers of Cassis de Dijon appealed to the European Court of Justice claiming that the German law violated the principle of the free movement of goods. We will not enter in the merits of the Court's decision but simply consider how the competing interpretations of Article 30 implied different institutional choices (also assuming here that the German legislation was struck down in spite of being non-discriminatory, which was probably not the case).

The German Government argued that only discriminatory measures are covered by Article 30 of the EC Treaty and that disparities in technical standards should be reduced by recourse to the procedure of harmonisation set out in Article 100. Moreover the German Government justified its regulation by reason of the protection of health and of consumers, and of the fairness of commercial transactions. For the German Government to accept the plaintiff's claim would, it argued, be to replace German law by French law in Germany. The reading of Article 30 proposed by the German Government corresponded to a traditional view of the EC Treaty as touching upon limited areas of traditional national policies. Though it was consensual that the Treaty pursued broader goals than traditional international trade treaties, a face reading of the Treaty, ignoring the dynamics of integration, pointed to a division of competences between the EEC and the Member States close to what in the USA was described as dual federalism: policy about commerce will be a matter for the Community, while the other policy powers, such as economic and social regulation, would remain in the hands of the States. Accordingly, the balance between the market and regulation was to be set by the States either on their own or through joint decisions in the Community political process. Hence, the German Government view was that Article 30 had to be interpreted as limiting the Court's powers of intervention to the prevention of protectionism. Decisions concerning the regulation of the market, except for cases where discriminatory barriers on exports or imports were created, were left to the States.

If this interpretation had been accepted it would have been for the German Government to determine the minimum alcohol content of liquers valid in its own national market, or in other words, in its share of the common market. Provided that national rules were non-discriminatory *vis-à-vis* products of other Member States, they could only be altered by the Community legislature under the harmonisation powers given to it by Article 100 (and now also

100A). Member States will remain responsible for regulating the characteristics of products but they could be supplemented by the Community legislative process acting under the harmonisation powers granted by Articles 100 and 100A where non-protectionist national measures directly affected the establishment or functioning of the common market. This corresponds to a constitutional model in which the core of regulatory powers will be kept in the hands of the Member States, now subject to the constraints of non-discrimination against foreign products.

The Court, however, did not follow the interpretation of Article 30 proposed by the German Government in *Cassis de Dijon*. The decision in the case is well known and has been cited many times: the Court accepted that, "in the absence of common rules relating to the production and marketing of alcohol . . . it is for the Member States to regulate all matters relating to the production and marketing of alcohol and alcoholic beverages on their own territory".[3] Moreover, "obstacles to movement within the Community resulting from disparities between the national laws relating to the marketing of the products in question must be accepted in so far as those provisions may be recognized as being necessary in order to satisfy mandatory requirements relating in particular to the effectiveness of fiscal supervision, the protection of public health, the fairness of commercial transactions and the defense of the consumer".[4] This was not, however, held to be the case with the German regulation. In the opinion of the Court, the German law was not "necessary" in order to attain the objectives desired: a reduction in the drinking of alcoholic beverages. The lower content of alcohol of Cassis de Dijon would not stimulate the consumption of alcohol, since there were many other products in the German market with lower alcohol contents. Although the Court recognized the usefulness of fixing mandatory limits for the transparency of commercial transactions, it considered that labelling could sufficiently protect this interest.

This interpretation has quite different institutional consequences. The State is only *prima facie* competent to determine the minimum alcohol contents even where it does not discriminate against foreign products. Whether that minimum alcohol content is "necessary" or not is an assessment to be made by the Court. In other words, whether market regulation is "necessary" or not is determined by the Court. The Court assumed the power of deciding whether or not a regulation is necessary to attain a certain social goal and even, with the introduction of the principle of proportionality, if that goal may justify the burden imposed by the regulation.[5] In the case of *Cassis de Dijon*, the Court replaced the German decision over minimum alcohol

[3] See para 8.

[4] See para 8.

[5] As discussed in the previous chapter, whether or not a regulation is justified and proportional is a judgment that the Court has made in accordance with what it deduces to be the European majority policy.

contents with its own. It considered that the German-defined minimum alcohol content was not necessary in the pursuit of any legitimate objectives (as defined by the Court) and, therefore, the minimum alcohol content should be left to market choice. Under this interpretation, two major institutional changes occur in the regulation and operation of the market. First, by introducing the judgement of "necessity" of regulation into the review of State policy-making (later supplemented with the concept of proportionality), the Court acquired *a priori* control over regulatory powers. It is for the Court of Justice to determine whether or not a certain regulation of the market is necessary. Once this occurs, a second institutional choice arises: after deciding to replace the State's judgement by its own, the Court, in deciding whether or not the regulation is necessary, decides between the market and the regulatory process in addressing the issue under regulation and allocating the resources at stake. If the Court upholds the regulation, resource allocation will depend on the choices taken by the regulator. If it strikes down the regulation, it will be the market, through voluntary market transactions, which will allocate the resources. Since the Court strikes down national regulations only with regard to imports[6] we will then have a competitive process between the national regulations to which the different national products would be subject. The competition between national products will, at the same time, be a competition between the different regulations to which they would be subject. The market would be the decision-maker on the "best" regulation.[7]

In the end, both results (upholding or striking down the national regulation) may require European legislation either to bring about harmonisation or to secure a certain level of market regulation. However, the existence of one situation or the other may generate different outcomes in the European legislative process. Those Member States who gain by the situation following the judicial decision are in an advantageous position in the debate at the European legislative level, especially if they enjoy a power of veto in the vote following the debate.

The *Cassis de Dijon* case law marked a phase in which the Court and the market became more important in the push for integration and harmonisation, and in changing the institutional balance of the European Economic Constitution. In this period the Court became directly involved in deciding the degree of regulation of the common market. In the previous chapter, it was described how this involvement occurred and the majoritarian content it assumed. At the same time, however, the limits imposed on State regulation by the case law on Article 30 and the deregulatory consequences at national level arising therefrom were linked to the pro-market political atmosphere and the revival of deregulatory theories. In the words of Norbert Reich: "The political focus has shifted from market failure to regulatory failure. Regulatory remedies that were designed to cure market defects are now made

6 See Chapter 3 above.

7 See the analysis of the Competitive Model below.

subject to market approval".[8] This, coupled with the continuous existence of numerous restrictions on free trade, was reflected in the Commission's White Paper in 1985, and in the new approach to harmonisation with the principles of mutual recognition, home country control and minimum directives. As the Court could not by itself harmonise all national legislation and eliminate all restrictions on trade, its role was perceived, under the strategy associated with the White Paper, as moving away from participation in the details of harmonisation to the legitimisation of a certain strategy of harmonisation. On the one hand, the few references made to the Court in the White Paper indicate—as Easson states—that "*no specific role* at all was perceived for the Court in the completion of the internal market by the 1992 target date":[9] the Court could no longer deal with the complexities involved in the harmonisation of detailed national legislation. On the other hand, the White Paper's policy is presented as a restatement of the case law of the Court: policy principles are drawn from the decisions of the Court and legitimised through them.[10]

Had it been fully applied, the new approach to harmonisation would have raised the principle of mutual recognition into a constitutional status, the basis of a constitutional economic model of regulatory competition among States. It would be for the market—where different national regulations will compete under mutual recognition—to assume a predominant role in economic integration and ex-post harmonisation (the better regulation in market terms would end up by being adopted by all Member States). However, mutual recognition did not became a general principle, and neither home country control nor minimum directives were pursued to the extent expected. The Court was required to intervene more and more frequently in this area of law in order to judge the validity of national regulations. It was thus entrusted with the work of harmonisation. At the same time, the developments in the Community legislative process and in the Court's case law (such as *Keck*) highlight the importance of the two other models of regulation focusing on Community or States' regulatory powers. This is a reflection of the different proposals put forward regarding the interpretation of Article 30 and regulation of the internal market.

Constitutional models and the legitimacy of European law

The institutional choices, regarding the allocation of regulatory powers, that can be detected in different interpretations of Article 30 and its co-ordination

[8] N. Reich, "The Regulatory Crisis: American Approaches in the Light of European Experiences", (1983) 3 *American Bar Foundation Research Journal*, 693.

[9] A. Easson, "Legal Approaches to European Integration: the Role of the Court and the Legislator in the Completion of the European Common Market", (1989) *Rev Integr Europ*, 100, at 101, emphasis added.

[10] See R. Dehousse, and G. Majone, "The Dynamics of European Integration: The Role of Supranational Institutions", Paper presented at the European Community Studies Association Third Biennial International Conference (27–29 May 1993, Washington, DC), at 11.

with Treaty rules on harmonisation may be represented in three ideal constitutional models of the European Economic Constitution: the centralised constitutional model, the competitive constitutional model and the decentralised constitutional model. The centralised model reacts to the erosion of national regulatory powers through Article 30 by favouring a process of market regulation by means of the replacement of national laws with Community legislation. The competitive model promotes "competition among national rules", notably through the principle of mutual recognition of national legislation. In the decentralised model, States will retain regulatory powers, but are, at the same time, prevented from developing protectionist policies. These models are heuristic devices. They are all present—and compete with each other—in the European Union. In the same way, all institutions with a regulatory role both participate in and help to shape the European model. The future of the European Economic Constitution is linked to the continuous interplay between the Constitutional models of centralisation, competition, and decentralisation. These, in turn, can be linked with three different visions of the European Economic Constitution and its legitimation.

The first argues that negative integration, deriving from the application of market integration rules, must be followed by positive integration which is legitimised through the development of traditional democratic mechanisms in the European Union.

The second argues for the constitutionalisation of negative integration. No traditional democratic developments are required for the European Union institutions since powers are left to the market. No transferal of powers to those institutions takes place. The market is conceived as the best source of legitimation of the European Economic Constitution. This vision protects market freedom and individual rights against public power.

The third vision still sees the highest source of legitimacy in national democratic legitimacy. The legitimacy of the European Economic Constitution derives therefrom and is thus conditioned. No other form of constitutional legitimacy that can be opposed to national democratic processes is foreseeable, or even defensible, in the European Union at this stage.

The disputes over Article 30 and European regulation are basically disputes over these different economic constitutional models and the different legitimacy they presuppose. Those arguing for an economic due process use of Article 30 and cost/benefit analysis favour an economic model of deregulation and regulatory competition, the constitutional legitimacy of which is founded upon the market limits to public power. Anti-protectionism readings of Article 30, on their side, tend to promote a decentralised model for the Union and to argue that national democratic processes are still the highest source of legitimacy to which neither market integration nor the Community legislative process can be opposed except in the case of national protectionism. The centralised model can be linked to those supporting harmonisation of national legislation either through a majoritarian use of Article 30 or through

Community legislation following deregulation at national level. The erosion of national regulatory powers is seen as a functional consequence of market integration (negative integration) that requires compensation at the Union level in the form of harmonisation (positive integration).

In the following sections the construction of the different economic constitutional models as heuristic models is aimed at identifying their benefits and shortcomings, and provide normative guidance in the decisions regarding Article 30 and other economic rules. The two basic conceptions underlying the debate on Article 30, economic due process versus anti-protectionism, will be related to the competitive and decentralised models. The names given to the models highlight some of their more relevant characteristics and are not to be understood as a perfect summary of the differences between them. For example, all models can be see as centralised, once the forces operating within each may lead to a single body of rules in the internal market. What is different is the process through which single rules arise, and, once they do, the flexibility and mechanisms of changing them. In the centralised model harmonised rules would be the outcome of decision-making by supra-national institutions within the framework of the European Union political process. In the competitive model, harmonised rules would be the result of competition among different initial national sets of rules, only the "best" surviving. Lastly, the decentralised model, in submitting the regulation of free trade to state legislation (as long as that does not discriminate according to nationality) may lead producers to make their products in accordance with the strictest of all rules and in this way guarantee access to the entire market: that would also lead to a *de facto* set of harmonised rules covering the entire internal market.

THE CENTRALISED MODEL OF THE EUROPEAN ECONOMIC CONSTITUTION (HARMONISATION)

The model of a centralised Union favours a process of market regulation by the replacement of national laws with Community legislation. Enhanced and more democratic mechanisms of decision-making at the European Union level are necessary in order to safeguard the regulation of the common market. National regulation is incompatible with the aim of an integrated market and should be replaced by harmonised or uniform legislation.

The supremacy of political integration over economic integration: from negative integration to positive integration

As described in Chapter 1 above, market integration rules have spilled over to the entire range of national regulatory policies. The consequences of this process have been deregulation at national level and, generally, a reduction in the political control over the economic sphere. The centralised model of the European Union answers to these developments by reintroducing political control over the economic sphere at the European level—in other words, by arguing that negative integration (the promotion of free movement by prohibiting national rules which create obstacles to trade) should be followed by positive integration (the enactment of harmonised rules at the European level). There are two basic assumptions behind this model: first, political control over the common market is only possible at the European Union level; secondly, political control over the economic sphere is legitimate. Those arguing in favour of such a model will tend to emphasise the need to complement the economic constitution with a political constitution. They will focus on the democratic structuring of the European political process. The important point is to establish forms of participation, representation and accountability in the European political process; if these are safeguarded, then the decisions of this process over the market are legitimate and sovereign.

This model still favours market integration by overcoming the obstacles to free movement which come from the existence of different national regulations to which products have to comply. At the same time it not only allows access to national markets but also guarantees equal conditions of competition in regard to the legal regimes to which products are subjected. Moreover, it maximises resources by pooling the expertise and regulatory instruments of all the States. Fundamentally, it requires the setting up of institutions responsible for harmonising legislation at the Community level. This is intended to guarantee co-ordination of Member States policies and public control over the market. [11]

Although all States may agree on the advantages of a common market and on the reciprocal opening-up of their markets, there are problems in achieving the collective action necessary for this purpose, due to the strong incentives for individual States to defect.[12] States often try to benefit from free trade while still protecting their own markets, the end result being that all States maintain measures protecting their markets and liberalisation of trade is not achieved.[13] To avoid falling into this trap, States have to establish co-operative agreements. Transaction costs and problems over information and enforcement make co-operation difficult, especially where there are no

[11] According to Ehlermann: "In the case of harmonisation for the purposes of establishing the internal market, four reasons may be identified . . .: (1) the removal of obstacles to basic freedoms; (2) the protection of essential interests that are threatened by the removal of obstacles; (3) the removal of distortions of competition which, although not obstacles in the above-mentioned sense, result in serious cost differences; (4) making it easier for individual firms or groups of firms to operate within the common market": C.D. Ehlermann, "Harmonization versus Competition Between Rules", (1995) 3 *European Review*, 333, at 334.

[12] See, for example, G. Garrett, "International cooperation and institutional choice: the European Community's internal market" (1992) 46 International Organization, 533, at 534.

[13] For an explanation of the "trade dilemma", ibid, at 537–8.

long-term relations.[14] The creation of institutions is fundamental in solving these problems because they diminish transaction costs;[15] collect and distribute information; increase transparency through monitoring; and can be given the power to enforce the co-operative agreements. The institutional structure and rules of the European Union reflect these concerns. Free movement rules and the jurisdictional structure of the Community were intended to reduce the risk of "free riders" and "trade dilemmas" and provide dispute settlement and enforcement mechanisms. However, the application of those rules has led to an erosion of national regulatory policies and generated a discussion on the policy framework to which the common market is to be submitted. Those promoting a centralised model (in the form of enhanced and more democratic decision-making at EU level) challenge the view that the common market should also favour a general deregulatory policy towards the market and defend, instead, the creation of new means of regulating the market at the European Union level. Political integration and, with it, increased positive integration is a form of regaining control over the economic order. The European Union is considered the new forum in which the traditional relation between the political and economic constitutions is to be reinstated.[16] The advantages of a centralised system are clear: it preserves the ability to regulate while, at the same time, allowing free movement. Community legislation allows for a higher degree of policy definition and choice at Community level than does either a model based on State legislation or market choice. Under State legislation (decentralised model) market integration may be blocked by the individual policies of Member States. Under a system of mutual recognition of national rules promoting competition among rules (competitive model), choices among competing rules are not a policy decision but, on the contrary, a market choice among different and competing policies.[17]

In a centralised model of the European Union, the institution entrusted with the role of regulating the market would be the Union political process. This would produce uniform legislation valid in all the Member States. However, the protection of free movement through uniform legislation is neither straightforward nor a perfect alternative. The European Union political and legislative process does not seem able to produce all the necessary legislation for the harmonisation of national laws. States may not be prepared to give up so much of their legislative powers (a fear which increases with the reduction of State control over the Community legislative process).[18] Moreover, it is not

[14] According to North, "free riders" and "prisoners dilemma" tend to occur in "one-shot" situations: D.C. North, *Institutions, Institutional Change and Economic Performance* (Cambridge, Cambridge University Press, 1990), at 12.

[15] Institutions provide stability in the "game", distribute information among the players, and provide a setting in which all players can meet and participate.

[16] On the relation between the political and economic constitutions in the EU see W. Sauter, *Competition Law and Industrial Policy* (forthcoming, Oxford, Clarendon Press, 1998).

[17] See below the analyses of these models.

[18] It may be that the increased supra-nationalisation of the decision-making process of the European Union will lead to a reduction of its supra-national normativism in a reverse process

necessarily good to have uniform legislation, since different national cultural and regulatory traditions may require different regulations, and innovation may be curtailed.

It may also happen that the choice for uniformity in the European Union political process may be to the benefit of some groups or States to the detriment of others. In this way, increased forms of traditional democracy at the European level may raise new democratic problems.

Problems with a centralised model of the European Economic Constitution

The regulation of the market through uniform legislation raises and intensifies at a micro-level the macro-problems of European integration: the relationship between the European Union legal order and national legal orders, with the corresponding conflicts over legitimacy, and the European integration versus national disintegration dilemma.[19] For the present purposes of analysis one can detect four problems in a centralised model of co-operation such as the one embodied in a full application of a centralised model of the Union. First, it does not leave room for national diversity. Secondly, it may lead to "market-freezing" and reduces legislative innovation and experimentation. Thirdly, it either assumes a developed sense of community or a developed system of enforcement capable of preventing more complex forms of evasion. Lastly, and mainly, it assumes that the Union political process is efficient or more democratic than the alternative institutions in regulating the common market. This is not so, due to several potential malfunctions in the European Union political process, much more complex than the issues normally addressed in the traditional "democratic deficit" literature and which result from the approach of the European Court of Justice in reviewing Community legislation. The following pages will try to reformulate old and new concerns with Community legislation into different types of democratic problems going beyond traditional democratic deficit questions and advocating a broader and more sophisticated approach of the European Court in the review of Community legislation.

The "European Union political process" here mainly refers to the European Community legislative process as defined in the Maastricht Treaty, in which the Council, the Commission and the Parliament participate. Although the European Union political process is different from, and broader than, the Community legislative process, the expressions are treated below as synonymous. This is because, for the purposes of analysing institutional

to that described by Weiler. See: "The Community System: the Dual Character of Supranationalism", (1981) 1 *Yearbook of European Law*, 267 and "The Transformation of Europe", (1990–91) 100 *The Yale Law Journal*, 2403.

[19] See C. Joerges, "European Economic Law, the Nation State and the Maastricht Treaty", in Renaud Dehousse (ed.), *The European Union Treaty* (München, C.H. Beck, 1993), 29, at 34.

malfunctions, the Community legislative process is not insulated: rather, legislative outcomes are a consequence of the operation of the global European Union political process.

Measuring European democracy

One main malfunction normally attributed to the European Union political process has been referred to as "legislative blockades" and, in a more sophisticated analysis, as the "joint decision trap".[20] This is normally related, in the democratic deficit literature, to the unanimity requirements (granting to a single State the possibility to block decisions) and the inter-governmental nature of the European Union political process. Coupled with these concerns is the low level of parliamentary control over the political and legislative processes in the European Union. This analysis is followed by arguments in favour of traditional majoritarian democracy at the European Union level, in the form of increased majoritarian decision-making and European Parliament powers. However both of these solutions are bound to raise other democratic problems.

Steps have been taken to facilitate the decision-making process and increase parliamentary control over the political and legislative processes. The Single European Act brought majority decision back to the core of decision-making in the Community legislative process,[21] reintroducing it in areas which affect the internal market. However, this has not led to truly democratic developments and has not sufficiently eased the Community legislative process. This was so for several reasons. First, the Commission has not enough resources to take on the degree of legislative initiative required by market integration (this was one of the reasons for the policies of mutual recognition, minimum harmonisation, and reference to standards). Secondly, States prefer to continue to decide through unanimity[22] (as they fear being in a minoritarian position themselves).[23] Thirdly, the Luxembourg agreements are still a "sword of Damocles" hanging over the European Union political process.

Following the Single European Act and the Maastricht Treaty, the European Parliament has been granted new powers (again reinforced in the new Amsterdam Treaty). In particular, under Article 189b Parliament and the Council must now agree for a decision to be adopted and Parliament, Council

[20] F.W. Scharpf, "The Joint-Decision Trap: Lessons from German Federalism and European Integration", (1988) 66 *Public Administration*, 239.

[21] This was done to overcome the Luxembourg agreements introduction of veto rights in the Community decision-making process.

[22] Scharpf cites Everling in saying that "in multilateral negotiations among a small group of governments over uniform regulations which will apply to all of them, unanimity seems a rational rule to follow for risk-averse participants even if they might benefit from majority decisions in the individual case": U. Everling, "Possibilities and limits of European integration", JCMS 1980, 217, at 221, cited in Scharpf, "The Joint-Decision Trap" (n.20 above), at 254.

[23] The possibility of a majority decision, however, can encourage opposing States to compromise. At the same time, the underlying fear of a return to the Luxembourg Accord rules or to be one day in a minoritarian position also drives the majority side to accept compromise. Furthermore, unanimous decisions may secure higher social compliance.

and Commission must all be in agreement for a decision to be adopted by majority voting. Though reinforcing the powers of the Parliament and introducing conciliation procedures this co-decision procedure has, in turn, also increased the complexity of the legislative process and likelihood of deadlocks.[24] In face of these small steps, majority decision-making and parliamentary control will continue to be dominant issues in the debates on European democracy and the reform of its political and legislative processes. Both concern democratic questions of over-representation of some nationals at the expense of other nationals.

The most sophisticated version of the problems of unanimity is that related to the analysis of the "joint decision trap" in the Community system which has been imported from the German federal system by Scharpf. Briefly, the "joint decision trap" occurs when the agreement of all levels of government (or all national governments) is required: since all national interests are satisfied and costs are shared (or transferred to EU level), "joint decisions have politically more attractive cost-benefit ratios".[25] However, this leads to an increase in expenditure on these programmes at the expense of potentially more efficient programmes.[26] States compete for funds independently of real needs, and their different positions are not taken into account. Furthermore, changes to the *status quo* are strongly limited by the requirement of unanimity, with negative consequences for the efficiency of public policies: "when circumstances change, existing policies are likely to become sub-optimal even by their own original criteria. Under the unanimity rule however, they cannot be abolished or changed as long as they are still preferred by even a single member".[27] This can also be presented, as Weiler demonstrates, as another aspect of the democratic deficit: "the ability of a small number of Community citizens represented by their Minister in the Council to block the collective wishes of the rest of the Community".[28]

In my view, effective majority voting is not however the necessary remedy for Europe's democratic problems and inefficient decisions. In effect, Scharpf mentions two conditions that set up the "joint decision trap" in the European institutional structure: "first, the fact that national governments are making European decisions and, second, the fact that these decisions have to be unanimous".[29] However, there is nothing to suggest that decisions taken by majority voting will prevent the inefficiencies of the "joint decision trap". Decisions taken by a majority of States will not take in consideration the distribution of costs and benefits in all States, but only in the States that compose that majority. Moreover, though Scharpf is right in pointing out that unanimity may

[24] Even taking into account the simplification of the co-decision procedure established in the Amsterdam Treaty not yet in force.

[25] Scharpf "The Joint-Decision Trap" (n.20 above), at 255.

[26] Ibid, mainly at 247–9 and 255–6.

[27] Ibid, at 257.

[28] J. Weiler, "The Transformation of Europe" (n.18 above), at 2467.

[29] Scharpf, "The Joint-Decision Trap" (n.20 above), at 267. See also at 254.

maintain a non-efficient *status quo*, majority voting may introduce the reverse problem: that is, once a majority is reached, a policy may be introduced that, though more efficient for the States which make up that majority, is less efficient in overall terms *vis-à-vis* the previous *status quo*, since the costs of the new policy for the States not making up the majority have not been taken into account. What changes under unanimity or majority rules is only the distribution of the costs and benefits of the potential inefficiencies in the decisions. Under unanimous voting the risk is that a decision will be taken only if it favours all States independently of the intensity of their needs, and that it will be maintained even though it favours only one State at the cost of the others. Under majority voting the risk is that a decision is taken or maintained even though the cumulative benefits it gives to the majority of States are less that the cumulative costs burdening the minority of States.

There is no single solution and what is required, at this stage, is a more comprehensive analysis of the different democratic inefficiencies in the European Union political process and the circumstances in which they are more likely to occur. The same analysis can be made of proposals for greater powers to be granted to the European Parliament. What from an European perspective can be seen as an increase in democracy, from a national perspective may well constitute a decrease in democracy (once nationals that previously controlled their national policies are now subject to the European majority).[30] It all depends on the political community taken into consideration for the application of the majority principle.[31]

The rules of the Treaty in its original drafting and subsequent revisions reflect these different concerns. The fear of majoritarian dominance is seen in several places, such as the requirement of unanimity in certain areas and for the alteration of Commission proposals (seen as independent) or in the complex system of qualified majority.[32] At the same time, majority rules also reflect the opposite concerns over minoritarian blocking or excessive representation.[33] These voting procedures are the constitutional expression of the fears of majoritarian and minoritarian biases, two types of institutional malfunction that may affect the European Union political process.

Majoritarian and minoritarian biases in the European Union political process

Taking on these majoritarian and minoritarian fears and on a broader analysis of the European Union political process, it is possible to highlight differ-

[30] See Weiler, "The Transformation of Europe" (n.18 above), at 2470.

[31] Ibid, at 2471.

[32] Which guarantees not just a simple majority of States but rules that the vote of the largest States is not sufficient to take a decision, and that the support of at least some smaller States is required. Other combinations, such as regional blocks, exist: neither the Southern nor Northern block is able to impose a decision on the other.

[33] In qualified majority rule, larger States have more votes through a "proportional" system involving a balance between population and economic power. Moreover, under qualified majority voting, the larger States in conjunction can never be outvoted.

ent institutional malfunctions in this process. These institutional malfunctions will give a broader picture of the different fears that dominate the debates on the European political process and its democratisation. Focus should be on the various problems of representation of interests in the European Union political process, calling the attention of the European Court of Justice to the legislative biases that may arise if the legislative process is dominated by certain interests. This would have consequences on the regulatory choices taken and on the distribution of their costs and benefits. Inspiration is draw from Komesar's definitions of majoritarian and minoritarian bias, in what can be considered as a development from two types of economic and legal theories of politics[34]—theories that emphasise the risk of the capture of the political process by small and organised groups (such as, "public choice" and interest group theories), and theories concentrating on the protection of minorities from the power of majorities either in a procedural or substantive manner (authors such as Ely and Dworkin).

The comparative institutional analysis developed by Komesar gives a more comprehensive understanding of the political process and of the operation of interests therein. He emphasises two types of fears: the power of the few over the many and the power of the many over the few.[35] The first carries the risk of a minoritarian bias, that is "an inordinate power of the few at the expense of the many";[36] the second a risk of majoritarian bias, that is: "an opposite response to the same skewed distribution of impacts which characterized minoritarian bias",[37] or, in other words, an inordinate power of the many at the expense of the few.

This picture becomes more complex in the European Union context in which two types of majoritarian and minoritarian biases are possible due to the different levels of decision-making and their inter-governmental or supra-national character: one constructed in terms of the balance of powers among States; and the other without taking into account States. In the first type, majoritarian bias consists of an inordinate power held by larger States at the expense of smaller States, and minoritarian bias consists of an inordinate power held by smaller States at the expense of larger States. In the second type, which is normally underestimated in the Community context, majoritarian bias consists of an inordinate power of the majority, evenly spread throughout all States large and small, at the expense of the few; and minoritarian bias consists of the fear of the European Union political process being captured by supra-national interest groups. We could call the first type vertical minoritarian and majoritarian biases, as they concern the relation between

[34] See N. Komesar, *Imperfect Alternatives—Choosing Institutions in Law Economics and Public Policy* (Chicago, The University of Chicago Press, 1994), in particular Chapters 3 and 7. See, also, from the same author, "A Job for the Judges: The Judiciary and the Constitution in a Massive and Complex Society", (1988) 86 *Michigan Law Review*, 657.

[35] Komesar, *Imperfect Alternatives*, (n.34 above), at 53.

[36] Komesar, "A Job for the Judges", (n.34 above), 671.

[37] Ibid, at 672.

States and the European Union political process; and, the second type could be called horizontal majoritarian and minoritarian biases as they derive from pressures which are spread throughout the Member States. Naturally this distinction is purely methodological, as in the Community legislative and political processes national and supra-national values and interests are frequently at play over the same issue. It is difficult to say if a specific outcome is the fruit of conflicting national interests, or the action of particularly strong and well organised interests groups.[38] Similarly, the interests of many States (possibly resulting in a majoritarian bias from a national interests' perspective) may correspond to the interests of some powerful supra-national interests groups (possibly resulting in a minoritarian bias from a cross-national interests' perspective).

Horizontal minoritarian bias: the over-representation of supra-national interest groups Legal studies on the Community legislative process have concentrated their analysis on the balance of powers among States portrayed in the voting mechanisms established by the Treaties and on the associated problems of efficiency and legitimacy. In contrast, little attention has been paid to the role of organised or specific interests in the Community political and legislative processes.[39] The fear that interest groups might capture the political process does not appear to have concerned those who framed the Treaties. According to Streeck and Schmitter: "especially in the 'neofunctionalist' image of 'Europe's would-be polity' and of the path to that polity, supra-national interest-group formation was expected to serve, in an important and indispensable sense, as a substitute for popular identification with the emerging new political community above and beyond the nation State".[40] A close collaboration between interest groups and European bureaucrats was envisaged.[41] "Interests were bound to be the Community's main constituency, and would provide the institutions with the 'elite systemic support' which is

[38] An example of this is the framing of the Single European Act. For a discussion giving a predominance to States' interests, see: A. Moravcsik, "Negotiating the Single European Act: National Interests and Conventional Statecraft in the European Community", (1991) 45 *International Organization*, 19. For an opposing view (based on neo-functionalism), see, D.R. Cameron,"The 1992 Initiative: Causes and Consequences", in A.M. Sbragia (ed.), *Euro-Politics—Institutions and Policymaking in the "New" European Community* (Washington, The Brokings Institution, 1992), 23. For a different example and more general conclusions on the mix of interests interplaying in the European Community legislative process see F. Snyder, "New Directions in European Community Law", (1987) 14 *Journal of Law and Society*, 167, at 172 and *New Directions in Community Law* (London, Weidenfeld and Nicolson, 1990), mainly at *56 et seq*.

[39] See D. Mitchell, "Interests groups and the 'democratic deficit' ", (1993) *European Access*, 14. For an exception in the legal field see, C. Harlow, "A Community of Interests? Making the Most of European Law", (1992) *55 MLR*, 331.

[40] W. Streeck, and P.C. Schmitter, "From National Corporatism to Transnational Pluralism: Organized Interests in the Single European Market", (1991) 19 *Politics & Society*, 133. Citation included is from Leon N. Lindberg and Stuart A. Scheingold, *Europe's Would-Be Polity: Patterns of Change in the European Community* (Eaglewood Cliffs, NJ, Prentice Hall, 1970).

[41] "From National Corporatism", (n.40 above), at 134.

required in the absence of public awareness or loyalties".[42] Interest groups were seen as essential in the functional process leading from economic integration to political integration.[43] Theories of integration have stressed their key role in the process of European integration[44] but this is not reflected in the legal studies of the political and legislative processes. Yet the role of interest groups coupled with other elements which are either general or specific to the European Union political process raise fears that, in some circumstances, Community legislation may be dominated by specific interests, and thus subject to a form of minoritarian bias.[45]

Risks of minoritarian bias are particularly strong when either the benefits or costs of a particular regulation are concentrated upon one group and its reverse costs or benefits upon a large majority. The skewed distribution of stakes will normally correspond to better organisation and information on the part of the group with higher stakes (where costs or benefits are concentrated).[46] Dispersed interests may be too difficult to organise; or not aware of their interests in the regulation; or not consider the cost or benefit sufficient to get them to act alone; or they may simply expect someone else to act. In contrast, the discrete character of a minority helps it to organise, the relatively high costs or benefits also spurring them into action. Because of the size of the group, information is available (comes from the proximity of those interests with the regulation) and is easily distributed among them.[47]

The technical nature of much Community legislation and the complexity of the decision-making process provides more opportunities for intervention by organised interests.[48] This is particularly so with economic regulatory law which is: "often viewed as concerning inherently technical matters and therefore deemed to require the co-operation, if not the consent, of the regulated

[42] D. Mitchell, "Interest Groups" (n.39 above), at 14, citing Lindberg and Scheingold, *Europe's Would-be Polity* (n.40 above), at 79.

[43] The role of interest groups in the integration process foreseen by functionalism theories is notably present in the book of Haas, *The Uniting of Europe* (Stanford, Stanford University Press, 1968 (first published 1958)); see, chiefly, at 9–10, 15 *et seq*. See also, L.N. Lindberg, *The Political Dynamics of European Economic Integration* (Stanford and Oxford, Stanford University Press and Oxford University Press, 1963), at 94.

[44] See Chapter 1 above.

[45] The control of decision-making by elites (including lobbyists) is presented as a fact by Haas: "The emphasis on elites in the study of integration derives its justification from the bureaucratised nature of European organisations of long standing, in which basic decisions are made by the leadership, sometimes over the opposition and usually over the indifference of the general membership. This gives the relevant elites a manipulative role which is of course used to place the organisation in question on record for or against a proposed measure of integration": *The Uniting of Europe* (n.43 above), at 17.

[46] See A.S. McFarland, "Interests Groups and the Policy-making Process: Sources of Countervailing Power in America", in M.P. Petracca (ed.), *The Politics of Interests: Interests Groups Transformed* (San Francisco, Oxford, Westview Press, Boulder, 1992), at 59, who refers to Olson as the major contributor to these studies,

[47] This picture of events may change if the majority is aware of their interests because of other factors such as catalic elements, political actors motivations or a generally high public awareness of the subject matter.

[48] See D. Mitchell, "Interest Groups" (n.39 above), at 15.

groups and other political clients".[49] Moreover, since specific interests affected by a particular regulation will tend to be in closer contact with those who regulate, their direct connection may create an interdependence between regulators and the regulated (capture risks).

This phenomenon is accentuated by the leading role played by the Commission in the legislative process. The Commission lacks a complete bureaucratic and technical machinery and has to depend heavily on the technical expertise of representatives of interest groups.[50] Furthermore, to enhance its powers as a European government the Commission must find support beyond the Member States. Thus it makes alliances with other forces: either Community institutions such as the Parliament and the European Court or supra-national groups and elite technocrats who support its policies[51] and its image of independence from national interests. If one adds to this the low political accountability of Commission members, and the Commission's strong bureaucratic characteristics, it may be feared that the Commission will be "captured" by interest groups[52] and that, consequently, its legislative proposals may suffer from some kind of minoritarian bias.[53]

The two institutions which traditionally represent majority interests also present problems in this respect. Both the Parliament and the Council have low political accountability. Dispersed majorities may not realise that their interests are adversely affected. Nor is public opinion aware of the powers of the European Parliament. As for organised interests, they are more aware of the powers Community institutions have over them, and may concentrate their efforts thereon in order to defend their interests and control information.

Finally, the influence of organised interests[54] is greater as decision-making moves from high level politics to low level politics.[55] Thus, the risk of minoritarian bias is greater with the delegation of legislative and executive powers

[49] F. Snyder, *New Directions in European Community Law* (London, Weindenfeld and Nicolson, 1990), at 35.

[50] Ibid, at 137. See also E. Kirchner, and K. Schwaiger, *The Role of Interest Groups in the European Community* (Gower, Aldershot, 1981), at 38.

[51] See K. Neunreither, "Transformation of a Political Role: Reconsidering the Case of the Commission of the European Communities" (1972) 10 *JCMS*, 233, at 236. See also Lindberg, *The Political Dynamics* (n.43 above), mainly at 98, where he says that the Commission has "encouraged the development of these groups".

[52] For a summary of Commission relations with interest groups and the reasons for that see Kirchner and Schwaiger, *The Role of Interest Groups* (n.50 above), at 9–10 and 43–7.

[53] However, according to Harlow, the Commission, itself, has also: "shown awareness of the need to counterweight to powerful corporate lobbies": C. Harlow, "A Community of Interests? Making the Most of European Law" (1992) 55 *MLR*, 331, at 339.

[54] See P.E. Peterson, "The Rise and Fall of Special Interests Politics", in *The Politics of Interests* (n.46 above), at 328.

[55] "High level politics" here means the direct participation of politicians committed to substantive policies and politically responsible *vis-à-vis* their constituency. "Low level politics" refers to all the different bureaucratic and technical actors either independent, autonomous, or related to political actors.

to the COREPER and the Commission, the creation of European agencies,[56] and the increased role of expert advisory and study groups. By contrast, the risk of dominance of the political process by supra-national interest groups is weaker in areas of conflicting national policies. As stated by Kirchner and Schwaiger: "if national policies become more divergent, greater difficulties occur for affiliates of European interest groups to agree to common policies".[57] In these cases, the input of national governments will also tend to increase and decision-making to move from low level politics to high level politics.

Horizontal majoritarian bias: the fear of majorities in a European polity In cases of majoritarian bias the risk is that the interests of the many, evenly spread throughout the Community, will be satisfied at an unproportional cost to the interests of the few. Such fears of horizontal majoritarian bias will tend to increase with the progressive replacement of national political communities by the European political community. The risk of such majoritarian bias comes from the nature of the democratic process where the "majority wins", independently of any cost/benefit analysis including both the minority and the majority. In the words of Komesar: "If we suppose that everyone understands and votes their interests then, in a political process which counts votes for or against but which does not consider the severity of impact or the intensity of feeling about the issue, a low-impact majority can prevail over a high-impact minority even though the majority will gain little and the minority is harmed greatly."

The conditions which give rise to such risks of majoritarian bias are not particular to the European Union political process and can briefly be described as the following:[58]

(1) The more public and understandable the subject matter, the more dispersed interests will be aware of their interests and ready to influence the political process.
(2) As it moves from low level politics to high level politics, the decision-making process is more accessible to majority influence.
(3) "The more discrete, insular, and immutable the minority, the more likely the existence of a stable majority willing to supress the minority".[59] This

[56] See G. Majone, *Independence vs. Accountability? Non-Majoritarian Institutions and the Democratic Government of Europe*, EUI Working Paper SPS No. 94/3 (European University Institute, Florence, 1994), at 11.

[57] Kirchner and Schwaiger, *The Role of Interest Groups* (n.50 above), at 5.

[58] This follows quite closely Komesar, "A Job for the Judges" (n.34 above), at 673.

[59] Ibid, at 675. He also says that: "because majoritarian bias supposes large per capita costs for the minority with much lower per capita benefits for the majority, slipping into the minority status carries dire results. In such a situation, members of the majority would want to feel secure that the significant negative impacts of this . . . action did not apply to them. To reassure members of the majority, the disadvantaged minority would have to be clearly defined. In other words, these minorities would have to be safe targets".

is because these characteristics of the minority reassure the members of the majority that they will not become a part of the majority themselves.

(4) These same characteristics of a minority make activation of the majority easier. "The more familiar a classification or source of difference the easier it is to draw the dormant majority's attention and move it to act . . . Simple symbols decrease the costs of communication, information, and organization, thereby making it more likely that the majority will be active rather than dormant".[60]

The more developed the European political process becomes and the larger its competencies, the higher will be the risk of such majoritarian bias and the attention that it should deserve in the review of Community legislation. The development of a European polity and growth of European policies will raise common interests and supra-national majorities as well as awareness of the relevance of the European political process in the defence of such interests. A good example of a policy easily subject to majoritarian bias is emigration policy, since it is a topic which is of public awareness and of interest to the majority and since the minority is strongly discrete, insular and immutable. Other cases will tend to occur in the European Union political process with regard to well-defined topics which affect a minority group or/and a single Member State, a possible example being the "Mad Cow Disease" issue.[61]

Vertical minoritarian and najoritarian biases The way in which the Community legislative process was conceived in the Treaties stressed the concerns about the vertical type of minoritarian and majoritarian bias, ie the fear that the Community political process could either be blocked by the smaller States or a single State, or be controlled by the more important States or a coalition of States. The blocking of decision-making by a minority of States (or a single State) or its control by the more powerful States, results in biased decisions being made in the European political process. The complexity of the European Union decision-making rules is intended to avoid the risks of vertical minoritarian and majoritarian biases. Outcomes are normally presented as representing a complex but balanced representation of all national interests. It has been said that the *ad hoc* nature of the Community decision-making process raises legitimacy problems from a traditional democratic standpoint but that legitimacy is then assured by the quality of the outcomes. Analysis of Community decision-making usually emphasises the problems of either deadlock or democratic deficit (minoritarian bias). Recent developments, however, suggest a more sophisticated analysis is required and that attention should also be given to risks of majoritarian bias.

[60] Ibid at 676.

[61] Either subject to majoritarian bias of the horizontal type described or of the vertical type to be discussed below.

Vertical minoritarian bias: the over-representation of a minority of States or smaller States The traditional problems of decision-making deadlock and the democratic deficit give rise to situations of minoritarian bias. The control of the legislative process by an institution in which some States can block the will of the majority or—by threatening to block, can get extra benefits for themselves from the majority—leads to minoritarian bias. Risks of minoritarian bias are particularly evident in areas where decision-making is submitted to unanimity and some States have clear national interests benefited by the *status quo*. Such minoritarian bias may be present either in an over-representation of the minority in the decision, or in the blocking of that decision (thus maintaining the *status quo* which favours the minority). This does not mean that the decision is necessarily inefficient, or that it should be struck down when and if the Court is called to review it. Decisions subject to an over-representation of minoritarian interests may nevertheless meet the criteria of efficiency or redistributive justice which they are legally required to meet. This may be quite frequent when such efficiency criterion is a Pareto optimal.[62]

Vertical majoritarian bias: the over-representation of the majority of States or most powerful States Although the problems of the democratic deficit and deadlock in the decision-making process have received much attention from academic commentators (albeit that they are not seen it terms of minoritarian bias) the risks of majoritarian bias[63] have often been ignored. This can no longer be the case, in view of the present and future developments in the European Union legislative process. The use of majority voting has been increasing, mainly in technical issues.[64] Even when consensus is reached, the process of reaching it under the shadow of veto is very different from the process of doing so under the shadow of vote (as is now the rule).[65] Furthermore, a majoritarian institution, the European Parliament, has an ever-growing input into the decision-making process. All this means we can expect a shift in attention from the problems of minoritarian bias to the problems of majoritarian bias. This will be further promoted by the institutional changes prompted by the accession of new Member States. For the Union, broadening may well mean deepening, as an increased membership will require enhanced decision-making mechanisms with increasing resort being

62 See Chapter 5 below.

63 As mentioned before, the feared outcome is that a majority will decide for its own benefit even if the costs imposed on the minority will be higher than the benefits which the decision will bring to the majority. In the words of Susan Rose-Ackerman: "a majority only tries to increase the net benefit of their members even at a cost of a greater harm for the minority". Thus, these decisions do not necessarily withstand cost/benefit analysis: *Rethinking the Progressive Agenda—The Reform of the American Regulatory State* (New York, The Free Press, 1992), at 50.

64 N. Nugent, *The Government and Politics of the European Community* (London, Macmillan, 1989), at 105.

65 J. Weiler, "The Transformation of Europe" (n.18 above), at 2461.

made to qualified majority voting; a reduced technical input for each individual State (with only the stronger national administrations being able to impose their voice in the legislative preparatory work); and enhanced majoritarian democracy mechanisms in the form of the increased participation of the European Parliament.

If the majority and the minority on a given issue are clearly defined, with no risks to the Member States of the majority of becoming part of the minority themselves, then the risk of majoritarian bias is much higher.[66] In the context of the European Union system this reasoning has to be enlarged to cover the choices of voting mechanism. If some of the states in a majoritarian position on one issue have minoritarian interests in the same policy area, they have an interest in safeguarding consensual decision-making in that area: so, even if there is a clearly defined majority on the individual issue, there may at the same time be another majority in favour of unanimous decision-making in the larger policy area which covers that issue. Of course, that will not be the case if that area has already been excluded from unanimous decision-making, since majoritarian states would then have nothing to loose. The majoritarian risk is also higher where the majoritarian position extends from the specific issue to the entire policy area under which the issue is discussed, since the risks of being in a minoritarian position in that policy area are minimal. The formation of these discrete and clear majorities is parallel to what Pescatore has defined as the creation of "*directoires*": "in the Community, the hegemonic intents, that we attempted to get rid of by creating a balanced institutional structure, have returned sporadically as attempts to form, according to variable constellations, what we call "*directoires*". Through these coalitions, the most powerful States have tried to shift the decision-making process towards their own interests. They are able in this way to decide issues as part of a small oligopolistic political constellation, inside of which they are more able to exercise a dominant influence than they could within an organised institutional system, subject to well defined, permanent and enforced rules".[67]

Regulatory areas are particularly susceptible to majoritarian bias, not only because more use of qualified majority voting is made there but also because such areas are progressively excluded from appeals over "national vital inter-

[66] See the discussion above on horizontal majoritarian bias.

[67] P. Pescatore, "L'Executif Communautaire: Justification du Quadripartisme Institue par les Traités de Paris et de Rome", (1978) CDE, 387, at 397, translation by the author. In the original: "*dans la Communauté, les tendances hégémoniques que l'on croyait avoir définitivement bannies, précisément par la création d'une structure institutionnelle équilibrée, ont resurgi sporadiquement sous la forme des tentatives visant à former selon des constellations variables, ce qu'on appelle des* 'directoires'. *Au moyen de telles coalitions, des Etats plus puissants essaient de polariser à leur profit le processus décisionelle. Ils réussissent ainsi à préjuger les problémes à l'intérieur de une constellation politique limitée, en quelque sorte 'oligopolistique', au sein de laquelle ils sont mieux à même de faire valoir leur prédominance que dans le cadre d'un système institutionnel organisé, soumis à des règles précises, permanents et contrôlables*".

est" policies and a majority may already be quite well-defined, independent of the particular interests of some States.[68]

Summary To sum up the risks of *horizontal* minoritarian and majoritarian biases in the European Union political process, one can first identify high risks of *horizontal* minoritarian bias in decisions that do not deal with conflicting national interests and which tend to move from high politics to low politics (thus being left to less accountable and more resource/information dependent institutions). Where this corresponds to a skewed distribution of stakes, with low stakes for a majority and high stakes for a minority, the minoritarian interests will probably be better organised and not confronted with the interests of the dispersed majority. On the other hand, the risk of *horizontal* majoritarian bias is higher where decisions (not dealing with conflicting national interests) either present the opposite distribution of stakes (high stakes for the majority; low stakes for the minority) or a discrete, insular and immutable minority and an active majority mobilised by some catalytic groups[69] or by the notoriety and accessibility of the topic.

Similarly, one can identify the circumstances in which vertical majoritarian bias is most likely to occur: where qualified majority voting is possible; where the majority is well defined *vis-à-vis* the minority because, for example, the issue at stake is the specific cultural or regulatory tradition of a single (or a few) Member State(s); where the separation between majority and minority holds for the entire policy area upon which voting is taking place; and where the majority has no interest in agreeing on that area as one protected by the "national vital interest" clause, or alternatively, where that area has been already excluded.

The analysis of the centralised model and the risks of institutional malfunction in the European Union political process has highlighted new possible areas and forms of increased activism for the Court of Justice. In the area of market regulation (with a focus on the free movement of goods), the characteristics of the area (such as the technical discourse and the low level politics), coupled with the changes taking place in the Union decision-making mechanisms themselves, underline the risks of horizontal minoritarian bias and vertical majoritarian bias in Community legislation. This requires a new type of judicial approach to market regulation and the free movement of goods, no longer dominated by a majoritarian outlook. The shift, in the ECJ case law on market integration, from a focus on the review of national regulation restricting free movement of goods to a focus on the review of national regulation restricting the free movement of persons may correspond to an

[68] Garret has argued the existence of such a majority comprising the interests and actions of France, Germany and the Benelux countries. We cannot assess here the correctness of this assertion, the important thing being to point out the situations where risk of majoritarian bias is more likely to occur. See G. Garret, "International Cooperation" (n.12 above); see at 552 and, generally, 546 *et seq*.

[69] On this, see Komesar, "A Job for the Judges" (n.34 above), at 674–5.

understanding that the risks of minoritarian bias (a State's control of the legislative process protecting a "selfish" interest) is higher in the area of free movement of persons (subject to unanimous decision-making) than in the area of free movement of goods (subject to majoritarian decision-making). However, the potential institutional malfunctions highlighted in the centralised model must be confronted with those present in the other models and in the judicial process.

THE COMPETITIVE MODEL OF THE EUROPEAN ECONOMIC CONSTITUTION (COMPETITION AMONG RULES)

The competitive model of the European Economic Constitution has its basis on a fully-fledged application of free movement and competition rules. These are intended to safeguard the market from public intervention and to promote competition among rules through the mutual recognition of national rules.

The supremacy of economic integration over political integration: the neo-liberal constitution

Ordo-liberalism and European integration

Neo-liberal or "laissez faire" interpretations of the free movement rules and of the European Economic Constitution owe much to traditional ordo-liberal theories and their contribution to both the initial debate on European integration and in the provision of a coherent theoretical framework for an understanding of integration.[70] The ordo-liberal aim is the creation of a free market, liberal economy, protected through constitutional principles. Ordo-liberals believe in a true market economy, from which power is excluded and in which outcomes are the result of voluntary market transactions. Constitutional protection is considered necessary to prevent public intervention (viewed in many respects as a means of exercising private power) and to protect undistorted competition.[71] The Economic Constitution serves to provide the framework and the programme through which the economic system develops. According to Gerber,[72] for Ordo-liberalism, "the economic constitution is to set out a framework of principles and ideals, and government policy is to implement

[70] See, C. Joerges, *The Market Without the State?—States Without a Market?: Two Essays on the Law of the European Economy*, EUI Working Paper LAW No. 96/2 (EUI, Florence, 1996), at 6.

[71] See, W. Röpke, *International Order and Economic Integration* (Dordrecht-Holland, D. Reidel Publishing Company, 1959), eg at 24. See also Hayek, *The Road to Serfdom* (first published 1944, London, ARK, 1986), at 172 or *Law, Legislation and Liberty*, vol. 1 (London, Routledge and Keagan Paul, 1973), at 2–3.

[72] See D.J. Gerber, "Constitutionalizing the Economy: German Neo-liberalism, Competition Law and the 'New' Europe" (1988) 42 American Journal of Comparative Law, 25, at 44–5.

these principles and seek to attain these ideals".[73] The main concern is a political one: the protection of a free and equal society. "Within society itself no power groups should be formed which would make it possible for others, individually or as groups, to be subjugated and exploited".[74]

Ordo-liberals and other neo-liberals have been active participants in the project of European integration; they trusted to Community law the process of constitutionalising a free market economy with undistorted competition. It should be recalled that these neo-liberal ideas developed as a reaction to recent German and European history. For Röpke, there was an inevitable connection between the aims of individual freedom and the avoidance of nationalism, on the one hand, and free trade and the prevention of State control of the economy, on the other. According to ordo-liberals and other neo-liberals, the failure of the initial device of separation of powers to achieve its aim of controlling power and government meant that a new device had to be created. That device was a federation of States with an international authority to limit governments' economic powers and assure international order without taking over the power of the States. The division of powers inherent in this form of federalism, "would inevitably act at the same time also as a limitation of the power of the whole as well as of the individual state".[75] Hence, a federation is seen more as a source of individual rights than as a source of common policies.

For ordo-liberalism, just as the political constitution constrains political decisions so should the economic constitution constrain economic decisions.[76] The application of this concept to the European Union implies as a first assumption the existence of an economic constitution dependent, according to ordo-liberals themselves, on a political decision.[77] At least for some, such a political decision can be seen in the EC Treaty: its free movement and competition rules are to be read as limiting public power and safeguarding

[73] These ideas coincide in some or many respects with other neo-liberal theories, most clearly so with Hayek's ideas; his main difference with ordo-liberals was probably over the lower relevance he gave to competition law. He is not the only one, however, whose ideas come close to ordo-liberal thinking. Thus, Buchanan's defence of free markets through the constitutionalisation of economics is similar to a significant part of ordo-liberalism. The same is true of "law and economics" authors, because of their shared views of the importance of inter-penetration between legal and economic processes but, even more strikingly, in the importance both give to private law and to the establishment of a fixed set of legal rights protecting voluntary market transactions and the expectations of economic agents. One can draw upon all these sources in considering the prospects of European Union law founded on a Economic Constitution, the main aim of which is to limit public and private power within the market, be that through the review of public regulation against a set of private economic rights and liberties, or through the application of competition rules to public and private behaviour.

[74] F. Böhm, "Rule of Law in a Market Economy", in Alan Peacock and Hans Willgerodt (eds.), *Germany's Social Market Economy: Origins and Evolution* (London, Macmillan Press, 1989), at 58. This was the aim of the liberal revolution to be preserved and pursued.

[75] Hayek, *The Road to Serfdom* (n.71 above), at 173.

[76] D.J. Gerber, "Constitutionalising the Economy" (n.72 above), at 47.

[77] On the dependence of the economic constitution on a political decision, see, ibid at 44–5.

competition in the free market.[78] The economic due-process reading of Article 30 is based on this understanding. The important factor is not the creation of a new political authority, but the thorough application of rules on free movement and competition. Moreover, it is feared by some that any developments towards greater federalism, even if made under a liberal compromise, necessarily involve the creation of a "nation state" model, with more and more competences allocated to the central level, and thus reproducing there the structure already in place in the nation states.[79] Economic freedom for all by limiting public and private power in the market is the aim. It is also the "clue to the delineation of policy measures".[80] Free movement and competition rules as economic freedoms set the limits, the requirements and the manner of public intervention. The limits are that there should be no encroachment upon individual freedom and private autonomy; the requirements, that private autonomy be enhanced, contracts protected and private competition safeguarded; the manner in which this should be carried out is by means of general and universal rules, which cannot be "captured" by private interests.

In this way, free movement and competition rules become the cornerstone of the European Constitution and the source of its legitimacy. As Mestmäcker argues the legitimacy of European law does not come from the State but from the individual rights which it grants against public power.[81] Therein lies a big advantage of neo-liberal constructions of the European Union: they legitimise both European law and the existence of a European Constitution without requiring additional "traditional" democratic developments.

For those who are used to considering constitutions a contractual organisation of political power and (in the Western constitutional tradition) as a

[78] For a early analysis of this kind, see K. Markert, "Concurrence et Politique Economique dans la CEE", in *La Constitution Economique Européenne, Actes du cinquième Colloque sur la Fusion des Communautés européennes organisé à Liège les 16, 17 et 18 décembre 1970* (La Haye, Martinus Nijhoff, 1971), 237. In the words of this author: "*cette économie concurrentielle n'est pas seulement le* moyen *choisi en vue de l'etablissement d'un système économique commun, mais en même temps l'objectif, à savoir l'ordre économique qui, dans un Marché commun achevé, est destiné à longue à déterminer le processus économique . . . Mais ce qui est le plus essential, c'est que lórdre concurrentiel voulu par ce Traité C.E.E. comporte également l'objectif de la protection de la liberté économique de l'individu*", at 241 and 243.

[79] See the critique by Voigt of Buchanan's proposal for a "true" European Constitution. According to Buchanan, this Constitution should ensure free trade and competition among producers and consumers, protect the economic liberties of individuals and firms and generate enough cross-national competition to prevent interference by special interests in the market forces, increasing efficiency and wealth maximisation. See J.M. Buchanan, "Europe's Constitutional Opportunity", in *Europe's Constitutional Future* (London, Institute of Economic Affairs Readings 33, 1990), at 11; and S. Voigt, "European Political Union—An Appropriate for Applying Constitutional Economics to Real-Life Problems?", (1994) 45 *ORDO*, 273.

[80] Peacock and Willgerodt, "Overall View of the German Liberal Movement" in *Germany's Social Market: Origins and Evolution* (London, Macmillan, 1989), at 10.

[81] E.-J. Mestmäcker, "On the Legitimacy of European Law", *RabelsZ* 1994, 615, mainly at 619 and 626. See, also, E.-U. Petersmann, "Proposals for a New Constitution for the European Union: Building-Blocks for a Constitutional Theory and Constitutional Law of the EU", (1995) 32 *CMLRev*, 1123, at 1127, 1132 and 1154.

charter of fundamental rights reflecting the different values within a political community, it may not seem acceptable to transform a Treaty directed at market building and "biased" by economic rationality into a European Constitution. In effect, such a Constitution is bound to suffer from a political and a democratic deficit. This will reflect on the legitimacy of European law itself, which will need to develop towards more democratic European Union institutions. For neo-liberalism, however, there is no democratic deficit once power is devolved, through the Treaty rules, to the market; that is, into the sphere of private relations. Private law transactions are seen as the real source of the contractual and democratic legitimacy of any society and, thus, of the constitution upon which it is founded. It is here that the great attraction for Europe of the political programme of neo-liberalism lies: it requires no further transfers of powers from Member States to supra-national institutions. There will be no more problems of democratic deficit or conflicts between centralisation and national sovereignty. Moreover, this solution eliminates the fear that the integration process will be controlled by the most powerful States. While a supra-national political authority may be controlled by stronger States, competitive market forces will apply equally to smaller and larger States.[82]

Fundamental freedoms and economic due process

In a reading of the EC Treaty as an ordo-liberal or neo-liberal European Economic Constitution, free movement rules gain the status of fundamental rights, or rather fundamental freedoms. They would thus play a major role in the definition of the limits imposed on political power and of the border set between the public and private sphere. According to Petersmann, fundamental freedoms are the sources of legitimation of market integration non-discriminatory competition, in that they increase individual autonomy equality and responsibility, control abuses of government and maximise economic welfare.[83] The result of this construction is that economic choices are no longer considered a matter of policy, but as a question of constitutional rights.[84]

A constitutional conclusion of this kind, albeit without the strong economic liberal "content" of ordo-liberal theories, is also asserted by Cruz Vilaça and Piçarra, for whom:

> "another important aspect of the constitutionalization of the Treaty, which also relates to fundamental rights is the one dealing with the recognition of the 'four fundamental freedoms' . . . as fundamental rights which guarantee to citizens of the

[82] J.M. Buchanan, "Europe's Constitutional Opportunity" (n.79 above), at 15.

[83] E.-U. Petersmann, "Proposals for a New Constitution of the European Union" (n.81 above), at 1154.

[84] See Petersmann, ibid. Also "Constitutional Principles Governing the EEC's Commercial Policy", in M. Maresceau (ed.), *The European Community's Commercial Policy after 1992: The Legal Dimension* (Kluwer, 1993), 21, at 35.

Community the right to pursue the economic activity to which those provisions refer and protect them above all from any interference with those freedoms by the sovereign power of the Member States".[85]

In a broader-ranging and stronger manner, Streit and Mussler have argued that by, "considering the Treaty establishing the European Economic Community of 1958 from the perspective of an economic constitution, there is sufficient evidence to argue that the Treaty provides a framework for a common market as a self-organising system".[86] Free movement rules are intended to allow for "an unimpeded self-co-ordination of economic actors", while self-control of economic actors and limits to economic power are assured through competition rules.[87]

The protection of these values is entrusted to the European Court of Justice, whose task as guardian of the Treaty and interpreter of its rules gives it the most important role in safeguarding the self-organization of the market and the "demarcation of the private and public sphere".[88] The test proposed by Wils for "measures having equivalent effect to quantitative restrictions" is a good example of such a judicial empowerment and of the transformation of Article 30 into an economic due-process clause . In his opinion:

> "The borderline between legitimate and illegitimate national regulation under Article 30 should reflect the *balance between* the desire for integration, that is, *the desire to limit the influence of national governments on people's activities* throughout the Community, *and the desire for government intervention*, translated—for practical reasons or reasons of principle—into a desire for national regulation".[89]

Other commentators have also reflected such a conception of the European Economic Constitution with regard to Article 30, in arguing, for example, that competition rules will be the dominant value in Article 30 in ensuring the "natural functioning of the market"[90] or that free movement rules should be raised to the status of fundamental freedoms guaranteeing open markets.[91] It is in the

[85] J.L. da Cruz Vilaça, and N. Piçarra, "Are There Material Limits to the Revision of the Treaties on the European Union?", in *Vorträge und Berichte des Zentrums für Europäisches Wirtschaftsrecht des Universität Bonn* (1995), at 9. See, also, I. Harden, "The Constitution of the European Union", (1994) *Public Law*, 609, at 619 and Streit and Mussler, "The Economic Constitution of the EC—From 'Rome' to 'Maastricht' ", (1995) 1 *ELJ*, 5, at 15 and footnote 45.

[86] Streit and Mussler, ibid, at 14. In more clear-cut language, and in a critical appraisal, Bob Hepple notes that "The Treaty of Rome 1975 was firmly based on a neo-liberal ideology". See "Social Values and European Law", (1995) 48 *Current Legal Problems*, 39, at 41.

[87] See Streit and Mussler, "The Economic Constitution" (n.85 above), at 14. Note that free movement and competition had been signalled by Bohm as the cornerstones for the protection of a free market economy: F. Böhm, "Rule of Law in a Market Economy" (n.74 above), at 55–6.

[88] Streit and Mussler, "The Economic Constitution" (n.85 above), at 14.

[89] Wils, "The Search for the Rule in Article 30 EEC: Much Ado About Nothing?", (1993) *ELR*, 475, at 478 (emphasis added).

[90] See M. Todino, and T. Lüder, "La jurisprudence 'Keck' en matière de publicité: vers un marché unique inachevé?", (1995) *Revue du Marché Unique Européen*, 171, at 171 and 193. See also M. Waelbrock, "La Constitution Européen et les Interventions des États Membres en Matière Economique, in In Orde, Liber Amicorum Pieter Verloren Themaat" (Devanter, Kluwer, 1992), 331, at 335.

[91] E.-J. Mestmäcker, "On the Legitimacy of European Law" (n.81 above), especially at 631.

light of these ideas that the principle of mutual recognition of national rules, introduced by the Court in *Cassis de Dijon* and included in the new approach to harmonisation (following to the 1985 White Paper), has been understood as promoting competition among national rules subject to market choice. This is the basis of the competitive model of the European Economic Constitution.

Mutual recognition, the new approach to harmonisation and competition among rules

The so-called "new approach to harmonisation" conceives the regulatory process as a competition among national rules. In this respect, it is founded on three bases: first, community legislation will only set basic standards or minimum requirements; secondly, mutual recognition of national rules;[92] thirdly, acceptance of reverse discrimination (ie Member States can impose higher requirements on their nationals). The new approach has four interrelated aims:

(1) to overcome the traditional obstacles to legislation at community level;
(2) to allow some autonomy and innovation on the part of the States in defining their aims and policies;
(3) to solve problems of implementation; and
(4) to promote the "best" legislation through a competitive process among the different national legislations.[93]

Such an idea is not totally new in the Community context. When the EC Treaty was drafted, there were two divergent opinions on whether the prior harmonisation of social policy was necessary. The French, who had the most protective social legislation, demanded the harmonisation of social legislation. The position of experts was against prior harmonisation, preferring "to rely on normal competitive forces to achieve it in the long run".[94] The final solution, however, was one of compromise, with Germany agreeing to introduce equal pay for women and the 40-hour week.[95]

In its White Paper of 1985 on "Completing the Internal Market" the Commission developed the Court's *Cassis de Dijon* decision[96] to establish a new general principle regarding the removal of technical barriers on goods

[92] Also known as "home country control".

[93] From a more ideological standpoint, the trust in the market and on an ex-post harmonisation process inherent in the new approach to harmonisation can be argued on three bases: the prevention of "rent-seeking" as harmonisation no longer takes place ex-ante at the political bargaining level, dominated by interests groups; the devolution of powers to the market, which increases free choice and the role of a "sovereign consumer"; and the belief in competitive forces. See H. Siebert, "The Harmonization Issue in Europe: Prior Agreement or a Competitive Process?", in *The Completion of the Internal Market* (Symposium 1989, Institut für Weltwirtschaft an der Universität Kiel), mainly at 57.

[94] E.B. Haas, *The Uniting of Europe* (n.43 above), at 516.

[95] Ibid, at 519.

[96] According to Dehousse and Majone, "The Dynamics of European Integration: The Role of Supranational Institutions", Paper presented at the European Community Studies Association Third Biennial International Conference, 27–29 May 1993, Washington DC, at 11: "the new

and services: "the general principle should be approved that, if a product is lawfully manufactured and marketed in one Member State, there is no reason why it should not be sold freely throughout the Community".[97] Mutual recognition is seen as "an effective strategy for bringing about a common market in a trading sense".[98] This is superior to the traditional harmonisation strategy in two respects: first, it avoids the difficulties and delays involved in Community decision-making; and secondly, it prevents the danger of over-regulation, allowing for more flexibility and innovation.[99] Its objectives are "building an expanding market and a flexible market".[100] Following this principle a company will only need to comply with one national rule for its products to be able to move freely throughout the entire common market. Firms could choose among the different national regulations, and consumers among the products complying with those different rules. This will create a competitive process among the different national rules: the choice of producers of where to produce and of consumers of what to buy will determine the "best rules". Legislative competition under a principle of mutual recognition places the major burden of deciding the regulatory level and uniform standards upon the market. As argued in the Padoa-Schioppa Report: "Consumers will become informed about different product qualities, and where regulations are inefficiently specified or excessively burdensome, producers in those jurisdictions will lose market share; the authorities will be induced to reconsider their regulations".[101] In effect, legislative competition, under mutual recognition, will not bring about the "best" legislation in regulatory terms, but in market terms. It is the market that becomes the decision-making institution which decides the regulatory framework.

A competitive constitutional model may—and often does—apply to much more than "competition among rules". The broader model will be one of competition among governments.[102] For Thomas Dye, federalism is not only competition between the central government and State governments but also among State governments themselves. The aim is twofold: to control the abuse of power in the same way that the horizontal separation of powers

strategy of mutual recognition . . . could be presented as the logical development of the laissez-faire doctrine developed by the European Court of Justice in the famous Cassis de Dijon judgment and in a number of related cases". Although Cassis de Dijon case law has served as a source of legitimation for the Commission's strategy, such case law cannot, as argued above, be said to be based in a *laissez-faire* doctrine. See also the discussion in Chapter 1 and citations therein.

[97] "Completing the Internal Market", White Paper from the Commission to the European Council, Brussels, 14 June 1985, COM(85) 310 final, para 58. See also para 77.

[98] Ibid, para 63.

[99] Ibid, paras 61 and 64. See also para 79.

[100] Ibid, para 62.

[101] Cited from book edition: Tommaso Padoa-Schioppa et al., *Efficiency, Stability and Equity* (Oxford University Press, 1987), 61.

[102] This expression belongs to Thomas Dye that proposes a model of American federalism as "competition among governments": T.R. Dye, *American Federalism: Competition Among Governments* (Massachussetts/Toronto, Lexington Books,1990).

does,[103] and to allow choice among different government policies: "competitive federalism envisions a marketplace for governments where consumers-taxpayers can voluntarily choose the public goods and service they prefer, at the cost they wish to pay, by locating in the governmental jurisdiction that best fits their policy preferences".[104] Competition among governments can, however, have many variants, depending on what things are submitted to the competitive process, eg regulatory law; labour law; tax policies; monetary policies; justice; and redistributive policies. A major shortcoming of the competitive process is that many elements which vary from State to State, and which influence the choice of government jurisdiction by consumers-taxpayers, are normally ignored by or cannot be submitted to the competitive process: our choice of jurisdiction (where we live) is also strongly influenced by elements such as the weather, being with the woman or man we love and the quality of football matches in a particular State.

Competition among governments also depends on the rules of competition. "Just as the market place requires rules—protection of property rights, enforcement of contracts, recognized rules of exchange, and a stable monetary system—so also intergovernmental competition requires rules".[105] These rules may vary, defining the limits and forms of the competitive process. Competition among rules does not necessarily require the mutual recognition of rules: one can give freedom of choice to consumers-taxpayers regarding the government jurisdiction under which they prefer to live or establish themselves, but deny the validity of more than one rule in one jurisdiction or even defend a discriminatory application of that rule. For example, a system where protectionist measures are admitted will still be a competitive system as long as consumers-taxpayers are free to choose in which protectionist or non-protectionist State to install themselves. In sum, competition among governments or legislative competition varies with regard to the subject and the manner of the competition.

The EC Treaty includes many rules limiting and defining competition among the States. For example:

(a) The entrusting to the Community of commercial policy prevents States from competing with each other in commercial relations with third States.
(b) Free movement rules and the non-discrimination principle ensure some of the mobility of consumers-taxpayers among States necessary for competition to be workable.
(c) Articles 118a(3), 129a(3) and 130t allow, subject to the Treaty rules, Member States to introduce more stringent requirements (but not lesser requirements) than those imposed by Community legislation, thereby

[103] Ibid, at 6. See also the analysis of ordo-liberalism and European integration above.
[104] Ibid, at 14.
[105] Ibid, at 26.

encouraging in these fields, only competition "to the top", not just among Member States, but also between Member States and the Community itself.

(d) Article 92 on state aids limits competition with regard to state support to undertakings.

(e) The role given to the Court of Justice in the interpretation of the Treaty rules prevents competitive interpretations and applications of Community rules among national jurisdictions.[106]

These are only some examples on how the competitive process depends on the rules of the competition. The decision to create a single currency, for example, means that monetary policy will no longer be subject to a competitive process. As stated by Reich: "competition between legal orders is as such neither efficient nor harmful. It is much more necessary to know the objectives, contents and form of the legal orders among which competition in a (quasi-) federal jurisdiction will take place".[107] Furthermore, it is necessary to decide in what to compete and under what rules. In the present analysis, the competitive model is linked to the neo-liberal vision of the European Economic Constitution which entrusts to the market the process of competition among national rules. In Community debates, competition among rules normally refers to regulatory competition under a principle of mutual recognition. But there are limits to this: mutual recognition can be decided by the Court of Justice or by Community legislation, but in either case there are some rules or standards that are excluded from competition under mutual recognition. These rules are either imposed uniformly on all States or submitted to a competitive process under a principle of non-discrimination (the basis of the decentralised model to be discussed below). The Court's *Cassis de Dijon* case law with its principle of mutual recognition and mandatory requirements, together with the Article 36 exceptions, could be said to have been the framework of the Court's decisions on what to submit to a competitive process in the market. The new approach to harmonisation is the basis for the decisions of the Community legislative process on what to submit to the same competitive process.

Minimum harmonisation envisages a competitive process under a rule of mutual recognition except in regard to "essential health and safety requirements".[108] Those essential "health and safety requirements" will be mandatory in all States. Once a product complies with those essential requirements it can enter any national market, the different national rules being recognised throughout the Community. The Community essential requirements can still

[106] Judicial institutional competition in integration systems is discussed by Oviedo with regard to the Mercosur: M. Oviedo, *Understanding Mercosur Legal Integration Challenges* (Typescript, Florence, 1997).

[107] N. Reich, "Competition Between Legal Orders: A New Paradigm of EC Law?", (1992) 29 *CMLRev*, 861, at 867–8.

[108] White Paper on "Completing the Internal Market" (n.97 above), para 65.

be submitted to a competitive process, but in this case only to bring them to a higher level: States may impose national requirements *stricter* than the harmonised Community essential requirements. In this case State intervention occurs in parallel with market-participation and not market-regulation. States will not regulate the market (no longer subject to its jurisdiction) but will impose a certain market behaviour on some of its participants (the ones subject to its jurisdiction); the State hopes that those participants will "win" competition in the market; in this way, so will that State rules "win" regulatory competition, through the operation of market forces. States can impose their own regulations on domestic products but must accept imported products in accordance with other regulations. The market will choose between products subject to different regulations and, in consequence, between the different regulations. This is the minimum harmonisation Directives' technique, co-ordinated with the acceptance of reverse discrimination (States discrimination against their own nationals).[109]

In reality, Directives allowing States to impose higher requirements on their nationals (and thus creating reverse discrimination) are an exception. The rule is normally that the requirements apply to both imported and domestic products with those conforming to those requirements benefiting from a market access clause.[110] Even when States are authorised to impose higher requirements upon their nationals, Community minimum standards will in fact also tend to be the national maximum standard. This suggests that neither the Community political process nor the Member States truly believe in the efficiency of the competitive model under a rule of mutual recognition. This suspicion is confirmed by two observations on the new approach to harmonisation in practice. First, until now the minimum requirements have not been

[109] Directives can confer three types of treatment on imported and domestic products once they satisfy the essential requirements prescribed therein: first, Directives can include a market access clause for all products (domestic and imported) complying with those essential requirements; secondly, Directives can authorise national regulators to impose stricter requirements to both domestic and imported products; thirdly, Directives can authorise national regulators to impose stricter requirements on domestic products only. An example of a market access clause is Article 12 of Directive 89/107/EEC on food additives (OJ 11.02.1989 L 40/27) whose para 2 states: "Member States may not prohibit, restrict or obstruct the *marketing* of food additives, food or food ingredients on grounds relating to food additives, if these comply with the provisions of this Directive, the existing specific directives and the comprehensive directive refered to in Article 3" (emphasis added). See also Article 10 of the Directive 89/108/EEE on quick frozen foodstuffs (OJ 11.02.1989 L 40/34). Examples of the second type can be seen on the Doorstep-selling and Package Holidays Directives. Article 8 of the latter states: "Member States may adopt more stringent provisions in the field covered by this Directive to protect the consumer". See Directive 85/577/EEC (OJ 31.12.1985 L 372/31), and Directive 90/314/EEC (OJ 23.06.1990 L 158/59). An example of the third type is actually prior to the "new approach to harmonisation": Article 15, para 1 of the Labelling Directive states that "Member States may not forbid *trade* in foodstuffs which comply with the rules laid down in this Directive by the application of non-harmonised national provisions governing the labelling and presentation of certain foodstuffs or of foodstuffs in general" (emphasis added). See Directive 79/112/EEC (OJ 08.02.1979 L 33/1).

[110] See S. Weatherill, "Regulating the Internal Market: Result Orientation in the Court of Justice", (1994) 19 *ELR*, 55, at 63.

very minimal: they have normally been defined at higher levels thus restricting the room for market choice. Secondly, it is not uncommon for Directives to allow States to impose stricter requirements upon domestic and imported products (creating a competitive process, but under a rule of non-discrimination).

The choice between EC regulation and mutual recognition depends to a great degree on the beliefs on economic regulation and public intervention. The shift in the political climate from regulation to deregulation;[111] and the need to convince some Member States (mainly the United Kingdom)[112] to approve the Single European Act and to progress further in the construction of the common market, led to the focus on mutual recognition when drafting the new approach to harmonisation. However, the lack of mutual trust among States (essential to mutual recognition),[113] and the importance in the Community legislative process of States with a strong regulatory tradition, led to a different state of affairs in the implementation of such approach.

Economic and constitutional analyses of competition among rules

For some, the major danger foreseen in a competitive model under a rule of mutual recognition is a process of deregulation. Companies and individuals will move to States with less strict regulations, since their products and services will be accepted all over the Community. Harmonisation will occur according to the lowest common denominator. Some arguments have been put forward against such predictions of a "race to the bottom". Two main reasons are given: first, States will tend to balance private and public good so that they end up obtaining an identical total optimal output; and secondly, the protection of one interest will raise market pressures for the protection of other interests, this further contributing towards identical optimal balances.

The States' "total output" comes both from public goods (eg environmental and consumer protection) and private goods (such as production output). Raising the output of a public good may involve costs to private goods and vice versa. There will be a point at which the marginal benefit from the increased output of a good will be out-weighed by the cost imposed on the other goods. This process will generate an equilibrium in order to preserve or improve the total national output. By looking specifically at public or private goods, one can detect a redistribution process among the different States. Such a process, however, will not reduce the net output generated by both private and public goods.

[111] See N. Reich, "The Regulatory Crisis" (n.8 above), at 1.

[112] See A. Moravcsik, "Negotiating the Single European Act" (n.38 above), mainly at 44.

[113] G. Majone, "Subsidiarity and Mutual Recognition: Implications for Local, Regional and National Politics in a Unified Europe", Lecture given at the inauguration of the fourth edition of the Master in Public Management of the Universitat Autònoma de Barcelona (18 December 1992), at 6, and *Market Integration and Regulation: Europe After 1992*, EUI Working Paper SPS 91/10 (Florence, European University Institute, 1991), at 20.

The increased protection of a certain interest (good) will also generate pressures in the opposite direction. Van Long and Siebert give the example of environmental protection.[114] According to them, an increase in the environmental protection of the home country will: increase wages in the foreign country and decrease them in the home country; increase real income in the foreign country (mainly from production relocation); and increase foreign country pollution levels (by the same production relocation). Such pressures will work on the home country to decrease its pollution tax and attract producers and on the foreign country to improve its environment and increase its pollution tax. This will generate a balanced regulatory level, and not deregulation.

In presenting such a defence of the market's ability to handle the balance between regulation and free movement, some assumptions are made which are difficult to identify in the Community context. First, these studies normally presuppose the same preferences by all individuals and identical technologies, endowments and preferences by all States.[115] In the Community this is far from true, the consequences being that market pressures may take long to act and that the outcomes predicted above may differ on the basis of different State assessments of how much net output comes from the increase in a certain good. Secondly, the approaches presented above are not valid where there are "spill-over effects" or free riders.[116] For example, if the public good consists of consumer protection and a company can move to another country and still send its products to the original country there will be no improvement in this State's production of public goods. In addition, if spill-over effects exist the market will not be sending the right signals to the States: for example, if cross-border pollution exists, the cost of lowering environment protection will not be felt (at least totally) in the country responsible for deregulation. Whenever a State is able to transfer, totally or partially, the costs of deregulation, the market is less efficient in producing the right regulatory outcome. From a policy perspective one can sum up by saying that competition is at its best when the regulatory costs and benefits accrue on the regulatory "author" and when competition is over "undifferentiated products which consumers are competent to evaluate".[117] Competition will be at its worst when there are market failures such as externalities (transference of costs) or asymmetric information (consumers will not be in condition to evaluate goods), or when competition is over public goods (the benefits from which may accrue to those who do not pay their costs).[118]

[114] See Ngo Van Long and Horst Siebert, "Institutional Competition Versus ex-ante Harmonization: The Case of Environmental Policy", (1991) 147 *Journal of Institutional and Theoretical Economics*, 296.

[115] See ibid, at 298 and 303.

[116] See ibid, 297 and 307. Also Siebert, "The Harmonization Issue in Europe" (n.93 above), at 67.

[117] G. Majone, *Market Integration and Regulation* (n.113 above), at 15.

[118] See: ibid at 16; Siebert, "The Harmonization Issue in Europe" (n.93 above), for example at 57–8 and 68; T.R. Dye, *American Federalism* (n.102 above), at 17–19; J. Pelkmans, "Regulation and the Single Market: An Economic Perspective", in *The Completion of the Internal Market* (n.93

Much of this economic jargon and analysis is about democratic questions. Such things as externalities or asymmetric information can and should be converted into constitutional discourse, comparing the market with the alternative institutions under yardsticks such as representation and accountability. Under the competitive model ("competition among rules"), as has already been noted, the institution responsible for deciding on regulations is the market. Not just any market, but a market in which competing products are each subject to a different regulatory framework, and where factors of production can move freely in choosing the regulatory framework they prefer. The question is then how representative and accountable the market is *vis-à-vis* other institutions to decide on the "best" regulation. It is probably the absence of such an analysis that explains the scepticism of lawyers with regard to competition among rules to which Reich refers.[119] Lawyers work with traditional and well-established principles, such as non-discrimination, which are disrupted by a competitive process in which competitors are subject to different rules because of the concepts of mutual recognition and reverse discrimination. We are used to think in terms of the authority and "empire" of law over the market, and not in terms of the authority of the market over laws. Competition among rules challenges our understanding of the law and its principles. Its studies reinforce the idea that economics and constitutional law are separate worlds. Both tend to remain prisoners of different rationalities. Economics is presented as operating according to the notions of rational actors' behaviour and a world of costless transactions. Law appears to assume that its power and authority allow it to transfer normative ideals into real world facts in some sort of causal relationship. Economics is associated with the goal of efficiency and law with normative ideals such as democracy. This is reflected in the studies of competition among rules, presented as promoting efficiency against legal values such as equality and democracy. Ascertaining the role of the market in competition among rules and subjecting it to an institutional analysis similar to that undertaken with other institutions allows us to depart from these limits and to construct a framework of analysis of the market and market failures in which law and economics can engage in a common discourse. The market is a decision-making institution providing a form of representation and accountability to be compared in different situations with the representation and accountability of the alternative institutions.

From a representative point of view, a market operating at its best will be a market where decisions are the result of voluntary transactions in which all the people affected participate, and in which all costs and benefits and alternative transactions are taken into account. Such a market would be an ideal decision-maker from the point of view of resource allocation efficiency. Of

above), mainly at 93 and an opposite view by H. Willgerodt, "Comment on Jacques Pelkmans 'Regulation and the Single Market: An Economic Perspective' ", in ibid, at 121.

[119] N. Reich, "Competition Between Legal Orders" (n.107 above), at 862.

course this ideal market will rarely, if ever, exist. But for our purposes what is important is not determining when the market is the "best" or even when it is "at its best", but rather when it is "better" than the alternative available institutions.[120]

What was described as the "best" market from a representative point of view may not be a good choice if the aim is not to attain resource allocation efficiency but to put into effect a redistributive policy. Here, voluntary market transactions may have to be replaced by imposed ones; and the process of representation may have to be enlarged from involving only those affected by the market transactions to one which includes all those who may gain something by interfering in the market decision (eg by taxing the market transaction). We will not enter here into the debate about who should decide between the aims of redistribution or resource allocation efficiency (on the basis of which the assessment of representation in the market will considerably vary); it should however be noted that regulatory law is normally about resource allocation efficiency.[121]

The aim is to assess the representativity of institutions with respect to all those affected by a given decision. Furthermore, "competition among rules" or "competition among States" respects States' policy autonomy. It is the respect for that autonomy which allows those affected by the policies to be able to choose. "There is no real competition, and hence no true responsiveness to individual preferences, if state and local governments are not free to pursue a wide range of policies. Policy variation among government is a requirement for genuine competitive federalism".[122] This means that the market should allow all those who benefit or suffer because of a certain policy or regulation to participate in market decisions. It is by comparing the degree and process of representation of these people in the market and in other institutions that we can decide when the market is the "better" institution.

The above analysis should help us in understanding the paradox of regulatory competition: if the market is regulated in a particular area it is because the market is not "trusted" in that area; why, then, submit that regulation to a decision of the market?; why submit regulations to the control of those being regulated?;[123] why should those who regulate the market trust in the market

[120] See Komesar's comparative institutional analysis: Komesar, *Imperfect Alternatives* (n.34 above).

[121] According to Susan Rose-Ackerman, "to echo a familiar theme in public finance, redistribution should be accomplished through a general system of taxes and transfers, not piecemeal through the complex of regulatory and spending programs": *Rethinking the Progressive Agenda* (n.63 above), at 18.

[122] T.R. Dye, *American Federalism* (n.102 above), at 20. Also on the same page: "states cannot serve as laboratories, and the innovative potential of federalism cannot be realized if the states are not free to pursue a wide range of policies".

[123] "Much can be said for submitting regulation to a preference test by those to be regulated—it is quite obvious that they will choose the "friedliest" regulator and thus create competition for the least strict or most supportive standards": N. Reich, "The Regulatory Crisis" (n.8 above), at 696.

to judge on that regulation? The answer is that the market which judges regulations is not the same as the regulated market. This must be so, because otherwise there would be a contradiction, in imposing a regulation on a market when the same outcome is expected from it (if the market is going to choose the product with higher standards, why impose these standards at all?). Submitting a regulation to market choice cannot mean submitting it to the choice only of those who will be regulated. A regulation affects many more people than just those who are directly regulated, and we have to look at the entire picture in order to assess the representative ability of the market.

The market responsible for choices in a competitive model is much more than the sum of voluntary market transactions. It also involves "voting with your feet", political votes and lobbying. The success or failure of a certain regulation or government policy under a competitive judgement may be dependent on a series of factors that can be described as follows:

(a) *What do people buy?*—If, for example, goods subject to regulation A by Member State A sell more than goods subject to regulation B by Member State B, then State B may alter its legislation in order to give its products equal conditions of competition and (hopefully) equal market success.

(b) *Where do factors of production go?*—If, for example, the labour law of Member State A provides a lower level of protection than the labour law of Member State B, capital may move to Member State A. On the other hand, labour may move to Member State B.

(c) *Where do consumers and taxpayers go ("voting with your feet")?*—If consumers and taxpayers (both individuals and companies) find the policy of Member State A better than the policy of Member State B (for example, because it gives them more protection, more freedom of choice, or lower taxation) and if they have the right to move to the jurisdiction that pleases them the most, this will put pressure on Member State B to take action (for example, by reducing the level of taxation or increasing consumer protection).

(d) *How do consumers and taxpayers vote and lobby?*—If consumers and taxpayers prefer the policy of Member State A to that of their own Member State, they may vote for a party proposing a new policy, closer to that of Member State A. They may also exert other forms of political pressure such as lobbying.

All these factors depend on the two essential assumptions of the competitive model: mobility and information.[124] It is essential that factors of production and consumers and taxpayers are mobile, in order for the market to send the right signals to the policy-makers. It is the mobility of factors of production and of consumers and taxpayers which indicates the preference of the people

[124] See T.R. Dye, *American Federalism* (n.102 above), at 15–17.

for one policy rather than another. It is also mobility that gives people the possibility to choose among jurisdictions with different policies and ways of life. Information is also necessary if market transactions are to send the right signals to the States on the opinions of the participants in the market process.

Let us imagine that with regard to product X, which is subject to different regulations in Member States A and B, I am ready to take a safety risk of level S1 if that means paying less than 10 ECU for the product. Let us suppose moreover that a safety risk of level S1 is accepted by the legislation of Member State A, but that Member State B imposes a higher mandatory safety protection of S2 which results in an increase in product costs, making product X cost more than 10 ECU. Here, my act of buying product X from Member State A and not that from Member State B would send the right sign to the policy maker: I prefer to take a higher safety risk (level S1) if that means paying less for product X. Now, let us imagine that I am not ready to accept the higher safety risk S1 but only the lower risk S2; and let us suppose that I do not have information allowing me to know that the safety risk of product X from Member State A is S1. In this case, I will still buy product X from Member State A because it is less expensive, since I do not know it has a safety risk higher than that which I am prepared to take. My lack of information will make me send the wrong signal to the policy-maker.

Comparative information is also essential for factors of production and for consumers and taxpayers to be able to move and to exert political pressure. Only when informed about different State policies can they move to the one favouring them most. Also, only if people have information on the policies of different Governments can the competitive process operate in giving people reasons and arguments for exerting political pressure through lobbying and voting. One can speak in this regard of the options of voice and exit,[125] and adjust these concepts to the different forms of expression people may have either within the jurisdiction to which they are subject to or by actually leaving that jurisdiction in favour of another jurisdiction. **Voice** refers to situations where choices are made or stances taken which express a preference for a certain regulation but do not involve leaving the jurisdiction (this includes voting and lobbying and also market transactions within that jurisdiction). **Exit** refers to situations where preferences for a certain regulation over another are expressed by moving to a different jurisdiction (and thus the relocation of factors of production and of consumers and taxpayers).

When the efficiency of the market is assessed, under the present constitutional analysis, in order to choose the "best" regulation, the possibilities of

[125] These concepts have been crafted by Hirschman in his well known book *Exit, Voice and Loyalty—Responses to Decline in Firms, Organizations and States* (Cambridge, Harvard UP, 1970). For two different examples in the use of these concepts see, Dye, *American Federalism* (n.102 above), at 17 and Weiler, "The Transformation of Europe" (n.18 above), at 2411. The use of these concepts here, however, does not fully coincide with that of these authors or with the original definition given by Hirschman, but includes all market transactions within a jurisdiction (for example, both buying a product and ceasing to buy it) in the domain of voice.

exit and voice in the market and in the political process[126] should be taken into account for all the different interests affected by the regulation. In this respect we must note a major difference between the European Union and other competitive systems such as the USA: mobility is not fully guaranteed. Not only is mobility traditionally much lower in the European context, but also it has not been guaranteed to all those affected by policies.[127] Free movement has been central to development of the "European market citizen" but, at the same time, has also remained attached to the market.[128] Factors of production are guaranteed free movement by the EC Treaty and the same applies to people who are linked to those factors or who are themselves acting as market agents (companies and liberal professionals under the rules of freedom of establishment and the freedom to provide services; and individuals as labour under the free movement of workers) but consumers have no such general guarantee.[129] This means that consumers' opportunities of exit are much more limited that those of other groups affected by a regulation. This may well support the present activism of the Court in the realm of free movement of persons,[130] in order to increase the input of other interests in the common market and in the competition among States it entails.

There are or may be other problems of representation in the market. Even among those that are able to move, not all have the same capacity for mobility: capital, for example, normally has much more mobility than labour. The same can be said of voice, where not all have the same opportunities: unemployed people have much less voice than unionised labour or organised capital, for example. Another problem is that those who are regulated can normally send a clearer and stronger signal to the political process than can those who are not regulated but nonetheless are affected by the regulation. For example, the signal sent by producers in moving to another State when they find pollution prevention standards too costly will be much more easily perceived by government authorities than the satisfaction of all those happy to live in an unpolluted environment. Externalities are also a common shortcoming of representation in competitive systems. Here the problem is that some people affected by a decision do not participate in that decision. It is

[126] In including all the factors that are at work or should be at work in a competitive process we should speak not only of economic market but also of political market.

[127] Much will depend now, in effect, on the interpretation and the development to be made of Article 8a, para 1 of the EC Treaty, introduced by the Maastricht Treaty, together with the new title on free movement of persons, asylum and immigration to be introduced by the Amsterdam Treaty (note that this title is linked in the Amsterdam Treaty to Article 7a—free movement of persons in the context of the internal market—and not to the broader provision of Article 8a—free movement of persons as a citizenship right).

[128] See M. Everson, "The Legacy of Market Citizen", in J. Shaw and G. More (eds.), *New Legal Dynamics of European Union* (Oxford, Clarendon Press, 1995), 73, mainly at 86 and 87.

[129] The Court of Justice deemed the freedom to provide services to include the freedom of consumers to purchase tourist services, in the well known Joined Cases 286/82 and 26/83, *Luisi and Carbone* [1984] ECR 377.

[130] See Chapter 3 above.

enough to give another pollution example: in this case cross-border pollution. Those who are harmed by cross-border pollution are outside the jurisdiction of the pollution regulator and thus cannot exert any form of voice or exit in the decision-making process. The pollution regulator will not be accountable to those most harmed by the low standards of its regulation.

The promotion of a constitutional model of competition among States under mutual recognition of national rules must depart from an analysis of the role of the market in such competition and take into account the constitutional questions embodied in such decision-making powers being allocated to the market. It requires an analysis of the representation and accountability of the market in different circumstances. The European Court of Justice must incorporate such reasoning when reviewing national and Community legislation and setting the balance between public regulation and market self-organisation.

THE DECENTRALISED MODEL OF THE EUROPEAN ECONOMIC CONSTITUTION (STATE REGULATION UNDER NON-DISCRIMINATION)

Competition among rules under non-discrimination

The decentralised model can be summarised as a system in which States retain regulatory powers, but are at the same time, required not to discriminate against foreign products or persons in their exercise of those powers. To a great extent, this is still a model based on competition. As already noted, competition among rules is not uniform; it can be structured in different ways, depending on the definition of the competition rules. In the *realm of powers left to the States*,[131] the American system can be seen as a good example of competition taking place under different rules.[132] This is also the case in Europe, depending on whether, for example, the principle of mutual recognition is applied or instead one accepts non-discrimination as the rule.

A model of competition among rules in which free trade is achieved under non-discrimination, is proposed by Edmund Kitch in a paper entitled

[131] We are not here describing the American model as a decentralised model, since that realm of powers can always be subject to Congressional pre-emption. Even if the commerce clause can also be seen as promoting a competition between national and state governments in the regulation of the market (Dye, *American Federalism* (n.102 above) mainly at 3 and discussion at 99), that competition has generally been decided in favour of national government. See, for example, P. Juillard, "Les orientations de la jurisprudence constitutionnelle de la Cour Suprême: établissement du marché unique et renforcement des libertés publiques", (1991) 59 Pouvoirs, 59, at 62.

[132] Competition under mutual recognition exists over legislative disparities (as mentioned before, matters such as different tax and corporate laws are subject to different regulatory regimes, such as the case of the famous Delaware corporate laws). In the other areas (as discussed in Chapter 3 above) the rule is non-discrimination, except in the period of economic due process, where in *Schollenberger* v. *Pennsylvania* 171 US 1 (last quoted in *Weaver* v. *Palmer Bros. Co.* 270 US 402) the Supreme Court developed a principle close to mutual recognition.

"Regulation and the American Common Market".[133] Kitch argues that regulation should be decentralised and that the states' power to regulate should only be submitted to a non-discrimination principle. He does not believe that decentralisation would erect barriers to trade, since this would be against the states' self-interest. A process of bargaining and co-operation among states would lead to free trade and more efficient regulation or deregulation.[134] We will call this model of competition based on a non-discrimination rule, the decentralised model in order for it not to be confused with the model of competition under mutual recognition which authors normally have in mind when they speak of "competition among rules" in the Community context.

In a decentralised model the process of competition will occur among different markets, each market controlled by its own set of regulations. The choice of producers and consumers as to which market to operate in and establish themselves in would be instrumental to States' decisions concerning regulation. It would, however, be for each State to decide on the regulatory scheme within that State, to which all market participants would be required to comply. Competitive pressures on the State would be present through consumers' desire to have either access to more products or alternatively to have higher standards of protection, and/or through the producers' desire to compete in markets with lower standards and, thus, lower costs.

In competition under mutual recognition we (consciously or unconsciously) choose among sets of different rules *within our own jurisdiction*. In competition under non-discrimination we choose by *moving among jurisdictions* with different rules. For consumers, the former offers more choice, the latter more protection. In a decentralised model, the role of market transactions in expressing preferences among legal orders is extremely reduced once consumers are not able to buy products subject to different rules (recall that in a pure model of this kind not even legislative disparities would be admissible). However, voice still exists in the form of voting and lobbying, provided the

[133] In A. Dan Tarlock (ed.), *Regulation, Federalism and Interstate Commerce* (Cambridge, MA, Oegeschlager, Gunn & Hain, 1981). See also his "Regulation, the American Common Market and Public Choice", (1982) 6 *Harvard Journal of Law and Public Policy*, 119.

[134] "The fact that there is decentralised authority over the laws and government practices affecting commerce does not mean that there will not be free trade. Free trade among decentralised authorities will result from voluntary co-operation, motivated by the fact that free trade will produce greater wealth for all to share. In the short run, this approach to free trade may cause significant instability, as each jurisdiction tries to establish a bargaining position through bluff, threat, and implemented threat. But in the long run, this system may provide more free trade than centralised authority because it places stronger incentives on each jurisdiction to promulgate efficient rules for both its internal and external commerce": "Regulation and the American Common Market" (n.133 above), at 13–14. Reich has noted that Kitch's argument is an argument against centralisation ("Competition Between Legal Orders" (n.107 above), at 866). But Reich has also argued that, by dismissing the need for positive integration (that is regulation at a centralised level) Kitch is in fact proposing deregulation (Reich, "The Regulatory Crisis" (n.8 above)). In fact, Kitch believes the federal legislator is a greater threat to an open market than the states themselves ("Regulation and the American Common Market" (n.133 above), at 46–7). Yet Kitch's theory is not in itself pro-deregulation since he accepts that states are still able to regulate subject to a principle of non-discrimination.

consumers and taxpayers have the information and the ability to compare their State's policies and outcomes with those of the other States.

In a decentralised system, the main regulatory institution will be the States themselves. While in the competition model (under a rule of mutual recognition) the market choices of consumers over what to buy, and of factors of production over where to produce will be essential in determining the level of market regulation, in a decentralised model the regulatory choices are mainly dependent on the exercise of political pressure on the States' political systems through voting, lobbying and the choice of jurisdiction.

Anti-protectionism

Protectionism is the main danger foreseen in allowing the Member States the power to regulate free trade. This was clearly the first concern in the minds of those who framed the EC Treaty, as indicated by the Treaty's emphasis on the prohibition of traditional trade barriers and discrimination on the grounds of nationality. However, with anti-protectionism readings of the EC Treaty, States are still understood as the legitimate source of policy-making and their powers should only be restricted when they use such policy-making to favour home nationals against foreign nationals.

One of the main arguments in favour of allocating the bulk of regulatory power to the States comes from their proximity to the different interests involved. This proximity makes States the most representative and accountable institution. If one takes into consideration only the interests directly affected by the regulation (those within that State jurisdiction) the State appears to benefit from an added democratic value in comparison with more distant institutions such as the European Union political process. The State is also seen as more able and efficient to assess the costs and benefits which a certain regulation or deregulation might impose on those affected by it within that State. This is so because of the States' knowledge of cultural traditions, market structures, social behaviour and history. They also possess the bureaucratic machinery capable of collecting the necessary information. As this machinery will be in charge of implementing the adopted regulation, there is a strong argument for State input in shaping it.

Another argument in favour of a regulatory role for the Member States is that they can more promptly assess and react to new problems as well as experiment with new policies. The States' political processes have decision-making procedures which are less complex than European ones, and in which ideological cleavages are not normally as strong as they are (albeit hidden) within the European Union political process. Moreover, decentralisation allows innovation and testing of rules in one or more Member States, the result of which can then be transposed to other States.

The State political process is also seen as not sharing, at least to the same degree, the democratic problems faced by European Union institutions. The reference to a democratic deficit in the European Union political process has been stressed over and over again, and will not be repeated here. But the argument for a decentralised model entails that the best safeguard of democracy is still the nation state. Reducing European Union competences and increasing national input will be the solution for the European democratic deficit.

The underlying idea of the anti-protectionism approach to the EC Treaty is that States should keep their policy autonomy while not being allowed to use it to advantage its own nationals at the cost of nationals of other Member States. The problem with anti-protectionism ideas is that it is not at all clear when a State its advantaging its own nationals at the cost of foreign nationals. Moreover, not all benefits accorded to home nationals at the cost of foreign nationals should be considered as protectionism.[135] The core of Members States' policy autonomy and sovereignty is that, in some cases, they may still favour their home nationals even at a cost for foreign nationals (the question is where and how). Finally, common problems and common goals among States require more than the national levels of decision-making can democratically offer and co-operation among these national decision-makers may not be possible or sufficient to supplement such democratic deficits.

Institutional malfunctions in state regulation of the common market

The main problem foreseen in submitting free trade and regulation to a completely decentralised model is the restrictions it would create for free trade. It is somewhat "naive" to expect free trade to come about simply because Member States have an interest in co-operating so as not to restrict free trade. High transaction costs in the bargaining process, the adoption of short-term policies, different market structures, minoritarian bias, the temptation to behave as "free riders": all these circumstances create problems for an idyllic vision of States' behaviour in the bargaining process which will lead to free trade.[136] Moreover, when Kitch puts forward his view he is basing his assumptions on federalist systems, especially the USA, where the pre-existence of a common market and of federal structures creates a framework within which the competitive and bargaining process which he envisages may be much more successful than with traditional trade relations. One can also say that in the European Union the progress on market integration is establishing a good ground for co-operation. However, many problems remain before co-operation can be complete and efficient.

[135] Some of these problems have already been addressed in the discussion on discrimination tests: see Chapter 2 above. They are again dealt with in the normative discussion of the test to be adopted with regard to Article 30 in Chapter 5 below.

[136] As is pointed out by Richard Collins: "Protectionist politics, high transaction costs when politicians are bargainers, free riders problems and great political temptations to burden outsiders have impeded trade agreements through recorded history": R.B. Collins, "Economic Union as a Constitutional Value", (1988) 63 *New York University Law Review*, 43, at 124.

If there were no transaction costs, and assuming the net benefits from free trade proclaimed in economic studies to be true, a decentralised model would be sufficient to achieve free trade: States could lose in some circumstances but would receive compensation from the States which gained from liberalisation. Unfortunately, reality is not a world of costless transactions. First, States may not have sufficient information to realise the net gains from free trade or to measure the costs and benefits. Secondly, politicians may not be able to explain to their constituents the gains to be had from liberalisation or compensation. Thirdly, States may not have the means and the time to co-ordinate so many different policies. Fourthly, even after agreement, the incentives for evasion remain strong (as States might want to try to win all the time), so more subtle and sophisticated obstacles may arise.

Even consensus on free trade gains and the need to eliminate obstacles to trade is not sufficient in itself: many obstacles to trade come from different assessments of what is the right policy[137] (something a decentralised model aims to preserve), so we need to decide when we are going to prefer to have a choice among different regulations (which create restrictions to trade) and when we are going to have free trade. Though States may agree as to the advantages of free trade and co-operation in general, they may not be able to agree as to when a specific regulation should be sacrificed in the name of free trade. This is because States correspond to different political communities, with different lifestyles and different notions of what is good and bad (for example, different risk aversion calculations). A State can make the best balance among all interests involved including out-of-State interests (those involved in imports, for example) but that does not necessarily lead to uniformity. Uniformity requires all States to set the same balance. Yet the optimal balance between free trade and the States' legitimate interests (such as consumer and environmental protection) may not be the same in different States. As has been pointed out before, not everyone gives the same value to the same interest. This means that the value given to consumer protection, for example, may vary in different States, according to consumer behaviour and the consumer's acceptance of higher or lower risks with the correspondent difference in costs. Uniformity is an interest that goes beyond the way in which each State is able to set the best balance among the different interests involved. Since the optimal balance in State terms can be different from State to State, uniformity requires some or all of the States to change that optimal balance. It requires co-ordination in order to avoid "free riders" and achieve a compromise among the different State balances. The balance between the general benefits arising from uniformity (such as economies of scale and greater consumer choice) and the optimal diversity coming from efficient regulation in State terms is at the heart of the regulatory decisions taken by the European Union political process. There must be a decision on when it is possible to

[137] See Chapter 3 above on the distinction between uniformity and optimal diversity.

choose among different efficient regulatory frameworks enacted by States (optimal diversity) and when uniformity should be preferred (securing free trade). This decision is difficult to achieve through a co-ordination process based on a case by case pattern (in which restrictions to trade coming from competition among rules under a non-discrimination rule are discussed issue by issue). It requires some form of political integration,[138] preventing evasion from individual decisions that do not benefit all, and convincing those harmed in specific cases that compensation is inherent in the values of solidarity and stability that compose the long-term framework of those decisions. Economic integration and trade liberalisation favour resource allocation efficiency and improve the economic situation of the integrated area. However, in political terms, economic integration requires that economic gains be fairly distributed among all States.[139]

Even in a context of optimal diversity (in which the goal is efficient State regulation) the States' political processes present representative problems in the regulation of the common market. Regulatory decisions are made taking into account national interests. Interests of nationals of other Member States are not normally taken into account. Even when national legislation is not enacted with protectionism intents or does not discriminate against foreign nationals, the institutional structure of the States' regulatory process tends, in any case, to favour home interests. Information, participation and regulatory traditions are controlling elements of the regulatory process that will naturally reflect domestic interests. This results in what may be called national bias and is an essential component of the test to be proposed, in the final chapter, to guide the application of Article 30 in the review of national measures.

Anti-protectionism approaches start from a consideration of the EC Treaty as a traditional commercial Treaty among States, establishing a trade agreement intended to prevent protectionist policies and to reduce barriers to trade. Member States can no longer develop "selfish" policies in trade or other areas covered by the Treaty. Apart from policies protecting their own nationals to the disadvantage of other nationals, however, policy-making is still seen as internal matter for each State. As will be discussed in more detail below, it is debatable if that is still the case in the European Union and whether Member States regulatory powers should not be seen as strictly interdependent and subject to participation by a larger political community (that, of all those affected by the State regulation within the single European market). Autonomous policy-making and diversity may still be protected values, but this is not the same as considering whether or not some kind of participation in and scrutiny of the national political processes by the broader political

[138] According to Lindberg, political integration consists in: "the development of devices and processes for arriving at collective decisions by means other than autonomous action by national governments": L.N. Lindberg, *The Political Dynamics of European Integration* (Stanford and Oxford, Stanford University Press and Oxford University Press, 1963), at 5.

[139] W. Molle, *The Economics of European Integration, Theory, Practice, Policy*, 2nd. edn. (Dartmouth, Aldershot and Brookfield, 1994), mainly at 425.

community (including all those affected by that State's regulation) is necessary. This does not mean that the judgement of the broader political community is to overturn the judgement of the regulating State, but that the former should have some form of representation of their interests within the regulating States' decision-making process.

5

Article 30 and the European Economic Constitution: Reforming the Market or the State?

CONSTITUTIONAL MODELS, GOALS AND INSTITUTIONS

In the previous chapter, different models of the European Constitution have been reviewed. As stated, all models have played, and will continue to play, a role in the shaping of the European Economic Constitution. At the same time, all models present institutional malfunctions varying according to the set of factors and values described. Treaty rules such as Article 30 should be understood and interpreted in light of these models. Some Treaty rules, for example, appear to promote a centralised model of the European Union (eg rules establishing common policies or harmonisation rules such as Article 100A) while others may be seen as favouring a decentralised model (eg the "limits" on Community powers and the subsidiarity principle of Article 3B).[1] The discourse among the alternative models of the European Constitution is both a reflection of and reflected in the interpretation and application of the Treaty rules. The debate on these rules should thus be based on these constitutional models, the institutions dominating them and the underlying values and goals. This will help in identifying the different institutional malfunctions that should be the object of the judicial review of Community and national legislation. Since constitutional models are only "ideal abstractions" and "heuristic constructions" they need to be transformed into constitutional criteria to solve the day to day normative conflicts faced by courts. The interpretation and application of legal rules is the field where constitutional models are transformed into constitutional criteria. What dominates this process is a discourse about goals and institutions.

Goals

Whichever institution is entrusted the regulation of the common market will have to balance a variety of goals reflected in European Union sources. The

[1] In this respect, see the Protocol on the application of the principles of subsidiarity and proportionality included in the recent Treaty of Amsterdam.

goal of achieving an optimal gain for society through balancing the interests of free trade with other EU and State interests (such as consumer and health protection) is present in the EC Treaty in both its original and its revised form. For example, in Article 2 of the EC Treaty as amended by the Treaty on European Union it states that the task of the Community should be:

> "to promote throughout the Community a harmonious and balanced development of economic activities, sustainable and non-inflationary growth respecting the environment, a high degree of convergence of economic performance, a high level of employment and of social protection, the raising of the standard of living and quality of life, and economic and social cohesion and solidarity among Member States."

This general statement is then developed throughout the Treaty, either in stressing the value of open markets and economic competition or in the expression of concern for, among others, economic and social cohesion and the protection of the environment and of national cultural traditions. In some cases, the Treaty even helps us rate those values (as with the references to high standards).[2] At the same time, it underlines the importance of State autonomy in the evaluation of those interests through the principle of subsidiarity and by leaving the bulk of regulation in the hands of the Member States.

There are often several possible positions that can be taken when a balance has to be set between the burden being imposed on trade and the protection of one or more legitimate interests of Member States (a particular regulation may of course aim at protecting more than one interest). It is not easy to determine the gain to society which can be expected from the different interests or the different degrees to which they are protected. Different individuals and institutions will make different assessments. Of course, if the intention is to determine the net gain to society, this can be found in the sum of individual gains and losses. But while voluntary market transactions express these preferences of the parties in the operation of the market (as long as we assume that the behaviour of individuals is guided by wealth maximisation), this cannot be the case in the regulatory process. Even if we assume that the aim of regulations is to achieve resource allocation efficiency by reproducing the hypothetical rational choices which individuals would make in a world without transaction costs, it will always be impossible to do this without introducing the values, hierarchy and methods of measurement of the institution responsible for the regulatory choice. Clearly the regulatory choices of a institution will depend closely on the interests of those represented therein, as well as on the mechanisms and values already internalised in that institution's decision-making process and the context in which and for which the decision is taken.[3] Where certain competencies are generally constitutionally allocated to a certain institution, this implies that (provided no severe institutional

[2] See, eg Articles 100a(4) or 130r(2).

[3] This is why decisions will vary even if the interests represented are the same.

malfunction occurs) it is the best "equipped" to perform that function (or, in other words, the most legitimate institution).

Furthermore, efficiency can be measured in many ways. Taking as a basis traditional standards of efficiency we find "Pareto superiority", "Pareto optimality", "Kaldor/Hicks efficiency" and "Pigou optimality". These can be seen as rules orienting decision-making procedures or decision-making outcomes.[4] With regard to decision-making outcomes, Pareto superiority is assured if no-one is worse off and at least one person is better off. Pareto optimality exists if there is no conceivable "state N" in which anyone will be worst off. A decision is Kaldor/Hicks efficient if those that are better off win sufficiently to be able to compensate the losers so that the losers are not worse off. Finally, Pigou optimality exists where there is a net benefit, that is, where those better-off win more that those worst-off lose. These standards of efficiency can also be used to orient decision-making procedures, in which case they can be described as follows: Pareto superiority is assured if the decision is not disliked by anyone and is preferred by at least one person; Pareto optimality occurs if there is no "state N" in which anyone would dislike the decision; Kaldor/Hicks efficiency exists if the decision is approved by the majority, but where there are mechanisms to compensate the opposing minority; Pigou optimality corresponds to simple majority decisions. In terms of voting schemes (and assuming people vote according to their interests, which is not always the case)[5] one can say that the Pareto degrees of efficiency are secured through the requirement of unanimity; Kaldor/Hicks efficiency and Pigou optimality are achieved through some sort of majority voting.[6] Of course, in doing so we assume that each vote represents an equal interest. We do not take into account the intensity to which interests are affected. However, the relation between efficiency outcomes and efficiency decision-making procedures highlighted in efficiency studies stresses the interdependence between goals and institutions. Goals are about satisfying peoples interests and institutions are about how they express those interests and promote their satisfaction. What goals do is to define the community of those to be represented in a certain decision and the degree of protection that those interests deserve. Goals are more about institutional criteria than about balancing values (that can be made in different manners depending on the institutions that perform such balance).

In national systems (one-level systems) the debate about goals is mainly a debate about efficiency and re-distribution or equity. In a two-level system, such as the European Union, this picture is altered by the introduction of the

[4] Coleman speaks of the distinction between teleological (or consequentialist) modes of justification and consensual modes of justification. See: J.L. Coleman, "The Foundations of Constitutional Economics", in Richard B. Mckenzie (ed.), *Constitutional Economics—Containing the Economic Powers of Government* (Lexington, Massachussetts, Toronto, Lexington Books, 1984), at 141. See also the description of Pareto superiority, Pareto optimality and Kaldor-Hicks efficiency at 143–4.

[5] See R.S. Summers, "Comment", in *Constitutional Economics*, (n.4 above), at 160.

[6] Qualified majorities will represent some intermediary forms of efficiency.

concept of national diversity and the different (and legitimate) judgements of efficiency which it implies. Depending on the value accorded to national diversity, efficiency may have to be measured in national terms and not European ones. The optimal balance between free trade and legitimate interests (such as consumer and environment protection) may not be the same in different States, since, as we have seen, not everyone gives the same value to the same interest. Thus, for example, the value given to consumer protection may vary in different Member States, according to consumer behaviour, and to the general acceptance of higher or lower risks. This means that the Member States can make the best balance among all interests directly involved, without this necessarily leading to uniformity. Uniformity requires all States to make the same balance. It is an interest which goes beyond the capacity of each Member State to make the best balance among the different interests involved; since the optimal balance in State terms can be different from State to State, uniformity requires that some or all of States change that optimal balance.

A cost/benefit analysis such as the one that has dominated the application of Article 30 could be said to promote efficiency by balancing the costs and benefits of all the interests affected by a national legislation. The problem with this conception is that, as mentioned, there is no single and objective answer regarding efficient outcomes. It all depends on the concept of efficiency adopted, the community of interests taken into account and the scale and measurement mechanisms of the institution balancing the costs and benefits of a certain measure. We may even agree that the aim of regulatory policies to be reviewed under Article 30 is efficiency but this will not tell us much if we do not clarify to which type of efficiency are we referring and which is the better institution to perform that test of efficiency and balance the costs and benefits of regulations. To review national measures according to a goal of efficiency under cost/benefit analysis is in reality to replace one judgement of efficiency (that of national governments) for another judgement of efficiency (that of the European Court of Justice). This is why goals are of no use without comparing the institutions empowered to achieve them. Furthermore, decisions to review national measures in order to protect certain values (such as efficiency or even anti-protectionism) are in effect decisions on who is better to balance the costs and benefits of such measures.

The recognition of the complexity and variety of the values which have to be taken into account in balancing the costs and benefits of regulations, and of the legitimacy of the different efficient outcomes reached through different institutions, requires us to shift the analysis to institutional choices.

Institutions

Authors have tended to present judicial decisions on the review of national measures as grounded in the protection of certain values (anti-protectionism, efficiency, market integration). However, much of this discourse about values hides certain conceptions about the institutions related to those values. Many discussions about substantive decisions are, in reality, institutional discussions.

Let us take one example in Community law regarding one of the most well established legal values: equality under the law. Both the interpretation that has been made of Article 30 and other free movement rules, and the new approach to harmonisation, have given rise to a phenomenon identified in Community law as reverse discrimination. Reverse discrimination in Community law occurs when a State discriminates against its own nationals in favour of nationals of other Member States. Two main factors have been behind such cases of discrimination: first, when a non-discriminatory national measure is struck down by the Court because it is capable of restricting free movement, it is normally so only with respect to imported products, thus creating discrimination against national products;[7] secondly, the new approach to harmonisation is intended to establish common minimum requirements and mutual recognition of national regulations while, at the same time, allowing Member States to continue to impose stricter requirements on their own nationals, therefore creating reverse discrimination. The Court of Justice has accorded only a limited protection against reverse discrimination. In a nutshell, reverse discrimination is prohibited by the Court of Justice if it falls within the scope of Community law; but if the situation is purely internal to the State the Court refuses to intervene.[8] This has raised some debate in the legal literature since it authorises discrimination as a consequence of Community law. Authors tend to see reverse discrimination as a violation of

[7] As the Court recognised in *Mathot*: "with regard to Article 30 of the EEC Treaty, it must be emphasised that the purpose of that provision is to eliminate obstacles to the importation of goods and not to ensure that goods of national origin always enjoy the same treatment as imported goods": (Case 98/86, *Mathot* [1987] ECR 809, para 7). Thus, imported books in France cannot be subject to minimum prices but national books can (see Case 229/83, *Leclerc* [1985] ECR 1 and Case 355/85, *Cognet* [1986] ECR 3232); Beer imported to Germany may contain some additives that German beer may not (see Case 178/84, *Commission* v. *Germany* (German Beer Purity Law) [1987] ECR 1227); Italian pasta will still have to be made from durum wheat though Italian consumers can buy pasta not made from durum wheat imported into Italy from other Member States (see Case 407/85, *3 Glocken* v. *USL* (Pasta) [1988] ECR 4233, and the follow up by the Italian Constitutional Court: *Ditta Punto e Pasta c. Sindaco di Vicenza*, Corte costituzionale, Sentenza del gennaio 1994 n.27).

[8] The heart of this approach is, then, the definition of what constitutes a purely internal situation, not falling within the scope of Community law. The case law of the Court appears to be dependent on two main criteria to ascertain the connection of a particular fact with the Community legal order: the degree of legal integration, and the existence of a link with another Member State or the exercise of free movement. Such reading, however, is not straightforward and many doubts and criticisms can be raised with regard to such criteria. See, for example: Case 115/78, *Knoors* [1979] ECR 399; Case 136/78, *Auer* [1979] ECR 437; Case 175/78, *Saunders* [1979] ECR 1129; Case 180/83, *Moser* [1984] ECR 2539; Case 229/83, *Leclerc* (Prix du Libre) [1985] ECR 1; Case 98/86, *Mathot* [1987] ECR 809; Case 207/87, *Guy Bekaert* [1988] ECR 2029; Case C–61/89, *Bouchoucha* [1990] ECR I–3551; Case C–90/61, *Baptista Morais* [1992] ECR I–2085.

the principle of equality.[9] However, the same has not occurred in the case of legislative disparities that are in substance identical to reverse discrimination as a violation of the principle of equality; the argument will be made here that it is hidden institutional analysis that explains why legal scholarship has been so defiant towards reverse discrimination when compared to the much more peaceful acceptance of a similar form of regulatory competition: legislative disparities.

Legislative disparities and reverse discrimination both have in common the fact that States have different legislation with regard to the same subject, and that they have to accept each other's regulation, according to the principle of mutual recognition. They differ in that, in the case of reverse discrimination, one State applies different regulations to products within its jurisdiction from different States, whereas in the case of legislative disparities the different States apply different regulations to products within their jurisdictions that will then compete in each other's jurisdiction. In the former, one State applies two different laws to identical situations under its jurisdiction by reason of mutual recognition. In the latter, two States apply their respective and different laws to identical situations. For example, with regard to goods, legislative disparities concern factors involved in the production and costs of a product but which do not "accompany it" to another State; reverse discrimination concerns the characteristics and circumstances of marketing a product that accompany it to another State market. Thus labour law, company taxes, wages and environmental protection laws on production site all give rise to legislative disparities if they differ (as they normally do) among Member States. Professional qualifications, product requirements and marketing conditions (such as laws on labelling, packaging and advertising) may give rise to situations of reverse discrimination.

Legislative disparity has generally been much more easily accepted within the EU legal context than has reverse discrimination. A *prima facie* reason is that where there exist legislative disparities, for a State to apply its law to foreign products would be an extension of its legal jurisdiction to situations occurring in another jurisdiction; on the other hand, all a Member State has to do to prevent situations of reverse discrimination is to apply its law to identical situations occurring within its jurisdiction. However, this distinction between legislative disparities and reverse discrimination is largely a formal

[9] For the debate on reverse discrimination see: G. Druesne, "Remarques sur le champ d'application personnel du droit communautaire: des 'discriminations à rebours' peuvent-elles tenir en échec la liberté de circulation des personnes?", (1979) 15 *RTDE*, 427; Greenwood, "Limits on the Free Movement of Persons in EEC Law", (1987/1988) *Yearbook of European Law*, 185; J. d'Oliveira, "The Community Case—Is Reverse Discrimination Still Permissible Under the Single European Act", in *Forty Years on the Evolution of Post War Private International Law in Europe* (5 Centrum voor Buitenlands Recht en International Privaterecht Universiteit van Amsterdam, Kluwer); S.D. Kon, "Aspects of Reverse Discrimination", (1981) 6 *ELR*, 75; K. Mortelmans, "La discrimination à rebours et le droit communautaire", (1980) *Diritto Comunitário e degli Scambi Internazionale*, 1; D. Pickup, "Reverse Discrimination and the Freedom of Movement of Workers", (1986) 23 *CMLRev*, 135.

one. Substantively, both situations are very similar: in both cases some products are submitted to a competitive disadvantage by reason of their jurisdiction of origin; in both cases "competition among rules" takes place (through the choice of where to produce and what to buy). Moreover, that formal distinction does not apply in the realm of Community law legislative policy and its constitutional review. Community law has jurisdiction to prevent both legislative disparities and reverse discrimination when harmonisation rules are drafted. We would argue that the relatively low level of legal controversy over legislative disparities—when compared to that raised over reverse discrimination—is due to the different representative ability of the market and national political processes in the two cases. In other words, not all interests affected will express their preferences either in the market or the national political process. It is the different institutional performance of markets and national political processes in both settings that explains the higher deference given to legislative disparities, and not any substantial difference regarding the principle of equality.

In cases of reverse discrimination the group of people affected by it and the jurisdiction of the policy-maker do not coincide. Representative problems exist here, in that people cannot take into account all the costs and benefits of the regulation. A regulation of a State implies a balance between the production of public and private goods. What happens when the State regulation is subject to competition among rules with reverse discrimination is that such balance is altered by the rules of another State. For example, if a State must allow into its market products coming from other Member States which contain some nationally prohibited additives, the increase, as predicted by that State, in the production of public goods (in terms of consumer and health protection) will not occur (at least, to the extent expected). As a consequence, those who stood to benefit most from the national regulation, will not exert *voice* (buying the product or political participation) or *exit* (moving from legal and economic jurisdiction) in favour of the regulation. On the other hand, those regulated and burdened by its costs will find themselves more harmed by the regulation because they will be competing with products not subject to the regulation. They will have ever-greater incentives to exert voice and exit against the regulation. These representative problems are the same as those which economists call "externalities" or "information costs". In constitutional terms, both representation and accountability suffer from institutional malfunctions of the market and the national political processes in these circumstances. Cases of reverse discrimination must, however, be distinguished from cases of legislative disparity. Here, the costs and benefits of the regulation are concentrated on the jurisdiction enacting it. The costs involved in a decision to lower labour standards (reducing the production of public goods but increasing the production of private goods) are not transferable to another State by virtue of reverse discrimination. Under mutual recognition associated with legislative disparities, national products and persons will still compete subject to different rules but the different national balances between costs and benefits implicit in those rules remain unaltered and there is no transfer of such costs or benefits between States. It is these different institutional settings that explain why a derogation from the principle of equality is more easily accepted in the case of regulatory competition arising from legislative disparities than in the case of reverse discrimination.

It must be stressed, however, that the existence of higher institutional malfunctions in the case of reverse discrimination than in the case of legislative disparities does not mean that reverse discrimination should not be authorised and that the Court of Justice should intervene to prohibit it. Reverse discrimination and the allocation of powers it trusts to the market in promoting regulatory competition should be compared with its institutional alternatives. Those arguing for the European Court to put an end to reverse discrimination ignore both the values of diversity and competition it promotes and the institutional comparison necessary to determine who should decide the issue. Since this judgement implies a balance among national interests, national institutions are better suited and have more legitimacy to make that decision. It should be for the institutions of Member States to decide whether to compete even if by creating reverse discrimination. The Court of Justice approach to reverse discrimination is based on its trust in national political processes and courts to deal with their own nationals, while the same is not the case with regard to foreign nationals. The different legal debates on reverse discrimination and legislative disparities and the criticism of the Court's decision to limit its protection against reverse discrimination in Community law, are not a result of any substantive differences regarding the principle of equality but of different judgements regarding the institutions applying that principle in different circumstances.

The same institutional analysis can be made of economic due process or non-discrimination approaches to Article 30. The economic due process interpretation of Article 30 proposes a shift in the burden of resource allocation efficiency. It distrusts regulatory processes and views in voluntary market transactions an institutional setting able to produce more efficient decisions. Non-discrimination tests, in turn, entail a distrust in national political processes. They do not give away a cost and benefit analysis, they only determine that, only where there is discrimination, national cost/benefit analysis is to be replaced by the European Court's cost/benefit analysis. If this is so, then the test should concentrate on the institutional dimensions of protectionism and when is that institutional shift to occur. Traditional protectionism readings would argue that only where national political processes discriminate against foreign nationals is the Court authorised to replace national governments. But it is doubtful whether, taking into account the context of European Union integration, those should still be the only cases where the Court can legitimately replace national government's cost/benefit analyses.

ECONOMIC DUE PROCESS VERSUS ANTI-PROTECTIONISM

The intermix between goals and institutions becomes clear in the analysis of the two main alternative concepts behind the different interpretations given of Article 30: economic due process and anti-protectionism. Economic due process is linked with the constitutional model of competition described in the previous chapter. This model aims at promoting free competition and a liberal economy and society, entrusting to the market the leading role in the allocation of resources. Other institutional alternatives are generally distrusted: either because transaction or information costs do not allow them to take all interests into account or because of the fear of the concentration of powers they might entail or the risk that they may be captured by particular interests. Anti-protectionism is linked with the decentralised constitutional model also described in the previous chapter. This model aims at preventing anti-protectionism while leaving intact States' regulatory autonomy. National diversity is fully safeguarded because States could still regulate as they saw fit as long as such regulation would not discriminate between nationals of all Member States. National political processes are still identified as the best and more democratic institution to pursue goals such as efficiency. They will only need to be corrected in cases of protectionism.

As stated before, in the case law on Article 30, deepening and broadening progressed together. The consequence was that almost any State measure could be submitted to judicial review under the *Dassonville* test. The stress, mainly until the *Keck* decision, has been on the inability of restrictive tests (such as discrimination) to control State activities affecting the free movement of goods, and on the need for greater judicial control over national regulations. In my view both cost/benefit and discrimination tests have been unable to provide a sound normative foundation for the Court's review of State regulation of the market. There has been a general acceptance of the different levels of discretion employed by the Court in its case law. In doing so, they have failed to address the institutional choice inherent in the replacement of a State's assessment of the costs and benefits of a measure by the Court's assessment of those costs and benefits. Nor have they broached the question of the European Economic Constitution that should underlie any interpretation of Article 30 and its review of market regulation. To decide when the Court should balance between the costs and benefits of a measure and when this should be left to the Member States is a choice closely dependent on the position one takes regarding the European Economic Constitution and its relation with the rules of free movement. We have highlighted two different conceptions of the Economic Constitution of the Community or the European Union behind the control of the application of the rules of free movement, and especially behind the control of the application of Article 30. As already mentioned, in *Hünermund*, Advocate-General Thesauro has, finally, clearly set out this constitutional dilemma:

"Is Article 30 of the Treaty a provision intended to liberalize intra-Community trade or is it intended more generally to encourage the unhindered pursuit of commerce in individual Member States?"[10]

The first concept can be summed up by the idea that the aim of Article 30 is to prevent State protectionism. The second concept leads to the transformation of Article 30 into a kind of "economic due process" clause. Article 30 will be the core element of an Economic Constitution of the Union built on the free market, open competition, and a particular view of what kinds of regulation are acceptable. According to this concept, judicial review of national rules under Article 30 should assess State intervention in the market.

Although, as stated above, these concepts are not necessarily reflected in different interpretations being put forward for Article 30[11] they encapsulate the normative dilemma underlying this area of the law and its relation with the European Economic Constitution.

THE OPEN CHARACTER OF THE EUROPEAN ECONOMIC CONSTITUTION

The neo-liberal conception of the European Economic Constitution and its transformation of Article 30 into an economic due process clause can be subject to two main types of critique. The first, that will not be developed here, is strictly normative; it concerns the substance of the ordo-liberals economic programme and their conception of the way in which the market and the political process operate. Several of these problems involved in a ordo-liberal conception of the Economic Constitution have been discussed above in the analysis of the competitive model of the European Economic Constitution.

The second critique, is largely descriptive. It is argued that neo-liberal constructions of the European Economic Constitution find no reflection in European reality. As the majoritarian approach and the *Keck* decision demonstrate, no such concept of the European Economic Constitution has been adopted by the Court.[12] Moreover, there is no correspondence between ordo-liberal economic constitutional concepts and the constitutional traditions of Member States. Nor are such concepts reflected in any really dominant way in the text, or even the genesis, of the EC Treaty.[13] Finally, the "constitutional reaction" of Member States at the Community level to the deregulatory devel-

[10] Opinion of Advocate General Tesauro delivered on 27 October 1993 in Case C–292/92, *Hünermund* [1993] ECR I–6787.

[11] Balance tests, for example, have been argued on grounds going from anti-protectionism to "economic due process".

[12] See Chapter 3 above.

[13] See F.W. Scharpf, *Negative and Positive Integration in the Political Economy of European Welfare States*, Jean Monnet Chair Papers 28 (European University Institute, Florence, 1995), at 8–9 and references therein. According to Joerges, this was recognised by ordo-liberals themselves; see, C. Joerges, *The Market Without the State—States Without the Market: Two Essays on the Law of the European Economy*, EUI Working Paper LAW 96/2 (Florence, 1996), at 6.

opments provoked at national level by market integration goes against any such ordo-liberal or neo-liberal constructions of the European Economic Constitution.

It is true that the broad scope granted by the Court of Justice to market integration rules (notably Article 30) has prompted deregulatory consequences at national level. Nevertheless, the constitutional steps undertaken by the Member States both in the Single European Act and the Maastricht Treaty, were, in part, devoted to complementing for the erosion of national regulatory powers caused by market integration rules. This was already visible in the Single European Act. It promoted the construction of an internal market and the development of free movement and free competition, while at the same time restoring (or reinforcing) political and public authority over that process (mainly by enhancing Community decision-making). The Single European Act extended Community competences by widening its fields of action. Even more importantly, Community powers to develop regulatory policies were enhanced by the introduction of a new Article 100a.

The Treaty of Maastricht has struck a further blow to the liberal concept of European integration. Though primarily concerned with currency and monetary stability (something close to the liberals' heart, as it is considered essential to the protection and efficiency of the free market economy)[14] the Treaty on European Union has in effect reinforced pre-existing interventionist elements and created new forms and mechanisms for public intervention. Moreover, the Treaty stresses not only economic efficiency, but also social and redistributive values. It therefore calls for a broader concept of the European Economic Constitution and its relation to political values.[15]

[14] See: F. Böhm, "Rule of Law in a Market Economy", in Peacock and Willgerodt (eds.), *Germany's Social Market: Origins and Evolution* (London, Macmillan, 1989), at 56; D. Gerber, "Constitutionalising the Economy: German Neo-Liberalism, Competition Law and the 'New Europe'", (1994) 42 *American Journal of Comparative Law*, 25, at 46; Peacock and Willgerodt, "Overall View of the German Liberal Movement", in *Germany's Social Market* (above), at 8–9. Although they would not necessarily agree with the manner in which currency stability is ensured under the Maastricht Treaty—through fixed exchange rates, and later a single currency. Buchanan, for example, argues for a competition model among all national currencies with free convertibility: J. Buchanan, "Europe's Constitutional Opportunity", in *Europe's Constitutional Future*, Institute of Economic Affairs Readings, No 33 (1990), at 13–14. See also, A. Peacock and H. Willgerodt "Overall View of the German Liberal Movement" (above), at 9.

[15] Arguing that the Treaty on European Union adopts a mixed-economy system, see F. Snyder, "L'Economia Mista e La Nuova Costituzione Economica Dell'Unione Europea", Bozza provisoria per presentazione al seminario su L'Economia mista, oggi, CE.R.IS.DI., Palermo, le 10 e 11 aprile 1992. See also: F.W. Scharpf, *Negative and Positive Integration* (n.13 above), at 7, and C. Joerges, "European Economic Law, the Nation-State and the Maastricht Treaty", in Renaud Dehousse (ed.), *The European Union Treaty* (München, C.H. Beck, 1993), 29, at 53. For an even stronger conclusion see S. Simitis, "Dismantling or Strengthening Labour Law: The case of the European Court of Justice", (1996) 2 *ELJ*. Broadly, according to Sciarra, although "at the origins of the Community, social issues were selected as mere functions of a well functioning market" there has been a growing importance and autonomy of social policies that no longer validates "such a mechanical consequence": S. Sciarra, *European Social Policy and Labour Law—Challenges and Perspectives*, Collected Courses of the Academy of European Law, vol. IV, Book 1 (*Kluwer Law International*, 1995), 301, at 311.

This is recognised and criticised by ordo-liberal authors such as Streit and Mussler.[16] They argue that Community competencies were not only extended, but that its discretionary powers in exercising those competencies were also increased. Public intervention and distortions of competition are seen as unavoidable. Several factors explain this result. The first, and most obvious, is that the Maastricht Treaty was the outcome of political bargaining involving, among other things, an ideological compromise between liberal and interventionist concepts of the economy and of European integration. Secondly, the form and scope of action now given to the Union corresponds to traditional forms and fields of action of the Member States (which had in any case been progressively eroded by the application of the EC Treaty). Conferring those powers on the Union, while submitting them to the principle of subsidiarity, can thus be seen as a return to the *status quo ante* with regard to the relationship between public power and the market. Thirdly, those powers can be seen as complementing the powers granted in the area of monetary and macro-economic policies: they allow co-ordination, and in some cases may be important elements in guaranteeing co-operation by Member States in the pursuit of the goals of economic and monetary union.

All this undermines the legitimacy of a neo-liberal interpretation of the Treaty free movement and competition rules and the consequent "economic due process" interpretation of Article 30. The developments promoted by the Treaty on European Union have even led one author to speak of "the constitutional primacy of cohesion over free competition in open markets [giving rise to] an obligation on the part of the Court of Justice to give effect to such primacy within the limits imposed by Article 164".[17] In a more limited manner, one can agree with this same author that there is an inherent conflict between structural policies and orthodox competition policy based on open markets.[18] Broadly, it is possible to speak of a conflict between the values of economic and social cohesion and free market competition which underlie the Treaties upon which the Union is founded. One can describe this as the European Union representation of the traditional European "constitutional parity between the protection of economic freedom and market-correcting intervention".[19] Again, we are left with the question of when the Court should decide upon the balance to be set among those values. This question will be addressed later in this chapter.

16 See Streit and Mussler, "The Economic Constitution of the EC—From Rome to Maastricht", (1995) 1 *ELJ*, 5, mainly at 21–2. For a different interpretation but focused on European Monetary Union provisions, see I. Harden, "The Constitution of the European Union", (1994) Public Law, 609. In his opinion: "The institutions and procedures of EMU represent not just a significant step towards further European economic and political integration, but also a constitutional step away from the unconstrained discretionary economic power of the 'Keynesian State'": at 616.

17 Fraser, "The New Structural Funds, State Aids and Interventions on the Single Market", (1995) ELR, 3, at 16. But see also 14–17.

18 Ibid, at 4.

19 Scharpf, *Negative and Positive Integration* (n.13 above), at 10.

THE EUROPEAN ECONOMIC CONSTITUTION AND ANTI-PROTECTIONISM

Protectionism can be understood in quite different manners and different anti-protectionism tests have been constructed.[20] This may be misleading in at least two ways. On the one hand, if the focus is on the purpose of protectionism, one becomes engulfed in endless disputes of legislative intent. This also results in ignoring decisions where the legislature did not have any protectionist intentions but where, due to institutional malfunctions (such as the control of information and expertise by national interests), there is, in practice, a protectionist outcome. On the other hand, if the protectionist effects of regulations are analysed, one becomes involved in defining the fine line separating material discrimination and the legitimate regulation of trade. This leads to criticisms of regulatory measures which arguably represent the best balance among all the interests involved, including those of importers and non-nationals.

In any case, critics of anti-protectionist interpretations of Article 30 and free movement rules normally argue that, "the major problem in accepting a discrimination criterion is that it can all too easily be circumvented by legislation which is on its face applicable to domestic and imported products alike".[21] A common argument against anti-protectionist theories is based on the difficulty of discovering the purpose of protectionism. It is impossible to reconstruct the decision-making process leading to a State's regulation and thus to uncover the real motivations behind them. Anti-protectionism theories have thus developed more objective criteria, capable of unmasking protectionist policies (the result of protectionist intentions or other institutional malfunctions). The first is that of formal discrimination. Measures that discriminate against nationals of other Member States are normally intended to protect home nationals at the expense of foreign nationals; these should not be accepted or should at least be subject to closer scrutiny. Nevertheless, many measures whose costs fall for the main part on foreign nationals have an appearance of formal equality in order to evade this first line of discrimination analysis. This leads to a second criterion of material discrimination or protectionist effects. In this case, the subject of examination is not intent or formal discrimination, but rather the effects of state measures. If state measures place a heavier burden on foreign nationals than on home nationals, they are considered to be materially discriminatory and as having protectionist effects; they should therefore be considered *prima*

[20] See, also, the discussion on discrimination tests in Chapter 2 above and the analysis of the decentralised model in Chapter 4 above.

[21] L.W. Gormley, "'Actually or Potentially, Directly or Indirectly'? Obstacles to the Free Movement of Goods", (1989) 9 *Yearbook of European Law*, 196, at 198. Also, in *Prohibiting Restrictions on Trade within the EEC* (Amsterdam, Elsevier Science Publishers BV), at 14. See also, for example, A. Mattera, *Le Marché Unique* (Jupiter, 1988), at 191–2; M. Waelbroeck, *Les réglementations nationales de prix et le droit communautaire* (Bruxelles, Editions de L'Universite de Bruxelles, 1975), at 27.

facie inadmissible. However, problems arise even here.[22] It is difficult to assess protectionist effects. For instance, a higher burden imposed on imports may not be so much a direct result of the legislation but more a consequence of the distribution of national and imported products in the market. To identify whether a legislative classification, having a higher impact upon imports than upon domestic products, is necessary or not inevitably involves policy judgements in relation to that classification; and almost all national legislation has a different impact on domestic and imported goods, as a result of imports having to comply with a different set of rules. These problems explain why a test based on protectionist effects either allows States to continue to develop sophisticated protectionist policies, or, in order to prevent such policies, becomes more like a balance test. Arguments based on the failure of classic anti-protectionism tests to prevent protectionism in practice are put forward to support proportionality as the best test to fight it.[23] For others, however, anti-protectionism is simply too restrictive, since the aim of the Treaty is to eliminate State restrictions on trade independently of whether those restrictions also affect national products.[24]

It must also be decided whether all measures having protectionist effects are invalid or whether the test for anti-protectionism should be complemented by criteria determining which measures with protectionist effects are valid. (For example, should there be a decision to uphold a protectionist measure whose benefits outweigh its costs against the alternative of a non-protectionist measure which has a lower net benefit or no benefit at all?). In effect, anti-protectionist theories are complemented by a balance test. In such cases, anti-protectionism is not the sole criterion used in reviewing State measures, but it is the *first*: if a state measure is found to be protectionist, it will then be submitted to cost/benefit analysis. As a consequence, the anti-protectionist test does not prevent a balance test, but limits its use by the Court: the proportionality of a measure will only be assessed if that measure is discriminatory or protectionist. This is a workable construction of Articles 30 and 36, one which recognises that it is impossible to avoid balancing. However, it does not avoid all the problems mentioned above in the initial assessment of protectionism effects. Moreover, it is bound to create some confusion between the test for protectionism and the assessment of proportionality. Most importantly, it raises a fundamental question: if the Court is the more appropriate and legitimate institution, in the second stage, to balance all the interests and values involved, why is this not always the case? In other words, *what gives the Court legitimacy in balancing the costs and benefits of protectionist or discriminatory measures, and why should this legitimacy not apply in other cir-*

[22] For a critique of the protectionist effects test, see D.H. Regan, "The Supreme Court and State Protectionism: Making Sense of the Dormant Commerce Clause", (1986) 84 *Michigan Law Review*, 1091, at 1130.

[23] See, for example, Mattera, *Le Marché Unique* (n.21 above), at 191–2.

[24] For example, Waelbrock, *Les réglementations* (n.21 above), at 28.

cumstances? This shifts the discussion into the area of comparative institutional analysis, since it demonstrates that *protectionism is not a substantive criterion upon which a review of national measures can be based, but is rather a factor of legitimation for the Court in applying a balance test.* The protectionism test does not tell us which measures are acceptable and which are not. Rather, it determines which measures are to be subject to balance and which are not. The issue is not one of avoiding a balance test; balancing will also take place under a protectionism or discrimination test. Instead, the question is when can the Court legitimately apply the balance test.

The concern over protectionism is relevant because it illustrates the mistrust with which Member States' legislative processes are viewed in certain circumstances. What we should therefore be looking for is a test to determine when the State is the best (or legitimate) institution to balance the costs and benefits of a measure and when, instead, the best institution is the Court. Concerns over protectionism can help us determine the circumstances in which we can or cannot trust States to regulate. In this sense, the test which will be set out at the end of this book can be related to a sophisticated construction of anti-protectionism as well as to anti-discrimination and improved representation for all affected interests. As will be argued, however, it involves a constitutional construction of the European Union and a broader body of values than those embodied in anti-protectionism.

BEYOND ANTI-PROTECTIONISM: THE POLITICAL ASPECTS OF EUROPEAN INTEGRATION AND THE CONSTITUTIONALISATION OF EUROPEAN COMMUNITY LAW

The above requires that we refine the critique of anti-protectionist concepts of European Community law by redefining the values involved in European integration and the character of Community law. The European Union and its legal order can no longer be explained as a free trade area or in terms of international trade law. The construction of the internal market, as well as of European integration and its constitutional foundations, involves a large body of new values which go well beyond those dated concepts of the Treaty.

As odd as it may sound, these new values may even justify some sort of protectionism. In an article entitled "The Selfish State and the Market", Gergen comments, "it is a maxim of constitutional law that states may not discriminate against citizens of other states to enrich their own citizens. But, like many supposed truths, this maxim is subject to exception. States may seek the advantage for their citizens in a variety of ways, some of which entail discrimination".[25] That states may discriminate in favour of their own nationals is often disregard in European discussions on the regulatory powers of

[25] M.P. Gergen, "The Selfish State and the Market", (1988) 66 *Texas Law Review*, 1097.

Member States and the effects on trade of such powers. However, the protection of nationals, even to the disadvantage of nationals of other Member States, not only forms part of the concept of state sovereignty that the European Union has not completely destroyed, but is also a function of the State's existence. The existence of States, as identifiable political communities, only makes sense as long as those political communities express a greater degree of solidarity with their members than with non-members. This solidarity necessarily results in some sort of preference or discrimination in favour of members of that political community *vis-à-vis* the members of other political communities. This problem is particularly acute in the European Union, since the effects of Community primary law have spilled over into areas of national law which do not principally concern the regulation of trade among the Member States. If the scope of the rules on free movement had remained within the realm of traditional international trade law, there would have been only a small risk of affecting general State policies and the values they embody. However, that is not the case, and an extended jurisdiction of Community market rules should result in an extension of the values to be taken into account in applying those rules. This includes the protection of a State's own nationals (for instance, the economic and social protection of weaker national social groups).[26]

As Gergen notes, referring to the interpretation given by the United States Supreme Court to the commerce clause, the conflict between a State's legitimate exercise of sovereign powers to protect (favour) its nationals and the requirement of equality among all Union citizens (nationals of all Member States) means that some State protectionism will have to be considered as legitimate and acceptable.[27] Clearly, two things are necessary to determine when protectionism or discrimination is acceptable: firstly a balancing of the costs of protectionism and the benefits of the State's legitimate interests; secondly, criteria to define which of these interests are preferred by the European Union and how they can be assessed in relation to their costs.[28] As stated, such criteria involves European constitutional values going beyond anti-protectionism. This cannot be assessed under an anti-protectionism test. The fundamental problem remains: if the only value protected by the free movement of goods is anti-protectionism, on which values should the Court base its decision when balancing the costs and benefits of protectionist or discriminatory legislation? It is better to recognise that a balance will always have to be set and thus to define who should make this decision in different situations. This will allow a larger body of values to be taken into account in the legal and judicial discourses. It will, for example, allow

[26] We understand the problems in introducing such reasoning through Article 36; and for that reason believe this problem must be addressed at its origins: the scope of Article 30 and other free movement rules.

[27] Gergen, "The Selfish State and the Market" (n.25 above), at 1101.

[28] From a pure legal dogmatic point of view, it also requires a more "elastic" interpretation of Article 36.

clearly recognition and discussion of the balance between free movement and social values: a question which the conflict between national regulations and Community internal market rules has brought to light.[29] Furthermore, it will promote a debate on those values and their position within the European Economic Constitution.

At the same time, however, it is argued that rather than going too far in restricting State powers, anti-protectionism does not in fact go far enough. The motivation for this criticism is also related to the constitutional transformation of the Community and the broad body of values it now represents. The anti-protectionist reading of the Treaties is based on an understanding of Treaty rules as regulating interstate conflicts. The concept of anti-protectionism is associated with commercial relations among States and the forms of regulation of international trade. It does not take into account developments in Treaty rules with respect to individual rights. Nor does it consider the creation of a European Constitution and a European citizenship. Furthermore, it does not reflect the complexity of the Union's goals, which go far beyond the establishment of a free trade area or even an internal market. Social and cultural values must be introduced into the "economics-dominated" discourse of free movement rules. In the same way, the development of political integration in turn requires the development of political rights. This is also a normal consequence of a Union whose aims are no longer wholly, or at least only, directed towards the satisfaction of the interests of its Member States, but towards the people of those States as citizens of the Union. The test adopted in the interpretation of Article 30 must mirror such development.

A CONSTITUTIONAL LAW APPROACH TO ARTICLE 30

Article 30: a fundamental political right

In the recent *Bosman* decision the Court once more restated the status of free movement rules as "fundamental freedoms".[30] As we have seen, ordo-liberal conceptions of the European Economic Constitution require that free movement rules be constructed as economic freedoms limiting both the competences and powers of States and supra-national institutions. Moreover, this is the basis of the legitimacy of European law and of its constitutional foundations.

As argued above, no such interpretation of the European Economic Constitution is reflected in the legal sources or in the political workings of the European Union. However, not reading the European Economic Constitution as a neo-liberal programme does not mean that Article 30 cannot be seen as

[29] See, P. Davies, "Market Integration and Social Policy in the Court of Justice", (1995) 24 *Industrial Law*, 49.

[30] Case C–415/93, *Bosman* [1995] ECR I–4921.

a fundamental economic freedom. Such economic freedom need not be given the *laissez faire* element for which the neo-liberals argue. It can instead correspond to the economic freedoms found in different national constitutions of European States the content of which has been defined by constitutional law theory and constitutional courts in a much looser sense than that by which neo-liberal "orthodoxy" understands free movement rules. This is not, however, what is being argued here. A European Constitution does require a body of fundamental economic rights or freedoms (limiting, if necessary, public intervention in the market) in parallel to those normally found in national constitutions; however, this is not the role in which to cast Article 30. There are two reasons. First, the status of the free movement of goods in the construction of the internal market and in the review of State regulation thereunder might make other values instrumental to that interpretation of Article 30. There is a risk of giving such fundamental economic freedoms a status higher than that awarded to other fundamental rights and values in the Community legal order. This would then exacerbate the spill-over of market integration values into other areas of the law. At the very least, it would increase the phenomenon to which Hepple refers when he states that "the normative hierarchy of national constitutional rights, international and European conventions on human rights, and the economic freedoms which form the foundation of the Community, has become confused and ambiguous".[31] Secondly, it would place an undue burden on Article 30, namely reviewing all kinds of public regulations in the market. It is this author's opinion that the construction of Article 30 as a fundamental right should instead focus on enhancing the representation of the interests of nationals of other Member States within national political processes.

Article 30 and the rules on free movement are essential instruments in the distribution of power within the Constitutional order of the Union, and they should be treated as such. In this sense, they can be seen as rules on competences within the European Constitution. The review of States' regulatory measures distributes power both between the Member States and the market, and between Member States and the European Union political process. Such a distribution of power should take into account concerns over the separation of powers and the body of values to be promoted through the creation and regulation of a single market. The concept of fundamental economic freedoms as well as the development of fundamental social rights[32] will play a role in the interpretation of this body of values. This, in turn, will have an impact on Article 30 whenever "balancing" takes place.

[31] B. Hepple, "Social Values and European Law", (1995) 48 Current Legal Problems, 39, at 46.

[32] In arguing for the development of European fundamental social rights (that however must be considered, already, as part of the "constitutional traditions common to Member States" to which the Court refers) see Hepple, ibid, and Blanpain, Hepple, Sciarra and Weiss, *Fundamental Social Rights: Proposals for the European Union* (Leuven, Walter Lëen Fonds, 1996).

Our current proposal, however, goes beyond a "rule of competences" conception of Article 30. By attributing to it a role of correction of national political processes *vis-à-vis* representation of the nationals of other Member States, we maintain a fundamental rights conception of the free movement rules. This proposal places the emphasis on the political values of non-discrimination, representation and solidarity between States, rather than on the market freedom of economic agents. Free movement will be a political fundamental right, not an economic fundamental right. This difference is based in two contrasting concepts of the constitutional development of the European Union and its legitimacy. Those arguing for an "economic fundamental rights" conception of free movement rules assume a European Constitution founded on market rules and legitimised by the limits it imposes on public power. On the other hand, we argue here for the open character of the European Economic Constitution, the economic model and powers of which will be the result of a discursive process.[33] At the same time, individuals acquire new rights to participate in that discourse, notably through the extension of their "voice" into the political processes of other Member States. In this way, the free movement rules will also promote the development of and criteria for solidarity among the Member States, while building upon the concept of European citizenship.[34] This would allow the European Union to develop its particular form of legitimacy, independently of a State model and traditional majoritarian democracy. Instead, it would be based on a concept of democracy for the European Union that "is not only or even mainly given by the majority rule applied to political decisions, but eminently by the existence of a public domain of free discussion".[35]

[33] Elements of which are already present in the relation between European Union legal order and national legal orders but need to be developed and enhanced. Moreover, much of the democratisation debate of the European Union should turn instead on how to make more democratic such a discursive process.

[34] The best basis for which may well be that recently proposed by Weiler in two articles: J.H.H. Weiler, "Does Europe Need a Constitution? Demos, Telos and the German Maastricht Decision", (1995) 1 *European Law Journal*, 219 and Weiler with Haltern and Mayer, "European Democracy and Its Critique", (1995) 18 *West European Politics*, 4. In these articles, European citizenship is conceived and valued as different from traditional State citizenship. It is not dependent on an organic link with a community but on a civic understanding of the European *demos* independent of belongingness to an ethno-cultural identity. The advantage of the co-existence of those two forms of citizenship (national—ethno-cultural; European—civic) is that they would mutually check each other, thus creating what Weiler defines as "critical citizenship". This conception fits well with the discursive model here being argued for the European Union Constitution. The next and extremely difficult endeavour is to define the model and forms of that constitutional discourse. In any case, the concept of European citizenship must have a fundamental role in the democratic structure of that constitutional discourse by promoting the broadest participation and representation possible, starting in national political processes.

[35] M. La Torre, "Constitution, Citizenship and the European Union", paper presented at the Conference on European Citizenship: An Institutional Challenge, EUI, (Florence 13–15 June 1996), at 20. For a critique to the "majoritarian avenue" see R. Dehousse, "Constitutional Reform in the European Community: Are there Alternatives to the Majoritarian Avenue", (1995) 18 *West European Politics*, 118.

Article 30: reforming national political processes

We have already defined the European Economic Constitution as an open constitution with different competitive values, ranging from free competition to economic and social cohesion. The judicial review of market regulation under free movement of goods rules will have to reflect a balance among those values. At the same time, we have also noted that there is an intersection on those rules of the division of powers between Member States, the Union and the Market. The complexity lies in the fact that the debates on *centralisation versus decentralisation*[36] and *regulation versus deregulation* overlap. The values at stake therefore get confused, with the risk that some will be ignored. The adoption of a cost/benefit or balance test for Article 30 entails the danger that such overlapping will be neglected, and the *centralisation versus decentralisation* question will be subordinated to the *regulation versus deregulation* decision, or vice versa. This is so because any Community judgement taken on a cost/benefit analysis of the reasonableness of States' policy choices immediately assumes the hierarchy of values, the mechanisms of measurement and the interests inherent to the Community system. Thus, immediately subjecting State measures to cost/benefit analysis is to subject the decision on centralisation versus decentralisation to a centralised decision on regulation versus deregulation. To argue otherwise is to believe that a cost/benefit analysis is an objective process. In fact, cost/benefit analysis depends on the institution that makes the decision and the context in which that decision is made. In other words, it is not possible to say that a State can keep its policy autonomy when its regulations pass a Community cost/benefit analysis, without at the same time overruling such policy autonomy.[37] Our proposal is to safeguard such policy autonomy by allowing States to perform different cost/benefit analyses, on the basis of different values and different measurement mechanisms. At the same time, limits and constraints should be imposed on that process, intended to introduce the interests of foreign nationals into these national policy-making processes.

[36] It would, perhaps, be more accurate to describe the dilemma as *integration versus disintegration*, because it refers both to positive integration (centralisation) and negative integration (free movement). Scharpf defines negative integration as "measures increasing market integration by eliminating national restraints on trade and distortions of competition" and positive integration as "common European policies to shape the conditions under which markets operate, on the other hand": Scharpf, *Negative and Positive Integration* (n.13 above), at 1.

[37] This is the dilemma faced by theories proposing a wide scope to be given to Article 30 in order to promote market integration and not economic deregulation (for a recent example see S. Weatherhill, "After *Keck*: Some Thoughts on How to Clarify the Clarification", (1996) 33 *CMLRev*, 885, notably at 896–7). These theories, proposing to maintain a cost/benefit test in the review of any State measures with an effect on market integration, though attractive in their refinement and their goal, in practice rule in favour of uniformity against diversity. They promote harmonisation through the judicial process, as appeared to be the policy of the Court of Justice prior to *Keck*.

Whichever institution is called upon to regulate the common market will come across a variety of goals reflected in the European Union sources, and will have to face different consumer and production traditions in all Member States. In setting regulation, the position and interests of all market agents (both producers and consumers) should be taken into consideration. As is clear from the different Treaty rules, the creation of an internal market is intended to enhance the gains arising from free trade, while at the same time safeguarding other legitimate interests. Burdens on trade are generally a less effective resource allocation, both for production (as illustrated, for example, by the loss of economies of scale and by companies being diverted from the optimal place of production) and for consumers (in the form of higher prices and fewer choices). Resources that could be better employed in other activities are lost. The costs of non-protection or less efficient protection of other goals depend, naturally, on those goals. For the protection of consumers or of the environment, for example, the costs of under-regulation are not simply the harm caused to consumers. They extend to the harm caused to competing companies which maintain higher standards and which lose trade, not as a result of a rational and informed decision by the consumer but because consumers are ill-informed. Equally important are the costs imposed on society itself in terms of such things as expenditure on health and social security, and the cost of cleaning the environment. In some cases (health care, for instance) these interests are highly unquantifiable. Their quantification must be made in terms of acceptable risks or, in other words, based on the maximum an individual will be willing to pay in order to diminish such a risk.

The criticisms of the "economic due process" and anti-protectionism theories of Article 30 demonstrated that the European Court of Justice is bound to balance all the values involved in the regulation versus deregulation and centralisation versus decentralisation debates, within the context of that article. Those criticisms also showed that the Court neither should nor can make that balance in all cases.

A second important conclusion is that different institutions may reach different and equally legitimate and efficient balances of the values concerned. The institutional setting, and the procedures according to which a decision is taken, thus lead to different outcomes. Since institutions differ, we must expect the results they produce to differ as well; but we should require that "balance" should be determined in each institution through consideration of all the interests affected.

One can conclude from what has been argued that a balance will always be made; the best way to take into account a broader body of European constitutional values is to recognise and openly undertake such balance; substantive criteria intending to limit balance (such as protectionist tests) are in effect hidden institutional criteria concerning when the Court should carry out the balance. One should therefore concentrate on developing a true institutional criterion, enquiring as to when it is legitimate for the Court to replace the balance of Member States; such criterion should take into account, as underlined, the need to increase the representation of nationals of other Member States in a State's political processes as well as respect for national diversity and policy-autonomy.

Since different Member States can produce different, efficient regulatory decisions, there must be a meta-decision on when is efficiency going to be pursued under diversity (maintaining different national rules) or when it is to be pursued under uniformity (establishing common rules). By attributing regulatory powers to Member States and the Community political process the Treaty seeks to set a balance between diversity and uniformity. Member States are expected to reach the best balance according to a diversity-efficiency concern, while, at the same time, the Community political process is expected to demand uniformity when this is necessary, and to reach the best balance in those terms. Since Member States alone (without co-ordination or a central institution) can never achieve the best balance in terms of uniformity, it is not legitimate to review the exercise of regulatory powers accorded to them under the Treaty by means of a uniformity test. Uniformity should not be achieved in this way, but through co-operation among States, market processes and, as intended in the Treaty, through the Community political process.

At the same time, we can no longer allow Member States to take decisions from a purely national perspective. State regulation is now almost always regulation of the common market as well. Within the framework of the European Economic Constitution, Member States should take all interests affected into account when regulating the common market. This includes out-of-State interests. Member States should be able to make different policy judgements. What we should not permit is that they ignore out-of-States interests in the making of those judgements. The policy autonomy of individual States should be linked to political solidarity among States and to the new political rights and status that a European Constitution will grant to all "European citizens". On the one hand, as Joerges comments:

> "The taming of the nation-state through democratic constitutions has the potential of ensuring that the common good will be defined in a legitimate way . . . [b]ut the legitimacy which the economic law of the democratic nation-state can claim, rests upon processes in which only the members of the national community participate . . . There is no built in protection against one-sided definitions of economic objectives and the common good".[38]

On the other hand , as the same author notes: "The logic of European integration cannot claim *a priori* superior legitimacy when it dismantles national concerns in the name of market integration".[39] One of the advantages of the present proposal is that it does not assume *a priori* that market integration is more legitimate than State regulation. Rather, it operates at the level of the

[38] Joerges, "European Economic Law" (n.15 above), at 12.
[39] Ibid.

correction of State legitimacy problems. It is not intended to replace national policy-making with market integration rationality, but to correct and improve national policy-making so as to expand its democratic basis. This would require Member States to internalise within their national political processes all the interests affected by their regulation of the common market or, alternatively, to include national interests which can represent out-of-State interests within their national political processes.

Whenever a State's political process can demonstrate some form of representation of all the interests affected by a decision, it is possible to expect the decision reached to meet a criterion of optimal-diversity. In this case, the operation of the State's political process will come close to its "ideal" form, as conceived in the Treaties.

The risk inherent in State regulations is that they will be *biased* by an institutional environment that often neglects, or simply cannot in practical terms take into account, the interests of nationals of other Member States. In contrast, positive harmonisation measures (in the form of Community legislation) may be required for the purposes of uniformity, but may suffer from the opposite *bias* of being decided in a institutional environment which tends to neglect the interests of consumers and producers in a minority of Member States (this is becoming more problematic as the use of majoritarian voting increases).

With respect to the review of State measures under Article 30, the risk is that national regulations will suffer from what could be called national bias. The basis for this would be the over-representation of national interests (with respect to out-of-State interests) in the State political processes. This does not mean that every decision made in this context is wrong or inefficient; it simply means that the political process suffers from an institutional malfunction which could allow the over-represented interests to benefit disproportionally at the expense of the under-represented interests.[40]

National bias is not dependent on legislative intent, but on institutional malfunctions. The most important factor is the presence of all interests involved in a regulatory decision within the structures of the political process which receives and processes information. If a legislature tends to ignore out-of-State interests, it is mainly because it does not consider and respond to those interests. The legislature is politically accountable to its own nationals (even if it is the "prisoner" of certain special interest groups, those groups are usually domestic ones). As a result, decisions will normally correspond to those interests. Even if out-of-State interests exert some pressure in the political process, this pressure will rarely be constant. It will thus be ineffective in face of the other interests.

This does not mean that the State political processes will always suffer from national bias. First, there are circumstances in which out-of-State interests are

[40] The language used here follows quite closely that developed in a different context by Komesar, *Imperfect Alternatives—Choosing Institutions* in *Law, Economics and Public Policy* (Chicago and London, The University of Chicago Press, 1994) (and see Chapter 4 above).

at least as well represented in the political process as are national interests. This may be, for instance, by reason of their economic importance in the national economy. Moreover, and more often, out-of-State interests may be the same as domestic interests. In this way, they will be represented through the corresponding domestic interests. National bias will only occur, in these circumstances, if a State discriminates between those joint domestic and non-national interests.

The test proposed

In this author's view, any solution regarding the interpretation and application of Article 30 in the review of State measures must take into account problems of legitimacy: decisions of Member States that affect the free movement of goods can thus be seen as affecting interests not normally represented in the national political process. At the same time, decisions by the Court on the validity of a regulatory measure under the rules of free movement of goods implies playing a legislative role, with all the associated risks.

We have argued that Article 30 does not direct the Court of Justice to review the degree of public intervention in the market and that, moreover, an interpretation in this sense would undermine the legitimacy and stretch the resources of the Court. We have also argued against a "hidden" uniformisation of national regulations through Article 30, as would result from the subjugation of State measures to "European-constructed" policy judgements. However, to interpret Article 30 as only prohibiting protectionist measures is no longer sufficient in the present stage of European integration. The existence of a common market and the political dimension of European integration means that all decisions which concern that market should take all affected interests into account. It is suggested that the Court of Justice should not second-guess national regulatory choices, but should instead ensure that there is no under-representation of the interests of nationals of other Member States in the national political process. As it will not be possible for the Court of Justice to carry out case by case assessments to identify such representative malfunction in the national political process, tests must be designed to identify suspect measures.[41]

In this regard, it is possible to individuate two types of interests affected by national measures which interfere with the free movement of goods: cross-national interests and national interests. For the former, the interests affected are uniform throughout the Community. For the latter, the interests affected

[41] Of course, measures discriminating against foreign interest are *prima facie* suspected of national bias. This does not mean that all these measures will be struck down. As noted, the test proposed only identifies when the Court is to be authorised to replace its cost/benefit analysis for that of Member States. Even if a measure is brought under balance review due to national bias, it may still pass the Court's cost/benefit test.

diverge throughout the Community. If the interests regulated by a national measure are equal in the different Member States, then there is no suspicion of over-representation of national interests or under-representation of the interests of nationals of other Member States. That is the case with many national measures regulating market circumstances, which may explain the bias in their favour illustrated in *Keck*. For instance, the interests affected by a regulation prohibiting door-step selling of educational material or by a regulation prohibiting the sale of sex articles in non-licensed establishments are not national or foreign in nature. The interests of nationals of other Member States will be represented in the national political process by the same national interests. However, there are also national measures on market circumstances that do not regulate uniform interests. Examples of this type of measure include those that impose geographical limits on the marketing of goods or which set price controls on traditional national products. Under this test, these would *prima facie* be caught by Article 30 without having to find proof of discrimination.

Rules on the characteristics of products often tend to affect divergent national and foreign interests. It is sufficient to think of all national measures that regulate the composition of traditional national products or which correspond to the particular forms of production established in a particular Member State. However, in the case of product requirements of a technical nature (such as rules on additives for example) which are not part of national production habits, the same risk does not arise. Legislation aiming to regulate a recently discovered environmental or health risk would be included in this category.

To sum up, if a national measure regulates uniform or cross-national interests it will not *prima facie* fall under Article 30. In this case, a national measure should only be submitted to a balance test by the Court if it is shown to be discriminatory. The outcome of this proposal will be that the Court of Justice will only review national regulatory policies where there is a suspicion of representative malfunction in the national political process with regard to nationals of other Member States.[42] In all other cases, national regulatory policies may only be reviewed by the European Union political process.

CONSTITUTIONAL MODELS AND THE LEGITIMACY OF EUROPEAN LAW

The institutional choices regarding the allocation of regulatory powers that can be detected in different interpretations of Article 30, and its co-ordination with Treaty rules on harmonisation, may be represented in the three ideal constitutional models reviewed in Chapter 4: the centralised, the competitive

[42] There may be other representative problems or institutional malfunctions in the national political process which, however, cannot be dealt in the context of Article 30. In many cases they are better dealt with by national courts.

and the decentralised models. All these visions of the European Economic Constitution, their legitimacy and the regulatory models they reflect on present problems and potential institutional malfunctions. At this point, no particular model has been adopted. Instead, the future of the European Economic Constitution probably lies in an ongoing discourse involving these different models. Lawyers should concentrate on the shaping of this discourse. An important effort is required in the area of constitutional legal theory. More than a new constitution, Europe needs a new constitutionalism.[43] European integration forces us to rethink constitutional legal theory. First, European integration, coupled with the process of globalisation and other economic and social phenomena, has stressed the need to rethink traditional economic models; it has highlighted the crisis of national economic models and has required that we conceive of new forms of constitutional relationships between public power and the economy.[44] Secondly, European integration not only challenges national constitutions (the usual terms of the debate); it challenges constitutional law itself. It assumes a constitution, without a traditional political community defined and presupposed by that constitution; or it requires a new form of political community. European integration also challenges the legal monopoly of States and the hierarchical organisation of the law (in which constitutional law is conceived of as the "higher law"). Moreover, supremacy of the law is also challenged by concepts such as "competition among States" or "competition among rules" in which the law is subject to a process of market competition. These and other questions require a new constitutional legal theory.

This new European constitutionalism must create a constitutional framework for the institutional and legal discourses already taking place in the European Union. It must provide a methodological tool for the constitutional analysis of the institutional alternatives of market regulation in the European market expressed in the three constitutional models described above. It must also develop criteria of legitimacy for those choices, and European law and its relationship with national law. While analysing Article 30 of the EC Treaty from the point of view of the European Economic Constitution, we have attempted to take two steps in the direction of this new constitutionalism. First, we have suggested the importance of institutional choices and comparative institutional analysis as an analytical framework for the institutional and legal discourses of constitutional relevance taking place in the European Union. Secondly, we have sketched an alternative form of legitimacy for European law and its relation with national law and democracy, based on the promotion of the political rights of participation and representation of European citizens in national political processes.

[43] See J. Weiler, "Does Europe Need a Constitution? Demos, Telos and the German Maastricht Decision", (1995) 1 *ELJ*, 219, mainly at 220.

[44] As stated by Harden: "the emergent principles of the [European Union] constitution involve a transformation of the relationship between the public power and the economy that has typified the twentieth century state": I. Harden, "The Constitution of the European Union", (1994) *Public Law*, 609, at 610.

Bibliography

ALEXI, Robert, *A Theory of Legal Argumentation* (Oxford, Clarendon Press, 1989); English translation of *Theorie der juristischen Argumentation* (Surkamp Verlag, 1978)

ALMEIDA, Moutinho, *Direito Comunitário—A Ordem jurídica Comunitária—As Liberdades Fundamentais na CEE* (Lisboa, Centro de Publicações do Ministério da Justiça, 1985)

ALTER, Karen J., *The European Court and National Courts—Doctrine and Jurisprudence: Legal Change in its Social Context, Explaining National Court Acceptance of European Jurisprudence. A Critical Evaluation of Theories of Legal Integration*, EUI Working Paper RSC No. 95/27

—— and MEUNIER-AITSAHALIA, S., "Judicial Politics in the European Community–European Integration and the Pathbreaking Cassis de Dijon Decision", (1994) 26 *Comparative Political Studies*, 535

ARNULL, Anthony, "What Shall We do on Sunday", (1991) 16 *ELR*, 112

BALL, Carlos A., "The Making of a Transnational Capitalist Society: The Court of Justice, Social Policy, and Individual Rights Under the European Community's Legal Order", (1996) 37 *Harvard International Law Journal*, 307

BENGOETXEA, Joxerramo, *The Legal Reasoning of the European Court of Justice* (Oxford, Clarendon Press, 1993)

BERLIN, Dominique, "Interactions Between the Lawmaker and the Judiciary within EEC", (1992) LIEI, 17

BERNARD, N., "Discrimination and Free Movement in EC Law", (1996) 45 *International and Comparative Law Quarterly*, 82

—— "The Rights of the Individual in the Internal Market: Rights to Free Movement or Rights to Deregulation?", Paper at the SPTL Conference, Cambridge, 17 September 1996

BETTATI, M., "Le 'Law-Making Power' de la Cour", (1989) 48 *Pouvoirs*, 57

BLANPAIN, HEPPLE, SCIARRA and WEISS, *Fundamental Social Rights: Proposals for the European Union* (Leuven, Walter Leen Fonds, 1996)

BÖHM, Franz, "Rule of Law in a Market Economy", in Alan Peacock and Hans Willgerodt (eds.), *Germany's Social Market Economy: Origins and Evolution* (London, Macmillan Press, 1989)

BOOM, Steve J., "The European Union After the Maastricht Decision: Will Germany Be The 'Virginia of Europe' ", (1995) 43 *The American Journal of Comparative Law*, 177

BUCHANAN, James M., "Europe's Constitutional Opportunity", in *Europe's Constitutional Future* (London, 33 Institute of Economic Affairs Readings, 1990)

BUENDIA SIERRA, José, "Las secuelas del caso 'Cassis de Dijon'. Libre circulacion de productos alimenticios y reglementaciones nacionales", (1989) 16 *Revista de Instituciones Europeas*, 135

BURLEY, Anne-Marie and MATTLI, Walter, "Europe Before the Court: A Political Theory of Legal Integration", (1993) 47 International Organization, 41

BURROWS, F., Free *Movement in European Community Law* (Oxford, Clarendon Press, 1987)

CAMERON, David R., "The 1992 Initiative: Causes and Consequences", in *Euro-Politics Institutions and Policymaking in the "New" European Community* (Washington DC, The Brookings Institution 1992), 23

CAPPELLETTI, Mauro and GOLAY, David, *Judicial Review, Transnational and Federal: Its Impact on Integration* EUI Working Paper (European University Institute, Florence, Sept 1981)

—— and —— "The Judicial Branch in the Federal and Transnational Union: Its Impact on Integration" in Cappelleti, Seccombe and Weiler (eds.), *Integration Through law*, vol 1, Book 2 (Berlin, New York, Walter de Gruyter, 1986), 261

CASSESE, Sabino, "La Costituzione Europea", (1991) 3 Quaderni Costituzionali, 487

CELONA, Giuseppe, *La Libera Circolazione Delle Merci E Il Mercato Unico Europeo Nella Giurisprudenza* (Milano, Giuffrè, 1991)

CHALMERS, Damian, "Repackaging the Internal Market—The Ramifications of the Keck Judgment", (1994) 19 *ELR*, 385

COLEMAN, Jules L., "The Foundations of Constitutional Economics" in Richard B McKenzie (ed.), *Constitutional Economics* (Lexington, Massachussetts, Lexington Books, 1984)

COLLINS, Richard B., "Economic Union as a Constitutional Value", (1988) 63 *New York University Law Review*, 143

COPPEL, J. and O'NEIL A., "The European Court of Justice: Taking Rights Seriously?", (1992) 29 *CMLRev*, 660

CORTESE PINTO, Emilia, *Ostacolli Non Tariffari Agli Scambi Nel Diritto Communitario* (Milano, Franco Angeli, 1985)

DANIELE, Luigi, "Non-Discriminatory Restrictions to the Free Movement of Persons", (1997) 22 *ELR*, 191

DAVIES, Paul, "Market Integration and Social Policy in the Court of Justice", (1995) 24 *Industrial Law Journal*, 49

DEHOUSSE, Renaud, "Constitutional Reform in the European Community: Are there Alternatives to the Majoritarian Avenue", (1995) 18 *West European Politics*, 118

—— and MAJONE, Giandomenico, "The Dynamics of European Integration: The Role of Supranational Institutions", Paper presented at the European Community Studies Association Third Biennial International Conference, 27–29 May 1993, Washington DC

DRAGO, R., "Note de Jurisprudence sur l'arrêt du Conseil d'Etat du 27 Juillet 1979, Syndicat national des fabricants de spiritueux consommés à l'eau", (1980) *Revue du Droit Public*, 214

DRUESNE, Gérard, "Remarques sur le champ d'application personnel du droit communautaire: des 'discriminations à rebours' peuvent-elles tenir en échec la liberté de circulation des personnes?", (1979) 15 *RTDE*, 427

DUE, Ole, "The Law-making Role of the European Court of Justice Considered in Particular from the Perspective of Individuals and Undertakings", (1994) 63 *Nordic Journal of International Law*, 123

DYE, Thomas R., *American Federalism: Competition Among Governments* (Massachussetts/Toronto, Lexington Books, 1990)

EASSON, A., "Legal Approaches to European Integration: The Role of the Court and the Legislator in the Completion of the European Common Market", (1989) *Rev Integr Europ*, 100

EHLERMANN, Claus-Dieter, "Harmonization versus Competition Between Rules", (1995) 3 *European Review*, 333

EMPEL, Martin van, "The 1992 Programme: Interaction Between Legislator and Judiciary", (1992) *Legal Issues of European Integration*, 1

EVERLING, Ulrich, "The Court of Justice as a Decision-making Authority" in Michigan Law Review (ed.), *The Art of Governance: Festchrift in Honor of Eric Stein* (Baden-Baden, Nomos, 1987), 156

EVERSON, Michelle, "The Legacy of Marker Citizen", in J. Shaw and G. More (ed.), *New Legal Dynamics of European Union* (Oxford, Clarendon Press 1995), 73

FINNIS, J., "Natural Law and Legal Reasoning", in R. P. George (ed.), *Natural Law Theory. Contemporary Essays* (Oxford, Clarendon Press 1992), 134

FORWOOD, Nicholas and CLOUGH, Mark, "The Single European Act and Free Movement of Goods—Legal Implications for the Completion of the Internal Market", (1986) *ELR* 11

FRAZER, Ian, "The New Structural Funds, State Aids and Interventions on the Single Market", (1995) *ELR*, 3

GALMOT, Yves and BIANCARELLI, Jacques, "Les réglementations nationales en matière de prix au regard du droit communautaire", (1985) 21 *RTDE*, 269

GARRETT, Geoffrey, "International cooperation and institutional choice: the European Community's internal market", (1992) 46 *International Organization*, 533

GERBER, David J., "Constitutionalizing the Economy: German Neo-liberalism, Competition Law and the 'New' Europe", (1994) 42 *American Journal of Comparative Law*, 25

GERGEN, Mark P., "The Selfish State and the Market", (1988) 66 *Texas Law Review*, 1097

GOLUB, Jonathan, "Judicial Cooperation Between National Courts and the European Court of Justice: the Politics and Patterns of Preliminary References", Paper presented at the 37th annual convention of the International Studies Association, San Diego, CA, 16–20 April, 1996

GORMLEY, Laurence W., "Actually or Potentially, Directly or Indirectly? Obstacles to Free Movement of Goods", (1990) Yearbook of European Law, 197

—— "Reasoning Renounced? The Remarkable Judgment in Keck & Mithouard", (1994) *European Business Law Review*, 63

—— *Prohibiting Restrictions on Trade within the EEC* (Amsterdam, Elsevier Science Publishers BV)

GREENWOOD, C., "Limits on Free Movement of Persons in EEC Law", (1987/88) *Yearbook of European Law*, 185

HAAS, Ernst B., *The Uniting of Europe* (Standford, Standford University Press 1968 (first published 1958))

HANCHER, Leigh, "State Aids and Judicial Control in the European Community", (1994) 3 *ECLR*, 134.

HARDEN, Ian, "The Constitution of the European Union", (1994) *Public Law*, 609

HARLOW, Carol, "A Community of Interests? Making the Most of European Law", (1992) 55 *The Modern Law Review*, 331

HART, H.L.A., *The Concept of Law* (Oxford, Clarendon Press, 1961 (rep. from 1972))

HARTLEY, Trevor C., "Five Forms of Uncertainty in European Community Law", (1996) 55 *Cambridge Law Journal*, 265

HAYEK, Friedrich A., *Law, Legislation and Liberty*, vol. 1 (London, Routledge and Keagan, 1973)

—— *The Road to Serfdom* (London, ARK, 1986 (first published 1944))

HEPPLE, Bob, "Social Values and European Law", (1995) 48 *Current Legal Problems*, 39

HEYDEBRAND u d Lasa, "Free Movement of Foodstuffs, Consumer Protection and Food Standards in the European Community: Has the Court of Justice Got it Wrong?", (1991) 16 *ELR*, 391

HOLMER, Peter, "Non-Tariff Barriers", in George McKenzie and Anthony J. Venables (eds.), *The Economics of the Single European Act* (London, Macmillan, 1991)

HOLMES, Justice, "The Path of the Law", (1897) 10 *Harvard Law Review*, 931

ISAAC, Guy, "La condamnation du regime français de publicité pour les boissons alcooliques", (1983) RTDE, 470

JENNY, Frédéric Yves, "Competititon and State Aid Policy in the European Community", (1994) 18 *Fordham International Law Journal*, 525

JOERGES, Christian, "Paradoxes of Deregulatory Strategies at Community Level: The Example of Product Safety Policy", in Giandomenico Majone (ed.), *Deregulation or Reregulation—Regulatory Reform in Europe and the United States* (London, Pinter Publishers, 1990), 176

—— "European Economic Law, the Nation State and the Maastricht Treaty", in Renaud Dehousse (ed.), *The European Union Treaty* (München, C H Beck, 1994), 29

—— "Taking the Law Seriously: On Political Science and the Role of Law in the Process of European Integration", (1996) 2 *European Law Journal*, 105

—— *The Market Without a State?—States Without a Market?: Two Essays on the Law of the European Economy*, EUI Working Paper LAW No. 96/2 (Florence, European University Institute, 1996)

JOHNSON, Esther and O'KEEFFE, David, "From Discrimination to Obstacles to Free Movement: Recent Developments Concerning the Free Movement of Workers 1989–1994", (1994) 31 *CMLRev*, 1313

JUILLARD, Patrick, "Les orientations de la jurisprudence constitutionnelle de la Cour suprême: établissement du marché unique et renforcement des libertés publiques", (1991) 59 *Pouvoirs*, 59

KALEN, Sam, "Reawakening the Dormant Commerce Clause in its First Century", (1987–88) 13 *University of Dayton Law Review*, 417

KEELING, David T. and MANCINI, G. Frederico, "Democracy and the European Court of Justice", (1994) 57 *MLR*, 175

KENNEDY, Duncan, "Form and Substance in Private Law Adjudication", (1976) 89 *Harvard Law Review*, 1685

KIRCHNER, Emil and SCHWAIGER, Konrad, *The Role of Interest Groups in the European Community* (Aldershot, Gower, 1981)

KITCH, Edmund W., "Regulation and the American Common Market", principal paper in A. Dan Tarlock (ed.), *Regulation, Federalism and Interstate Commerce* (Cambridge, Massachussetts, Oelgeschlager, Gunn and Hain)

—— "Regulation the American Common Market and Public Choice", (1982) 6 *Harvard Journal of Law and Public Policy*, 119

KIWIT, Daniel, *Path-dependence in Technological and Institutional Change—Some*

Criticisms and Suggestions, Diskussionsbreitag 10/95 (Jena, Max-Planck-Institut zur Erforschung von Wirtschaftssystemen, 1995)

KOMESAR, Neil K., "In Search of a General Approach to Legal Analysis: A Comparative Institutional Alternative", (1981) 79 *Michigan Law Review*, 1350

—— "A Job for the Judges: The Judiciary and the Constitution in a Massive and Complex Society", (1981) 86 *Michigan Law Review*, 657

—— *Imperfect Alternatives—Choosing Institutions in Law, Economics and Public Policy* (Chicago & London, The University of Chicago Press, 1994)

KON, Stephen D., "Aspects of Reverse Discrimination in Community Law", (1981) 6 *ELR*, 75

KOOPMANS, Thijmen, "The Role of Law in the Next Stage of European Integration", (1986) 35 *ICLQ*, 925

LEITÃO, A.R., "Quelques réflexions politico-juridiques autour de l'élimination des mesures d'effet équivalent: unité du marché commun, principe logique ou principe organique?", (1986) *Revue du Marché Commun*, 21

LENAERTS, Koen, "Constitutionalism and the Many Faces of Federalism", (1990), 38 *American Journal of Comparative Law*, 205

LINDBERG, Leon N., *The Political Dinamics of European Economic Integration* (Standford and Oxford, Stanford University Press and Oxford University Press, 1963)

LINDE, Hans, "Due Process of Law Making", (1876) 55 *Nebraska Law Review*, 197

LISTER, Charles, "The Naming of Foods: The European Community's Rules for Non-Brand Food Product Names", (1993) 18 *ELR*, 179

LOPEZ ESCUDERO, Manuel, "La jurisprudencia Keck y Mithouard: Una Revision del Concepto de Medida de Efecto Equivalente", (1994) *Revista de Instituciones Europeas*, 379

LUDER, Tilman and TODINO, Mario, "La Jurispredence 'Keck' em matière de publicité: vers un marche unique inachevé", (1995) 1 *Revue du Marché Unique Européen*, 171

MACCORMICK, R. Neil, "Beyond the Sovereign State", (1993) 56 *MLR*, 1

MADURO, Miguel Poiares, "Reforming the Market or the State? Article 30 and the European Constitution: Economic Freedom and Political Rights", 3 ELJ 1997, 55

—— "Keck: The End? The Beginning of the End? Or Just the End of the Beginning?", 1 IJEL 1994, 30

—— MAILLO, "Regulatory Reform in the European Union—A View From the European Court of Justice", CD-Rom from the Fourth Biennial Conference of the European Community Studies Association, 11–14 May (Charleston, South Carolina, 1995)

MAJONE, Giandomenico, *Market Integration and Regulation: Europe after 1992*, EUI Working Paper, SPS 91/10 (European University Institute, 1991)

—— "Subsidiarity and Mutual Recognition: Implications for Local, Regional and National Politics in a Unified Europe", typescript of a lecture given at the inauguration of the fourth edition of the Master in Public Management of the Universitat Autònoma de Barcelona, 18 December 1992

—— *Independence vs Accountability? Non-Majoritarian Institutions and the Democratic Government of Europe*, EUI Working Paper, SPS No. 94/3 (European University Institute, Florence, 1994)

MALTZ, Earl M., "How Much Regulation is Too Much—An Examination of Commerce Clause Jurisprudence", (1981) 50 *George Washington Law Review*, 47

MANCINI, G. Federico, "The Making of a Constitution for Europe", (1989) 26 *CMLR*, 595

—— "Crosscurrents and the Tide at the ECJ", (1995) *Irish Journal of European Law*, 120

—— "The European Court of Justice, Trade in Services and Trade-related Aspects of the Protection of Industrial and Intellectual Property Rights", in Davies, Lyon Caen, Sciarra and Simitis (eds.), *Principles and Perspectives on European Community Labour Law* (Oxford, Oxford University Press, 1996)

MARE, Thomas de la, *Judicial Cross-Fertilisation in the European Community*, Thesis submited for the degree of LLM at the European University Institute (February, 1995)

MARENCO, Giuliano, "Pour une interpretation traditionelle de la notion de mesure d'effet equivalent a une restriction quantitative", (1984) *CDE*, 291

—— "Competition Between National Economies and Competition Between Business—a Response to Judge Pescatore", (1987) 10 *Fordham International Law Journal*, 420

MARKERT, Kurt, "Concurrence et Politique Economique dans la CEE", in *Constitution Economique Européenne, Actes du cinquième Colloque sur la Fusion des Communautées Européennes organisé a Liège les 16, 17 et 18 décembre 1970* (La Haye, Martinus Nijhof, 1971)

MASCLET, J.C., "Les articles 30, 36, et 100 du traité à la lumière de l'arrêt 'Cassis de Dijon' ", (1980) 16 *RTDE*, 611

MATTERA, A., *Le Marché Unique Européen* (Jupiter, 1988)

—— "De l'arrêt Dassonville a l'arrêt Keck: l'obscure clarté d'une jurisprudence riche en principes novateurs et en contradictions", (1994) *Revue du Marché Unique Européen*, 117

MCFARLAND, Andrew S., "Interest Groups and the Policy-making Process: Sources of Countervailing Power in America", in Mark P. Petracca (ed.), *The Politics of Interests: Interests Groups Transformed* (Oxford, Westview Press, Boulder, San Francisco, 1992)

MENGOZZI, Paolo, "Il Principio dell'investitore in una Economia di Mercato e i valori del Diritto Communitario", (1995) 1 *Rivista di Diritto Europeo*, 19

MESTMAECKER, E.J., "Can there be a European Law?" (1994) 2 *European Review*, 1

—— "On the Legitimacy of European Law?", (1994) 58 *Rebelsz*, 615

MIRE, Pierre le, "Note—Keck", (1994) 1 *AJDA* (*L'Actuallité Juridique, Droit Administratif*), 54

MITCHELL, Duncan, "Interest Groups and the 'democratic deficit' ", (1993) 2 *European Access* Apri1, 14

MOLLE, Willem, *The Economics of European Integration (Theory, Practice and Policy)*, 2nd edn, (Aldershot and Brookfield, Dartmouth Publishing Company, 1994)

MORAVCSIK, Andrew, "Negotiating the Single European Act: National Interests and Conventional Statecraft in the European Community", (1991) 45 *International Organization*, 19

—— "Preferences and Power in the European Community: A Liberal Intergovernmentalist Approach", (1993) 31 JCMS, 173

MORTELMANS, Kamil, "La discrimination à rebours et le droit communautaire", (1980) *Diritto Communitário e degli Scambi Internazionale*, 1

—— "Article 30 of the EEC Treaty and Legislation Relating to Market Circumstances: Time to Consider a New Definition", (1991) 28 *CMLRev*, 115

MOUTINHO DE ALMEIDA, *Direito Comunitário—A Ordem Jurídica Comunitária—As Liberdades Fundamentais na CEE* (Lisboa, Centro de Publicações do Ministério da Justiça, 1985)

MUSSLER, Werner and STREIT, Manfred, "The Economic Constitution of the EC—From 'Rome' to 'Maastricht' ", (1995) 1 *European Law Journal*, 5

NEUNREITHER, Karlhein, "Transformation of a Political Role: Reconsidering the Case of the Comission of the European Communities", (1972) X JCMS, 233

NGO, Van Long and SIEBERT, Horst, "Institutional Competition Versus ex-ante Harmonization: The Case of Environmental Policy", (1991) 147 *Journal of Institutional and Theoretical Economics*, 246

NORTH, Douglas, C., *Institutions, Institutional Change and Economic Performance* (Cambridge University Press, 1990)

NUGENT, Neill, *The Government and Politics of the European Community* (London, Macmillan, 1989)

OLIVER, Peter, *Free Movement of Goods in the EEC*, 2nd edn. (London, European Law Center, 1988)

—— Free Movement of Goods in the European Community, 3rd edn. (London, Sweet and Maxwell, 1996)

OVIEDO, Marcelo, *Understanding Mercosur Legal Integration Challenges* (typescript, Florence, 1997)

PADOA-SCHIOPPA, *Efficiency, Stability and Equity* (Oxford, Oxford University Press, 1987)

PAUL, Joel, "Free Trade, Regulatory Competition and The Autonomous Market Fallacy", (1994) 1 *Columbia Journal of European Law*, 29

PEACOCK, Alan and WILLEGERODT, Hans, "Overall View of the German Liberal Movement", in Peacock and Willegerodt (eds.), *Germany's Social Market: Origins and Evolution* (London, Macmillan Press, 1989)

PELKMANS, Jacques, "Regulation and the Single Market: an Economic Perspective", in Horst Siebert (ed.), *The Completion of the Internal Market* Symposium 1989 (Institut für Weilwirschaft an der Universitaet Kiel)

PENTLAND, "Political Theories of Integration: Between Science and Ideology" in Lasok and Soldatos (Eds.), The European Communities in Action (Bruxelles, Bruylant, 1981)

PESCATORE, Pierre, *Le Droit de l'Intégration* (Genève, A W Sijthoff—Leiden, 1972)

—— "L'Executif Communautaire: Justification du Quadripartisme Institué par les Traités de Paris et de Rome", (1978) *Cahiers de Droit Européen*, 387

—— "Public and Private Aspects of European Law", (1987) 10 *Fordham International Law Journal*, 373

PETERSMANN, Ernst-Ulrich, "Constitutional Principles Governing the EEC's Commercial Policy", in M. Maresceau (ed.), *The European Community's Commercial Policy after 1992: The Legal Dimension* (Kluwer 1993), 21

—— "Proposals for a New Constitution for the European Union: Building-Blocks for a Constitutional Theory and Constitutional Law of the EU", (1995) 32 *CMLRev*, 1123

PETERSON, Paul E., "The Rise and Fall of Special Interests Politics", in T*he Politics of Interests—Interest Groups Transformed* (Boulder, San Francisco, Oxford, Westview Press, 1992)

PIÇARRA, Nuno and VILAÇA, Cruz, *Are There Material Limits to the Revision of the Treaties on the European Union* (Vortragsreihe des Zentrum für Europaeisches Wirstschaftsrecht des Universitaet Bonn, 1995)

PICKUP, David M.W., "Reverse Discrimination and Freedom of Movement for Workers", (1986) 23 *CMLR*, 135

PIRES, Francisco Lucas, "Legitimidade da Justiça Constitucional e Princípio da Maioria", in *Legitimidade e Legitimação da Justiça, Colóquios no 10º Aniversário do Tribunal Constitucional* (Coimbra, Coimbra Editora, 1995)

PLOETNER, Jens, *The European Court and National Courts—Doctrine and Jurisprudence: Legal Change in its Social Context, Report on France*, EUI Working Paper RSC 95/28 (European University Institute, Florence, 1995)

POSNER, Richard A., *Economic Analysis of the Law* (Boston/Toronto/London, Fourth Edition, Little, Brown and Company, 1992)

POUND, Roscoe, "Law and Federal Government", in *Federalism as a Democratic Process* (New Brunswick, Rutgers University Press, 1942)

RASMUSSEN, *On Law and Policy in the European Court of Justice: A Comparative Study in Judicial Policymaking* (Dodrecht, Boston, Lancaster, Martinus Nijhoff, 1986)

—— "Between Self-Restraint and Activism: A Judicial Policy for the European Court", (1988) 13 *ELR*, 28

RAWLINGS, Richard, "The Eurolaw Game: Deductions from a Saga", (1993) 20 *Journal of Law and Society*, 309

REAGAN, Donald H., "The Supreme Court and State Protectionism: Making Sense of the Dormant Commerce Clause", (1986) 84 Michigan Law Review, 1091

REICH, Norbert, "The Regulatory Crisis: American Approaches in the Light of European Experiences", (1983) 3 *American Bar Foundation Research Journal*, 693

—— "Competition Between Legal Orders: A New Paradigm of EC-Law?", (1992) 29 *CMLR*, 861

—— "The 'November Revolution' of the European Court of Justice: Keck, Meng and Audi Revisited", (1994) 31 *CMLRev*, 459

ROMANO, Roberta, "The Political Economy of Takeover Statutes", (1987) 73 *VA L Rev*, 113

—— "The State Competition Debate in Corporate Law", (1987) 8 *Cardozo L Rev*, 709

RÖPKE, Wilhelm, *International Order and Economic Integration* (Dordrecht-Holland, D Reidel Publishing Company, 1959)

ROSE-ACKERMAN, Susan, *Rethinking The Progressive Agenda—The Reform of The American Regulatory State* (New York, The Free Press, 1992)

SANDALOW, Terrance and STEIN, Eric, "On The Two Systems: An Overview", in Terrance Sandalow and Eric Stein (eds.), *Courts and Free Markets* vol.1 (Oxford, Clarendon Press, 1982)

SCHARPF, Fritz W., "The Joint-Decision Trap—Lessons from German Federalism and European Integration", (1988) 66 Public Administration, 239

—— *Negative and Positive Integration in the Political Economy of Welfare States*, Jean Monnet Chair Papers, 28 (European University Institute, Florence, 1995)

SCHEPEL, Harm and WESSELING, Rein, "The Legal Community: Judges, Lawyers, Officials and Clerks in the Writing of Europe", (1997) 3 *ELJ*, 165

SCHMITTER, P.C. and STREECK-WOLFGANG, "From National Corporatism to Transnational Pluralism—Organized Interests in the Single European Market", (1991) 19 Politics and Society, 133

SCIARRA, Silvana, "European Social Policy and Labour Law—Challenges and Perspectives", in *Collected Courses of the Academy of European Law*, vol IV, Book I (Kluwer Law International, 1995), 301

SHAPIRO, Martin, "Comparative Law and Comparative Politics", (1980) 53 *Southern California Law Review*, 537

SIEBERT, Horst, "The Harmonization Issue in Europe: Prior Agreement or a Competitive Process?", in Horst Siebert (ed.), *Completition of the Internal Market*, Symposium 1989 (Institute fuer Welwiryschaft an der Universität Kiel)

—— and VAN LONG, Ngo, "Institutional Competition Versus Ex-ante Harmonization: The Case of Environmental Policy", (1991) 147 *Journal of Institutional and Theoretical Economics*, 296

SMITIS, Spiros, "Dismantling or Stengthening Labour Law: the Case of European Court of Justice", (1996) 2 *European Law Journal*, 156

SNYDER, Francis, "New Directions in European Community Law", (1987) 14 *Journal of Law and Society*, 167

—— *New Directions in Community Law* (London, Weidenfeld and Nicolson, 1990)

—— "L'Economia Mista e la Nuova Costituzione Economica dell'Unione Europea", Bozza provisória per presentazione al seminario su "L'Economia Mista, oggi", CE R IS DI, Palermo, le 10 e 11 aprile 1992

STEIN, Eric, "Lawyers, Judges and the Making of a Transnational Constitution", (1981) *American Journal of Internatinal Law*, 1

—— "Uniformity and Diversity in a Divided-Power System: The United States Experience", (1986) 61 *Washington Law Review*, 1081

STEINER, J, "Drawing the Line: Uses and Abuses of Article 30 EEC", (1992) 26 *CMLRev*, 749

STEWART, Richard B., "Environmental Regulation and International Competitiveness", (1993) 102 *The Yale Law Journal*, 2039

STONE, Alec, *Constitutional Dialogues in the European Community*, EUI Working Paper RSC No. 95/38, (European University Institute, Florence, 1995)

—— Judicialization and the Construction of Governance, EUI Working Papers RSC No. 96/59 (Florence, 1996).

STUART, MacKenzie, Lord, *The European Community and the Rule of Law* (London, The Hamlyn Lectures, Stevens & Sons, 1977)

SUMMERS, Robert, "Comment", in Richard B. MacKenzie (ed.), *Constitutional Economics* (Massachussetts, Lexington, Lexington Books)

SUNSTEIN, Cass R., "Lochner's Legacy", (1987) 87 *Columbia Law Review*, 873

—— "Protectionism, The American Supreme Court and Integrated Markets", in Roland Bieber, R. Dehousse, John Pinder, Joseph Weiler (eds.), *1992: One European Market? A Critical Analysis of the Commission Internal Market Strategy* (Baden-Baden, Nomos), 127

—— "Incompletely Theorized Agreements", (1995) 108 *Harvard Law Review*, 1733

TEUBNER, Gunther, *After Legal Instrumentalism?—Strategic Models of Post-Regulatory Law*, EUI Working Papers No. 100 (European University Institute, 1984)

TRIANTAFYLLOU, Dimitri, "Les règles de la concurrance et l'activité étatique y compris les marchés publiques", (1996) 1 *RTDE*, 32

UNGER, Roberto Mangabeira, *The Critical Legal Studies Movement* (Cambridge, Massachussetts and London, Harvard University Press, 1983 (rep. 1986))

VAN HUFFEL, Michel, "Le champ d'applications de l'article 30 du Traité de Rome et les arrêts Keck et Mithouard, Hunermund et Clinique: la nouvelle liberté de la libre circulation des marchandises ou 'l'enfer c'est les autres'?", (1994) *Revue Européenne de Droit de la Consommation*, 94

VOGEL, David, "Protective Regulation and Protectionism in the European Community: The Creation of a Common Market for Food and Beverages", Paper prepared for the biennial conference of the European Studies Association, Virginia, George Mason University, May 1991

VOIGT, Stefan, "European Political Union—An Appropriate Case for Applying Constitutional Economics to Real-Life Problems?", (1994) 45 ORDO, 243

VOLCANSEK, Mary L., *Judicial Politics in Europe: An Impact Analysis* (New York, Lang, 1986)

—— "Supranational Courts and the Legalization of Politics", in *Law Above Nations* (Gainesville, University Press of Florida, forthcoming)

WAELBROECK, M., *Les réglementations nationales de prix et le droit communautaire* (Bruxelles, Éditions de l'Université de Bruxelles, 1975)

—— "La Constitution Européenne et les Interventions des Etats-Membres en Matière Economique" in *Orde Liber Amicorum Pieter Verloren van Themaat* (Deventer, Kluwer, 1982), 331

WAELBROOK, D., "La compatibilité des législations nationales indistinctement applicables aux produits nationaux et importés avec les règles européennes de libre circulation des marchandises", (1983) *CDE*, 241

WEATHERILL, Stephen, "Consumer Safety Legislation in the United Kingdom and Article 30 EEC", (1988) *ELR*, 87

—— "Regulating the Internal Market: Result Orientation in the Court of Justice" (1994) 19 *ELR*, 55

—— "Comment on Case C–415/95, Bosman, Judgment of the European Court of Justice of 15 December 1995", (1995) 33 *CMLRev*, 991

—— "After *Keck*: Some Thoughts on How to Clarify the Clarification", (1996) 33 *CMLRev*, 885

WEILER, Joseph H.H., "The Community System: The Dual Character of Supranationalism", (1981) 1 *Yearbook of European Law*, 267

—— "The Transformation of Europe", (1990) 100 *Yale Law Journal*, 2403

—— "Problems of Legitimacy in Post 1992 Europe", (1991) 46 *Aussenwirtschaft*, 411

—— "Journey to an Unknown Destination: A Retrospective and Prospective of the European Court of Justice in the Arena of Political Integration", (1993) 31 *JCMS*, 417

—— "A Quiet Revolution—The European Court of Justice and Its Interlocutors", (1994) 26 *Comparative Political Studies*, 510

—— "Does Europe Need a Constitution? Demos, Telos and The German Maastricht Decision", (1995) 1 *European Law Journal*, 219

—— "The Reformation of European Constitutionalism" (1997) 35 *JCMS*, 97

—— and HALTERN, Ulrich, and MEYER, Franz, "European Democracy and Its Critic", (1995) 18 *West European Politics*, 4

WHITE, Eric, "In Search of the Limits to Article 30 of the EEC Treaty", (1989) 26 *CMLRev*, 235

WILLEGERODT, Hans, "Comment on Jacques Pelkmans 'Regulation and the Single Market: An Economic Perspective'", in Horst Siebert (ed.), *The Completion of The Internal Market*, Symposium 1989 (Institut für Weltwirschaft an der Universität Kiel)

WILS, P.J. Wouter, "The Search for the Rule in Article 30 EEC: much ado about nothing?", (1993) *ELR*, 475

WITTE, Bruno de, "Community Law and National Constitutional Values", (1991) *LIEI*, 1

Index